Welcome to the Big Lan

THE COUNTRY AND THE GAME

THE COUNTRY AND THE GAME

30,000 Miles of Hockey Stories

RONNIE SHUKER

SUTHERLAND HOUSE

TORONTO, 2024

Sutherland House
416 Moore Ave., Suite 304
Toronto, ON M4G 1C9

First edition, October 2024

If you are interested in inviting one of our authors to a live event or
media appearance, please contact sranasinghe@sutherlandhousebooks.com
and visit our website at sutherlandhousebooks.com for more information.

We acknowledge the support of the Government of Canada.

Manufactured in Turkey
Cover designed by Jordan Lunn
Book composed by Karl Hunt
Map composed by Shea Berencsi

Library and Archives Canada Cataloguing in Publication
Title: The country and the game : 30,000 miles of hockey stories / Ronnie Shuker.
Names: Shuker, Ronnie, author.
Identifiers: Canadiana (print) 20240414179 | Canadiana (ebook) 20240414187 |
ISBN 9781990823879 (hardcover) | ISBN 9781990823886 (EPUB)
Subjects: LCSH: Hockey—Canada—Anecdotes.
Classification: LCC GV848.4.C3 S58 2024 |
DDC 796.9620971—dc23

ISBN 978-1-990823-87-9
eBook 978-1-990823-88-6

Contents

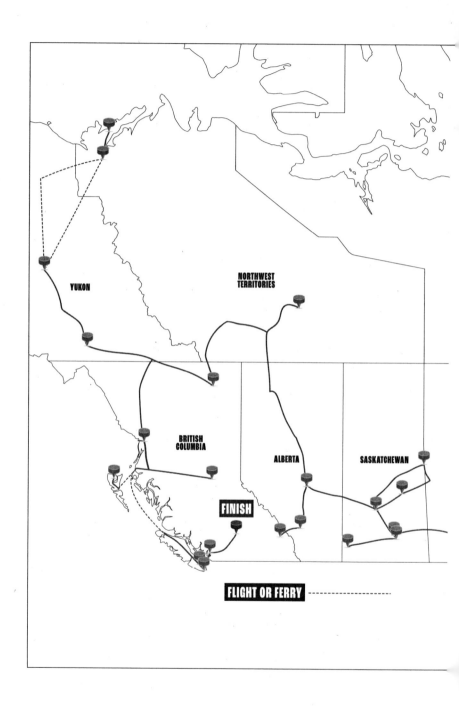

YUKON

NORTHWEST
TERRITORIES

BRITISH
COLUMBIA

ALBERTA

SASKATCHEWAN

FINISH

FLIGHT OR FERRY -----------

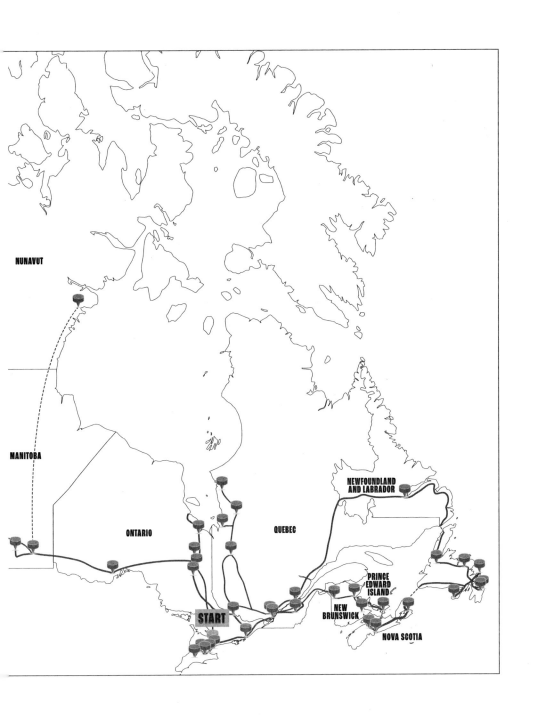

For my father

See you in the stands, Pops

Newfoundland and Labrador: Let the Game Begin

Shinny begins in the street. —Doug Beardsley, "The Sheer Joy of Shinny"

HOCKEY IS A game without end. One rink leads to another, one shift rolls into another, one period into another, one game into another, one season into the next, until it all just becomes one lifelong game.

The cycle restarts every September. For those of us who grow up in the game, who learn to skate as soon as we can walk, who start playing hockey before our first day of school, January is just the midpoint of a season that begins four months earlier. Come September, after the dog days of summer and the dead months of the hockey calendar, school starts anew and hockey begins afresh. The rhythm of this tandem, school and hockey, sets the pace for our lives, until school gives way to work, leaving hockey to carry on alone, resetting our internal calendar every September to the start of another hockey season, to a life of the ice.

It is a late September morning, the fiftieth anniversary of Canada's victory over the Soviet Union, as I make for Montreal. I wasn't yet even an idea when the Summit Series took place in 1972, so I have never quite understood the place it holds as perhaps the seminal moment in Canadian history, as hockey's hagiographers are wont to call it. But it makes for a damn good departure date. So, on September 28, 2022, fifty years to the day Paul Henderson scored the goal that saved Canada from nationwide mourning, I pack my backpack, hockey gear, food, supplies, and two spare tires into my four-wheeled friend, Gumpy, named after legendary goaltender Lorne "Gump" Worsley, and entrust him to shepherd me on my way. I then leave my home in a suburban satellite orbiting the center of the hockey universe, and head east along the Macdonald–Cartier Freeway, Highway 401.

In preparation for the road trip, I've mapped out a route that will touch three oceans and run through every province and two of the three territories, with a flight mixed in to Nunavut. The plan is to take the backdoor into Labrador, through eastern Quebec, and carry on to Newfoundland. Once in St. John's, at the easternmost end of the Trans-Canada Highway, I'll head west—and north—hitting up hockey towns all along the way. The goal: drive across the country, and watch, talk, and play hockey wherever the road leads to the ice.

Joining me for this leg of the ride is globetrotting goaltender Adrian Mizzi. In 2005, Adrian happened upon his first international beer-league tournament, playing for something called the Malta Pirates in Dubai. The Travelling Goalie was born. Since then, he's played hockey at the End of the World in Ushuaia, Argentina, at the Roof of the World on the Changthang Plateau, India, and wherever else his seminomadic existence has led him, goalie gear in hand, flag-stitched stick bag in tow.

"Dubai changed my life," he likes to say. "I found something. I really found my true calling."

It was in India that our paths first crossed. We'd each flown into the disputed territory of Jammu and Kashmir, where it is Canada cold in winter and where hockey, not cricket, is the preferred art of play. With over a hundred other like-minded traveling players from around the world, we piled into a caravan of taxis for a four-hour ride along switchbacks through the Indian Himalayas, with nothing but goofy gallows humor and Kama Sutra innuendo between us and a one-way express ticket to oblivion. Rather than erect guardrails, India's ministry of transportation had opted for riotous road signs to encourage safe driving: "Drive, don't fly," "Be soft on my curves," and, my personal favorite, "Life is a journey. Complete it!" We then shivered ourselves to sleep in our spartan homestays in a local village, warmed only by the hospitality of our gracious hosts, who gladly gave their guests everything of what little they had. All this to set the Guinness World Record for the highest altitude hockey game ever played. There, on a nearby unnamed floodplain in nowhere northern India near the border with Tibet, Adrian and I etched our insignificant names into obscure hockey history. I became the first person to score a goal in an organized hockey game over fourteen thousand feet, albeit a garbage goal that a limbless hamster could've nudged over the goal line, while Adrian became the only goalie to stop a penalty shot while inhaling fumes from an organically powered generator behind his net.

"I was one hundred percent certain it was diesel," Adrian says. "But after the second period, I was told it was yak shit."

From Toronto, Highway 401 is clear all the way to the provincial border, as is Autoroute Guy-Lafleur the rest of the way to Montreal, where we stop for the night. From there, it is another 668 kilometers (415 miles) to Baie-Comeau, our eyes pulled left and right between the Laurentian Mountains and the St. Lawrence River for the better part of nine hours. There we connect to Route 389.

Aside from Quebec's giant dams, signs of civilization are few along Route 389, only a couple of waystations to sleep, eat, and refuel, or just to pass through and pick up a postcard. The only road signs are those that list the slowly shortening distance north to Labrador and those for the monolithic Jean Lesage, René-Lévesque, and Daniel Johnson hydroelectric generating stations. The road is 566 kilometers (352 miles) of dirt, gravel, and periodic pavement dotted with old-school, red SOS telephone booths that look out onto mile after mile of spruce forest and taiga as the road rises, falls, and winds its way through the Groulx and Severson Mountains. It is also crisscrossed with railway crossings for the Quebec North Shore

& Labrador Railway mining train, which ships minerals south from the region's mines. Before the road was built, it also hauled hockey players from Labrador City down to Sept-Iles, Quebec.

When we make it to Labrador, the Big Land as they call it here, we connect to the Trans-Labrador Highway, which cuts through 1,247 kilometers (775 miles) of rugged frontier. Roads like this are what make the game possible in many parts of Canada. In Labrador, the highway was a game changer for communities along its route. Before it was completed in 1992, teams from the fly-in-only towns of Labrador City, Churchill Falls, and Happy Valley-Goose Bay, where Adrian and I are headed, were rarely able to travel beyond the bounds of their own town. With the Trans-Labrador, the distances are still significant, but no longer insurmountable. Midweek games between towns remain out of the question, but teams can now travel between communities for weekend games and tournaments. For most players in Canada, those living south of the Trans-Canada, this is something they can take for granted.

When we reach Happy Valley-Goose Bay, we head straight for E. J. Broomfield Memorial Arena, where Roxanne Dyson is busy rallying the community in support of one of its own. After young Aiden O'Keefe first beat his leukemia, a year earlier, Roxanne organized a parade upon his return. When the family got home to Happy Valley-Goose Bay, after the long drive from St. John's, where the boy had received treatment, the local hockey association, police force, and fire department were all waiting for Aiden in the parking lot of the arena. People held up welcome signs as police cars and fire trucks escorted him and his parents to the family's home just down the road from the rink. There were tears of joy and high-fives of happiness.

When Aiden relapsed, just a couple of months before we arrived, he was flown to Sick Kids Hospital in Toronto. Roxanne went right back at it again, ordering helmet stickers and rolls of orange tape so that Aiden's friends and teammates could support him as he received further treatment.

"He should be here trying out for his team right now," she says. "But he's not. He's in a hospital bed. He's having a rough time."

As Roxanne speaks, she pauses every so often to collect herself, wiping away tears as she brushes her black hair off her jacket.

"It's one of those families that you see here every day at the arena," she says, "that you pass, that you sit with, that work the canteen, that is just here."

Roxanne and I are sitting across from each other at a folding table in a kitchen at the back of the arena. Beside me is Craig Penney.

"Like Steve Penney of the Montreal Canadiens," Adrian pipes in with a 1980s reference.

"Yup, there you go," Craig says. "The old goalie."

Although his thick Newfoundland tongue betrays his roots, Craig has lived more than half his life in Labrador, flying Twin Otters for Air Borealis and running the local hockey program. I can sense his gratitude for Roxanne and other volunteers, like the woman who's operated the canteen for the past twenty-five years. Without them, hockey wouldn't happen here. As the geographical center of the region, with the highest population and largest airport, Happy Valley-Goose Bay is the hub of Labrador, both for places like Labrador City and Churchill Falls to the west as well as for the region's isolated communities north and along the east coast. Yet it has no definable economic identity, no discernible industry, other than the remnants of an old World War II (later NATO) airbase that is now a shared civilian and military airport. Not like Labrador City, the region's unofficial capital and economic center.

"It's a money town over there, a janitor makes over $120,000 a year," Craig says. "Lab City is mining, Churchill Falls is hydroelectricity, and we're . . ."

"Other," Roxanne says.

"We used to be military, right?" Craig continues. "We used to have a base. Germans, British, Italians. The base is still there, but none of them are there. A lot of buildings have been torn down, so it doesn't look like much of a base now."

Yet when it comes to the game, Happy Valley-Goose Bay is a hockey town like any other across Canada, the kind of place where the door handle of the local Tim Hortons is shaped like a hockey stick, where an elaborate roadside memorial down the Trans-Labrador honors a local hockey fan, where tournaments are named after local hockey lifers, and where displays in the arena remember people from the local hockey community, including a coach killed while driving the highway to a tournament in Labrador City. But hockey doesn't come easy here, nor anywhere in the region. Distance and money are the main issues. To send just one team from Labrador to the annual provincial championships in Newfoundland costs about as much as a new compact car, the same amount dished out in prize money every year for a high-stakes men's tournament in nearby Sheshatshiu that draws in ex-pros.

"Oh geez, there's NHLers that come in for that," Craig says.

After about an hour, Craig gets up to leave. His beer-league crew, the Huskies, a collection of pickup players that has been running since the 1970s, are set to play their first game of the season.

"Safe travels now," Craig says. "Take your time going down that road. There's a bit of wildlife on it."

"We haven't seen any yet," Adrian says.

"Well, that's good. You don't need to meet a thousand-pound bull moose out on the road."

A few days later, while Adrian and I were driving through Newfoundland, I received a text from Roxanne: "I hope your journey is treating you well. I just wanted to reach out to let you know that young hockey player Aiden O'Keefe lost his battle with cancer Monday night. Our hockey community and Labrador are devastated. We had a moment of silence Monday night, and he passed away just moments after."

When we reach the end of the Trans-Labrador Highway, after it funnels us out of the forest and onto the coast, Adrian declares he is just about done with Labrador. Everywhere we've stopped, he's tried to get us on the ice. When we hit Labrador City, it was a holiday, so the arena was closed. After a day of hockey tryouts in Churchill Falls, the arena shut down for the night. In Happy Valley-Goose Bay, Adrian lobbied hard with the Huskies' organizer, only to be turned away because all the spots were full. Farther down the Trans-Labrador, Port Hope Simpson had no arena, and neither L'Anse-au-Loup nor Blanc-Sablon, at the highway's end, had any ice in theirs yet. While waiting for the ferry to Newfoundland, Adrian finds out the arena in St. Barbe, on the other side of the Gulf of St. Lawrence, isn't open.

"It's been nine days since I've been on the ice. That's like an eternity for me," he says. "I'm so depressed I'm thinking about chucking my hockey bag into the ocean."

Then, while aboard the ferry, the tide suddenly changes. There will be hockey waiting for us when we get to Newfoundland. Just a five-hour drive down Highway 430 from the dock in St. Barbe to Hodder Memorial Arena in Deer Lake. The first of many such games to come.

On game day, there is an anticipation that comes with knowing there's going to be hockey that night. It gives the drive to the arena, however long or short, a distinct feel to it. As a kid, it was always pure excitement. As a teenager, it was a mix of nervousness and dread. Now, as an adult, it is a blend of gratitude and contentment.

Eager to get on the ice, we arrive early. Soon players begin pouring into the dressing room, mostly twenty- and thirty-somethings, greeting and kibitzing with us in a show of Newfoundland hospitality and humor.

There is a rhythm to hockey that goes well beyond the ice. There's the rhythm of grabbing your gear and going to rink, the rhythm of the dressing room, the chirping, the teasing, the self-deprecation. There's the rhythm of hockey talk, that curious kind of conversation that can instantly build bonds between players who know little about each other beyond the game. Then there's the rhythm of the game itself, a sixth sense of timing required to make a well-timed pass or a perfectly placed shot or just being in the right place at the right moment. Throw the rhythm of hockey out of whack, and it is hard to get it back. Like a taskmaster drummer who doesn't let the band take a break, hockey moves forward, and you either keep up or lose the beat. In a game set apart from all others because of its sheer speed, it is hard to catch up once you fall behind.

It takes Adrian and me a while to find our rhythm and keep up with the Newfoundlanders. The pace is quick, the tempo consistent, their skill level high. But it feels good to get on the ice. The drive to the rink, the dressing room barbs, the greetings and introductions on the bench, the game itself, the postgame banter, it all makes Hodder Memorial Arena feel like our own home rinks.

After the game, seven of us head over to Langer's, just steps from the arena. When we walk into the bar, still wet from the sweat that wrings out of your pores long after a game, Langer's is almost empty. Owned by local boy Darren Langdon, there are several framed photos of him by the bar, the largest an action shot from his only season with the Vancouver Canucks.

Life was good for Langdon when he opened his bar in his hometown in 1998. He was in his fourth season with the New York Rangers, having played with the likes of Wayne Gretzky and Mark Messier, earning $1 million in salary. So he decided that every time he scored a goal, a round of beers would be on the house. But then a funny thing happened. His scoring touch suddenly disappeared. Langdon had scored fourteen goals by the time he opened his bar, but he would score just three more over his final seven seasons.

Adrian buys a round for everyone, while I grab a water and sit down at a table with Noah Burnett, who's wearing a black hoodie from the *Ice Road Truckers* TV show.

Just twenty-three years old, Noah has owned his own rig since he was eighteen. Usually, he stays in Atlantic Canada, with the odd trip to Quebec or the Prairies. But every winter, he makes for the Northwest Territories, where he spends six to eight weeks driving back and forth between Yellowknife and the region's diamond mines, hauling equipment along the world's longest heavy haul ice road, the Tibbitt to Contwoyto Winter Road. I have time on an ice road in Northern Ontario planned ahead of me. I want to hear more.

"There's something almost romantic about it," Noah says. "It's a spot very few people get to see, some of the most beautiful country you'll ever drive through on the right night with the Northern Lights. You don't get those opportunities every day to go do something like that, so I jumped at the chance to do it. I just love the area, love the road."

While driving the ice road, Noah has no time for hockey, other than catching his Ottawa Senators on satellite radio. But at home in Deer Lake, he never allows work to interfere with play. The camaraderie of the dressing room, the tug of the ice, the pull of postgame badinage and beers at Langer's, everything that brought Adrian and me to Hodder Memorial Arena on our way to St. John's, Noah makes sure to make time for it all.

"You gotta have at least a night or two off to go out and see your buddies and all that stuff," he says. "I'm no superstar or nothing. It's just the ambience of the room."

After finally getting on the ice in Deer Lake, Adrian and I carry on to St. John's, stopping halfway in Gander, once home to the world's largest refrigerator. When the United States closed its airspace on 9/11, thirty-eight planes were diverted to Gander. Overnight, the population nearly doubled. Food donations poured in, and every shelf in town was emptied to feed both the residents and the sudden surge in visitors. But the town needed somewhere to put all that food. So with flight crews filling the local hotels and visitors taking up every spare bedroom and pullout couch in town, games at the Gander Community Centre were postponed so that the rink could be transformed into a giant walk-in fridge. For five days, the arena helped feed the town until everyone was allowed to go home.

In St. John's, we find a hotel beside the city's main arena, home to a revolving door of minor pro teams that have called the province home since it opened in 2001. For its first twenty years, the arena was known as Mile One Centre, named to mark the easternmost point of the Trans-Canada. But like so many urban arenas, it's since been given a corporate callsign. In this case, from a fast-food chicken chain. But in the spirit of its christening as Mile One Centre, Adrian and I decide it would mark the perfect start to our quest.

"I was supposed to be—you're not gonna believe this, and no one else will, but I know—the Leafs' number one pick. They went with George Ferguson. And I'm gonna tell you something else . . . how I knew it."

After a couple of days of shinny and downtime, Adrian and I have driven to a raised bungalow in Mount Pearl, a quiet neighborhood outside St. John's. We hadn't even made it past the door when Terry Ryan Sr., not one for formalities, launched into his draft story.

"You want us to take our shoes off?" Adrian asks once we are inside.

"Yeah, take your shoes off for fuck's sake. I don't want any Ontario dirt in here!"

We follow Terry Sr. up a short flight of stairs and into the living room, his thick thatch of silver hair stark against a black T-shirt with the logo for something called Goons Gym Fight Club. He sits down in a lounger near his wife, Gail, while Adrian and I take seats opposite him on the edge of a musty sofa.

"I was ranked the second-top skater that year, cause not only was I fast, but I could slash," he says. "You know what slash means? Cut east-west. I could fly."

About half an hour later, with his father still working his way through his draft story, Terry Jr. walks in, wearing a Blue Collar Whiskey hoodie, along with flip-flops and ripped jeans, ballcap turned backward, headphones around his neck.

"I'm giving the boys the whole shot," Terry Sr. says. "Now I'm getting to the good stuff."

"Is this the first story?" Terry Jr. asks as he plops himself onto a sofa to our right.

"No, we're well into it now."

Terry Sr. turns back to us and continues. The memories flood back so quickly that he speaks in fragments.

"And I'll tell ya—and I'm gonna get to that story—who loved me, who absolutely loved me! Johnny Bower. That's who told me. 'You're our number one pick.' In Maple Leaf Gardens."

Before being invited into the Ryan home, all I knew of the two Terrys was that they shared the same name. But it didn't take me long to learn their workarounds, "Senior" and "Junior," and to figure out that neither puts on any airs nor pulls any punches, especially with each other.

As Senior continues weaving his draft yarn, he digresses to another story about a former teammate, Mike "Worm" Veisor, who was drafted right after him in 1972 and went on to play in the NHL.

"I never played a game in the NHL, that always sort of bothered me," Senior says. "I said to him, 'Worm, was I good enough to play in the NHL?' And his words were . . ."

"Jesus," Junior mutters under his breath.

"Newf, fuck yes."

"Okay, get back to the story for fuck sakes!"

Other than their hockey credentials, I know little of either Terry. In many ways, it turns out, they are mirrors of one other. Each was a minor-league journeyman, neither a big-league success, but they made the most of their pro careers, and both are born storytellers.

Terry Sr. played his junior hockey with the Hamilton Red Wings in the early 1970s before being drafted into the NHL. He spent the rest of the decade playing minor pro in the United States for teams like the Suncoast Suns, Winston-Salem Polar Twins, Lansing Lancers, Muskegon Mohawks, and Kalamazoo Wings, followed by six years of senior hockey in Newfoundland. He was drafted by the Minnesota North Stars in 1972 but never played a game with them. The closest he came to the NHL was one season with the Minnesota Fighting Saints of the World Hockey Association. After his career ended, he came home to Newfoundland and became a French teacher. In 2000, he was inducted into the provincial hockey hall of fame.

"Dad, is this gonna end at the end of your professional career or what?" Junior asks.

"I'm gonna end it now."

"I came in twenty minutes ago. I just wanna see what the boys are doing on their trip."

"Alright, Terry. Let's go downstairs then."

"No, just wait. When was that ending? Where was that gonna end?"

"It's gonna end here."

"Terry, there wasn't even a question," Gail says. "He just started talking."

"He tells the story and he starts at the beginning of his career," Junior says to us before turning back to Senior. "Dad, these are snippets of stories."

"Well, that's me. I love to talk."

"Anyway, guys," Junior says, "how was your trip into St. John's?"

Adrian recounts our route from Toronto to St. John's as we follow the two Terrys downstairs to the basement. Framed photos and newspaper clippings line the Ryan Wall of Fame along the stairs, many of them of Terry Jr., who took a similar path on the ice as Terry Sr. He spent the first part of the 1990s playing junior hockey with the Tri-City Americans and then the rest of the decade bouncing between the Montreal Canadiens, who drafted him eighth overall in 1995, and their farm team, the Fredericton Canadiens. Like his father, he went on to play minor pro for several teams scattered throughout the United States before coming home to play senior hockey.

There was a time when Terry Jr. was better known, by his own admission, for being one of the biggest draft busts in NHL history, with only eight games played and just thirty-six minutes in penalties to show for it. But in those eight games, plus several more in the preseason, Terry Jr. made his mark, one he's since parlayed into a successful post-playing career in the arts, much of it while playing senior hockey all over Newfoundland and becoming a Canadian ball hockey legend with the men's national team. He's done stunt work, tried his hand at stand-up comedy, completed a bachelor's degree in folklore, authored two books, written screenplays, started up a podcast, and worked both behind and in front of the camera on film sets, including his role as the chirpy Newfoundland hockey player Ted Hitchcock in the Canadian comedy series *Shoresy*, a part he was born to play.

Although he had "hands," as they say in hockey parlance of skilled players who could score, Terry Jr. made a name for himself with his fists. The stories he's written with them are larger than life, whether it was dipping his hands in hot sauce before a game to sting the eyes of an opponent during a fight or knocking out his own teeth with a sledgehammer while drunk. At six-foot-one and just a shade over two hundred pounds, Terry Jr. isn't an imposing man. But as the stories tumble out of him, flashes of the freewheeling, fearless, hair-on-fire eighteen-year-old who went looking for trouble, and never backed down when he found it, come over the reinvented forty-five-year-old before us, including a trifecta of fights with Tie Domi, former heavyweight champion of the NHL.

"The first time was kind of a bet," Terry Jr. says. "Back here, I knew none of my buddies would actually think that I'd do it if I said, 'What the fuck, I'll fight him.' I was eighteen. But in my mind, unless he kills me, I win."

By then, Domi had already made a name for himself in the NHL, making the heavyweight belt gesture after a fight with Bob Probert, the toughest fighter in the league at the time. With 1,329 penalty minutes and 89 fights to that point, Domi was starting his first full season with the Toronto Maple Leafs and was looking to put on a show for the hometown fans when he found Terry Jr. in a scrum during a preseason game. Seven years his junior, Terry Jr. more than held his own.

"He was a legend and I figured I'm one of his first fights with the Leafs," Terry Jr. says. "Then the next year, he spun me around and said, 'You owe me one.' And I was like, 'Oh, I guess I do. Yes, I do.' And the third time . . ."

"He never put you down, though," Gail says.

"The third one he did," Terry Jr. says.

"Terry, you did alright," Terry Sr. says. "You did alright."

Terry Jr. did score a goal in the NHL, a deflection off his skate during a preseason game against the Boston Bruins. But it never comes up, even though the game sheet is on the Ryan Wall of Fame (along with a framed newspaper clipping showing the first Domi mix-up). Every story is about his fists, a basement blitzkrieg through his three fights with Domi, his two fights with Darren Langdon, his fights in senior hockey, and his fights on film. And he's still fighting, with telltale marks on his face and a sore arm from his most recent scrap to show for it. A year after our visit, Terry Jr. would play one game for the local minor pro team, the Newfoundland Growlers, as an emergency replacement—twenty years after his final pro game. In front of his hometown fans at the former Mile One Centre, he would start the game, get into a fight in the third period with a player twenty-two years younger, and leave the ice to a standing ovation.

Adrian and I watch and listen as Senior and Junior, standing opposite each other, go back and forth.

"You fought a lot of guys who were bigger than you," Senior says.

"I didn't fight to win, I was fightin' not to lose," Junior says. "I was fightin' to put on a show for the crowd."

"I know."

"You grab here," Junior says as he grabs Senior and pulls him close.

"And you control him."

"Even if it's Langer or anything," Junior says. "Like, you get in tight."

"There's an art to it."

"You know hockey fights. Holy fuck, Senior."

Father and son continue, reliving and reenacting Terry Jr.'s fights right there in the middle of the basement. By the time Terry Jr. finishes, he seems as spent as he must've been after the fights themselves.

It isn't until Terry Jr. leaves that I take a good look around the basement. Above stacks of books and DVDs on the floor, jerseys of every sort and stripe, many with logos I don't recognize from the two Terrys' careers, are strewn pell-mell across chairs, over the room's three sofas, on the wood-panel walls, from light fixtures and behind lamps, even from the curtain rods over the windows. There are autographed wood sticks from Wayne Gretzky and Bobby Hull, the kind the Hockey Hall of Fame would encase in glass. Here we are free to hold them.

Yet half of what is in the room isn't even about hockey. There are stacks of records, cassette tapes, CDs, and music magazines everywhere, with a slew of posters, photos, and records of the Beatles. Below the TV is a large photo of Johnny Cash, guitar in one hand, middle finger upraised in the other. If it were a hockey stick he was holding, it could've easily been a photo of Terry Sr., who bears a passing resemblance to the Man in Black.

"I started collecting music when I was about twenty," Terry Sr. says. "I met Elvis, I met Sinatra, I went out with Liza Minnelli as a date." All three chance encounters were doors that hockey opened.

As Terry Sr. inches his way through the basement, stories continue to spill out of him. We follow him along the Ryan Wall of Fame, willing captives to his tales, and back up the stairs to the front door, where Gail is patiently waiting for him to wrap it up so that they can go grocery shopping. He points at photos and clippings of either himself or his son, or both, schmoozing with athletes and actors. Ted Williams, Pete Rose, Wesley Snipes, Arnold Schwarzenegger, Walter Gretzky, Dennis Rodman, Terry Sr. has a story for them all. But it is the ones about his son that take the edge off his gruff exterior for a moment and bring out a softness in him.

"It's funny how life works," he says. "Here's a guy who was a top pick in the NHL and he's an actor? How in the hell did he get this? He's like the renaissance man. And he's really good."

As we slowly make our way upstairs, Terry Sr. asks Adrian about his own journey through the game. Adrian assumes the storytelling reins and begins at the beginning: Dubai, the Travelling Goalie, hockey in the Himalayas, his quest to play hockey in fifty countries before he turns fifty, which stands at forty-three and counting.

"Wow, that's fascinating, man," Terry Sr. says to Adrian and then turns to Gail. "Jesus, I could sit down with the boys all day."

"We'll be back," Adrian says.

"Yeah, you'll be back. As long as you don't get eaten by a crocodile in Uganda, then I won't get a chance to talk to you. Oh my god, boys, it's been a real pleasure. We've got friends for life now."

Every fall, without fail, the emails would start trickling in to the sports department at the *Telegram*, the St. John's daily. As the hockey season began to rev up, so would the inquiries from across the province. "Are you doing The List again this year?" "Is The List out yet?" "When is the List coming out?"

For more than thirty years, until its curator retired, the sports department at the newspaper managed Newfoundlanders Away, a weekly list that kept track of players who left the province to pursue a career in hockey, whether in the United States, overseas, or elsewhere in Canada. Sometimes The List was long; other times it was short. But it was always a must-read. Because when it comes to hockey, Newfoundlanders follow their own, whether it is a player from Corner Brook or St. John's or a pair of players from Bonavista.

From Mount Pearl, Adrian and I begin the drive west on the Trans-Canada. About two hours in, we turn onto Highway 230 and follow it northeast to the end. Bonavista is the slightly pared-down version of "O buona vista!" meaning "Oh happy sight!" These were the first words uttered by Giovanni Caboto when he landed on the tip of a peninsula on Newfoundland's northeast coast in 1497 and whose Anglicized name, John Cabot, now rests upon the local arena.

Around these parts, though, a couple of hockey players come quicker to mind than some long-dead Italian explorer. The names Michael Ryder and Adam Pardy carry a lot of weight around Bonavista. Only thirty-one Newfoundlanders have ever made it to the NHL, and only three have won the Stanley Cup, so having two NHL players, one a Stanley Cup champion, from a small town like Bonavista is about as unlikely as an encounter with an unfriendly Newfoundlander.

After retiring from the NHL, Ryder settled in St. John's. Pardy did, too, but his family is still back in Bonavista, including his parents, who own a guesthouse in town where we bunk for the weekend, and his older brother, Todd, who played senior hockey against Terry Ryan Jr. With his brother on vacation, Todd offers to give us a tour of Bonavista.

"My car probably smells like hockey gear," he says. "But jump in."

On the outskirts of town, Bonavista greets visitors with a pair of billboards outside Cabot Stadium: one of Ryder, dressed in the bold black and gold of the Boston Bruins, and the other of Pardy, in the fiery red and yellow of the Calgary Flames. All across Canada, signs like these, praising local NHL progeny, are often the first thing tourists see on their way into town: Sidney Crosby and Nathan MacKinnon in Cole Harbour, Nova Scotia; Jordan Binnington in Richmond Hill, Ontario; Claude Giroux in Hearst, Ontario; Jordin Tootoo in Rankin Inlet, Nunavut; and Zach Whitecloud in Sioux Valley Dakota Nation, Manitoba. Radisson Saskatchewan's Bill Hajt is probably the only player in the world to have had both a welcome sign and his own personalized fire hydrant. Kelvington and Foam Lake, Saskatchewan, portray the players they've catapulted to the NHL on oversized hockey cards, while the tiny farming community of Foxwarren, Manitoba, proudly lists the five it's produced on its welcome sign. It is through these and other players that many people learn the bits of small-town Canadian geography they know. After all, if not for Bobby Orr, few would know about Parry Sound, Ontario, and if not for Gordie Howe, even fewer would've ever heard of Floral, Saskatchewan. It is only because of Ryder and Pardy that I can now place Bonavista on a map.

Todd drives us to the other side of town, where the water tower looms over Bonavista near the cemetery.

"Michael Ryder Place is up here," Todd says as he drives past the cemetery. "And this is Adam Pardy Drive."

Ryder and Pardy are not alone in having a stretch of asphalt named after them, although only all-time greats get a multilane highway: Wayne Gretzky Parkway in Brantford; Autoroute Guy-Lafleur outside Montreal; and the Gordie Howe Bridge in Saskatoon. Hall of Famers, coaches, checking centers, and others have been so honored, even fighters—there is a Jody Shelley Drive in Yarmouth, Nova Scotia, named for a player who racked up 1,538 penalty minutes in just 627 NHL games.

Both Ryder and Pardy are important sons not only to Bonavista but to all of Newfoundland. Ryder won the Stanley Cup in 2011 with the Bruins and retired in 2015 with the most points ever in the NHL by a Newfoundlander, while Pardy, after nine seasons in the NHL, signed for one last hurrah at age thirty-four with the fledgling Newfoundland Growlers of the East Coast Hockey League. It was a storybook ending for a player from a province full of storytellers. Pardy ended his career by winning the league title, the Kelly Cup, in the team's first season.

"First pro championship in Newfoundland history," Todd says. "I'm a Leafs fan, so I'll take it."

"We are too," Adrian and I say in unison.

"Oh, you are, eh? My dad is a diehard Leafs fan. Oh my god, he's nuts. He's worse than me. Thinks they're gonna win the Stanley Cup every year."

"So you became a Leafs fan because of your dad?" I ask.

"For sure, yeah. I got brainwashed."

"I think that's how it happens for everybody."

"It's the only way," Adrian adds.

Our mutual pain shared, Todd drops us off at our guesthouse.

"Welcome to France!" says Fab Guérin. "First time in Saint-Pierre & Miquelon?"

"First time anywhere in France," Adrian replies.

After leaving Bonavista, Adrian and I had driven down to the town of Fortune on the Burin Peninsula and left Gumpy in the parking lot at the ferry terminal for the ride across Fortune Bay. When we docked two hours later, we were greeted by Fab, a portly Frenchman in his early fifties, who'd taken the day off to show us around France's lone remaining

North American outpost from its battles with Britain and to let us in on the archipelago's long-standing archrivalry.

"Half the people in France have heard of Saint-Pierre & Miquelon, the other half have never heard of it," Fab says. "But of those who've heard of Saint-Pierre & Miquelon, about half of them think we live in the Caribbean with heat and all kinds of sunshine, like St. Maarten, while the other half think we're freezing because they think we're close to Greenland, even though we're at the same latitude as Paris."

Officially a territorial collectivity, Saint-Pierre & Miquelon is a group of islands off the southern coast of Newfoundland. Described in its visitors' guide as "France, like nowhere else," it has its own time zone (half an hour ahead of Newfoundland), runs on the Euro, and has all the accoutrements of France. There are Renaults, Peugeots, and Citroëns on the stoplight-less streets, as well as croissants, baguettes, and Bordeaux in the shops, and the same tricolor flag and the language, although not quite continental French. The streets are narrow, some even cobblestoned. Parking is a similar free-for-all as it is in Paris, and following the French fashion, the signage says STOP, not ARRÊT as in Quebec. Yet in many ways Saint-Pierre & Miquelon is less like its French compatriots and more like its Canadian cousins. It is 3,818 kilometers (2,373 miles) from the nearest city in France, but just 19 kilometers (12 miles) from Newfoundland. Its colorful homes, a tradition stemming from when fishers would paint their houses the same color as their dories, look like those in St. John's. Its short summers, long winters, and fierce winds are akin to Atlantic Canada's, as are its tiny fir trees, white-tailed deer, foxes, rabbits, and wild horses. Its terrain is even rockier than the Rock's, so there are many above-ground tombs in the cemetery. There are also many Canadian products in the stores, including those dietary mainstays that the territory shares with Newfoundland: cod, salmon, and lobster. And then there's hockey.

"When I go to Canada, I say we're French," Fab says. "But when I go to France, I say I'm Canadian."

After checking us into our hotel, Fab takes us on a tour of the island of Saint-Pierre, where most of the six thousand people live, and then over to the Patinoire de Saint-Pierre to show us around the only indoor arena. When we walk in, the rink is empty and the ice is thin. Adrian had been planning to make Saint-Pierre & Miquelon flag number forty-four on his stick bag, only to find out days before we arrived that the Zamboni had been sent to Montreal for repairs. The first few layers of ice had been laid down, but the icemakers could alchemize no more until the Zamboni returned. As I talk with Fab, beside a No Spitting sign in English, l can see Adrian looking longingly upon the ice from the players' benches.

The ice is covered in logos, not in the jumbled stew of a European hockey jersey, but neatly arranged around the center circle. Two catch my eye: one is the head of a large cat, fangs bared, eyes dilated; the other is a sophisticated winged crest with a three-mast ship set inside the French flag.

The Cougars and the Missiles.

With only enough players for the two-team Ligue de Hockey de Saint-Pierre et Miquelon, the history of pro hockey on the archipelago boils down to one decades-long rivalry, which extends well beyond the ice. Allegiances are pledged within families and passed down from generation to generation, to either the green and black of the Cougars or the blue and yellow of the Missiles.

"Normally one family is one team, and it's the same for soccer, so it's crazy," Fab says. "There's a guy in the eighties, Cougar, and his daughter who was maybe twenty-five or thirty at that time. The Missiles scored a goal and she applauded because it was a nice goal. He slapped her in the face because she was not allowed to applaud for a goal for the Missiles. Some people are crazy."

"So would the Cougars and Missiles be like Toronto and Montreal?" I ask.

"Some nights it's more like Montreal and Boston."

After a late afternoon siesta, Adrian and I meet Fab for dinner at a local restaurant, with plans to carry on to a bar to watch the Maple Leafs and the Canadiens play their first game of the season.

"I got hooked with traveling to play hockey," Adrian says. "It's so easy to get hooked on this. You're gonna meet friends, right? Like, we came here and we met you and now we're having a meal together, talking about hockey, and we're gonna go watch a game."

"It's an easy connection," Fab says.

Fab's connection to the game came through Canada. During World War II, his grandfather was stationed in the French army at Signal Hill in Newfoundland, patrolling Bell Island and St. John's Harbour for German U-boats. With the war drawing to a close in 1945, he got to see his first NHL game. It was in Montreal, at the fabled Forum, and Maurice Richard was on the ice. When he returned to Saint-Pierre & Miquelon after the war, he was asked to be part of the committee to form a hockey team here. With no arena at the time, they practiced and played outside. It wasn't until 1956 that the archipelago got its first indoor arena and could start a league.

I ask Fab to paint us a picture of the hockey culture in Saint-Pierre & Miquelon. As president of the hockey federation, he has just the example to relay in his not-quite-fluent English.

"I used to go out with a girl twenty-five years ago, and we were with her grandmother one time at the other arena, the old one," Fab says. "The older arena, the boards were wood, and no plexiglass. People could lean on the board watching the game, so you can grab a player. There was a team from Bonavista playing the Cougar, and the grandmother of my ex was crazy about the Cougar. There was a big guy playing for Bonavista with a big beard. She took a lighter and she light. Out of the arena for two years!"

I would've said it was a very Canadian thing for that little old lady to do, but I'd never heard of a Canadian hockey fan trying to set an opposition player on fire.

Despite small numbers and limited internal competition, players from Saint-Pierre & Miquelon often make the jump to France's top league, the Ligue Magnus, as well as the national team. Many earn a reputation for being heavy hitters and physical players, for playing like Canadians. There is some truth to that. After all, they are the descendants of fishers, not cherry pickers, and they come from a little-known rocky outcrop in the

Atlantic Ocean, far from the boulevards and side streets of Paris or the vineyards in the French countryside. Like Newfoundland in Canada, Saint-Pierre & Miquelon is known in mainland France as *le Caillou* ("the Rock"), and the players it sends there are referred to as *les gars du cailloux* ("rockmen") by their teammates.

"Arnaud Briand, he's the guy with the best career from Saint-Pierre," Fab says. "He was named the French national team captain and was voted France's best player for two years."

A dual citizen born in Sydney, Nova Scotia, Briand represented France at ten World Championships and four Winter Olympics. Although years removed from his playing days, Arnaud remains a legend back home. He now lives in Montreal but still has family in Saint-Pierre & Miquelon, and he was visiting while we were there. So Fab had wrangled up his childhood buddy and told him to meet us at the bar, where we could watch the game.

"I guess he's a Canadiens fan," Adrian says.

"I hope so," Fab says. "So it's going to be two against two. I'm not alone anymore. Shall we go? We're going to see the Habs win tonight."

When Arnaud arrives in the middle of second period, he and I get talking while Adrian and Fab chirp each other and yell at the TV. Born just two months apart in 1970, Fab and Arnaud were inseparable as kids. Both fell for the game through their grandfathers, watching the Canadiens on the CBC feed from Newfoundland every Saturday night. That is how Fab taught himself English. As kids, they learned to play the game through road hockey on the hilly streets of Saint-Pierre, eventually graduating to the ice at the Patinoire de Saint-Pierre when it opened in 1984, Fab as a goalie and Arnaud as a high-flying forward. Arnaud worked his way up to the Ligue Magnus in France, where he played for all but two of his sixteen seasons. (Fab had a brief stint in the Ligue Magnus, too, in the late 1980s.) Although Arnaud is a Cougar and Fab a Missile, the two remain close friends.

"We're the same age," Arnaud says. "We used to play hockey together, we used to play soccer together, and we used to be in the same class together at school. We used to go to his place to play hockey on the swimming pool. His parents had a swimming pool, and they put some boards and some wood to cover it."

Arnaud and I both glance at the TV. The Canadiens' young guns Nick Suzuki and Cole Caufield are buzzing the Leafs' goaltender.

"Oh, no, take your guy!" Fab shouts.

"Suzuki, eh?" Adrian says.

Maybe it was because Arnaud had been raised in Saint-Pierre & Miquelon, and not Canada, but he'd proven that players can have a long and successful pro career outside the NHL and make a good living elsewhere in the world.

"From nineteen years old to thirty-five, I was a professional hockey player, full time," he says. "I went back to school briefly, but I got a salary to play hockey. Not millions or anything. Good time. My house was paid, my car, my kids' school paid, university paid, so just play hockey. Not bad. You have fun, you have friends, you drink some beer. I had a nice time."

"Yes, Caufield again!" Fab shouts. "Two-two. Uh buh buh buh bing!"

"That's not a good goal," Adrian says of the Leafs' goaltender. "That would bother the shit out of me."

I look over my shoulder to watch the replay, then turn back to Arnaud.

"How did you know you wanted to be a hockey player?"

Arnaud points at the TV.

"We grew up with that," he says. "Somebody ask me, 'Why you play hockey?' Look what I was watching on TV. It was the beginning of Gretzky and the Nordiques. And I said, 'I want to do that.'"

When Arnaud leaves, I turn back to the TV to watch the end of the game. The Canadiens and Leafs trade goals in the third period. Then, with time ticking down and the game tied, Fab gets to gloat.

"Seventeen point nine seconds," he says. "Game over!"

Adrian berates the Leafs' goalie. "Oh, fuck off! That's shit! Fucking useless! That's the way the fucking Leafs' season is going to be. That's the fucking Leafs."

Under the blare of Bruce Springsteen's "Born in the USA" pounding from the bar, Adrian then turns to Fab. "You're loving it, eh?"

"Of course!"

"Born to lose," Adrian says. "That's the Leafs. Why do I watch this shit?"

The Maritimes:
Origin Road

In the matter of origins, hockey is riven by dispute. At times the riving has been rancorous. If it were a road we were talking about, it would be a riven, rutted, rancorous road. Its shoulders would be narrow. Its corner would be blind. Never on any road would you have seen so much heaving, or roadkill. —Stephen Smith, *Puckstruck*

I N 1935, THE Herder family, who published the St. John's *Telegram*, donated the Herder Memorial Trophy to crown an annual provincial senior hockey champion. It would become the Stanley Cup of Newfoundland. These were the heydays of hockey in Newfoundland, but they were also the days before the Trans-Canada, so the only way to get anywhere was by train. Teams would have to travel as long as two days to play each other, as the Corner Brook Royals did in 1935, traveling thirty-two hours by train to St. John's, to win the inaugural Herder Cup.

After returning to Fortune, it takes Adrian and me an easy ten hours by road to drive across the Rock to Port aux Basques on Newfoundland's west coast to grab the ferry to Nova Scotia.

Eight hours later, groggy and grumpy from a listless sleep on the cleanest piece of filthy ferry floor we could find, we head south on Highway 125.

Our destination is Sydney's Centre 200 arena, home of the Cape Breton Eagles, the most-traveled team in the Quebec Maritimes Junior Hockey League. We have a rendezvous with John Hanna Jr., the team's assistant general manager.

John knows the rigors of the road well. He rode the bus for four years with the Ottawa 67's, winning the Memorial Cup in 1984. He then returned home to play for the Cape Breton Oilers, the farm team of the firewagon Edmonton Oilers at the time. The script was there to be written: local boy comes home to star with the minor pro team in his hometown. Even though he had seven goals and sixteen points in twenty games, John decided to turn down the team's contract offer and call it a career.

"I knew my limitations," he says. "I was a career minor-leaguer. My mom and dad were always, 'No, get your education.'"

"Further than either of us ever got," I say.

Adrian played junior hockey, while I didn't even make it that far. Yet for whatever reason in Canada, it is always former players who came within striking distance of the NHL who seem to have to apologize for their careers. If the NHL were Mount Everest, John's career would've taken him to base camp, while Adrian and I would've made it no farther than a dirty hostel in Kathmandu.

After a tour of the Eagles' training room, dressing room, and offices, John takes us over to the John Junior Hanna Concourse, named for his father. Above the entranceway to the seats hang photos and jerseys of inductees into Sydney's Hockey Heritage Hall of Fame. Among them are several Lebanese players, including John's close friend Fabian Joseph, cousin Kevin Morrison, and his dad.

We follow John outside to the casino right next door, where the old Sydney Forum once stood. Like so many young Lebanese rink rats born and raised in Sydney, John's father spent much of his childhood at the old barn on the edge of the town's Lebanese neighborhood, known locally as the Gaza Strip, despite that being in Palestine. A mural on the casino shows what the arena looked like before it was torn down. In it, kids are walking to the rink with their gear, many coming from the strip, an area of about six blocks near the arena. When Lebanon split from Syria after World War I, dozens of Lebanese families came to Canada and settled in Sydney. Some, like John's grandfather, the first John Hanna, worked at the coal mine or the steel plant. Many others opened businesses on the strip.

"The old joke was that the Lebanese couldn't play hockey," John says, "because every time they went into a corner, they wanted to open a store."

In its day, the Sydney Forum had a hatch at the back where workers would dump snow after cleaning the ice, forming a snowbank that kids from the strip would climb up to sneak into the arena for after-hours hockey. It was here that John's father honed the skills that would propel him to Broadway, with the New York Rangers, paving the way for other Lebanese players to the NHL.

John turns and points toward Townsend Street, about a block south of the casino.

"That's the Gaza Strip right there," he says as we walk toward it. "The area is a little old and beat up right now."

Overgrown grass between a row of gray-shaded warehouses gives it the rundown look of a deserted industrial area. Two-foot-high weeds sprout around a lonely parking meter in front of a brown and gray boarded-up barber shop.

We continue walking, past the local Rona outlet and over train tracks. We cross the street to the Steel City Sports Bar & Steakhouse, a local Lebanese-owned haunt where older Eagles fans gather before games. We turn right at Kay's Kozy Korner and make our way to the center of the neighborhood, the gray-brick Cedars Club. There, the Hanna, Joseph, Haddad, Livvi, Abbass, and other Lebanese families who'd settled on the strip and stayed generation after generation celebrate birthdays and weddings, or just get together. Closed at this early morning hour, the club is still a staple of the strip.

"They used to have pictures of people like my father and Kevin Morrison and Fabian Joseph," John says. "I had a little picture in there. Anyone from the strip who was involved in the hockey world was in there."

John then leads us into the residential part of the strip. Here, too, homes have been color-coded for fishers returning home. Some of the houses are painted beige or gray, others in pastels of green, yellow, red, or blue, many with white shutters and doors. A few are white, like the Joseph family home. In all, the Josephs had fourteen children, the last of whom would be drafted by the Maple Leafs and go on to win two silver medals for Canada at the Winter Olympics.

"Of course, the story goes it took his mom and dad fourteen tries to finally get a superstar," John says. "And that was Fabian."

Nearby is a large white house that has a sizeable yard next to a parking lot. It was here that John's grandfather had settled and where John's father was raised. Houses like this were called Hanna Blocks, bigger buildings with many family members living in them. The Hannas had an outdoor rink on the property where the men would play hockey after dinner. As a kid, John's father tried to play, too, but was always shooed away.

"My dad's sister, who was a bigger lady, she used to come out, put her fist up, with a purse in one hand, 'You let him play or you're all getting it!'" John says. "That's how he got his start in hockey. If he didn't have his big sister looking out after him, he might never have played."

On our way back to the arena, John pulls out his phone to show us a photo of his father's hockey card. On the front, against a black-and-yellow background, is a waist-up photo of John Hanna Junior, in Rangers red, white, and blue. Clean-shaven with short dark-brown hair, he had the shy half-smile of someone who knew he belonged in the NHL. On the back of the card is a caricature of a player in an Arab headdress and robe, bearing down with the puck on a terrified opponent.

"It says he's the first player of Syrian extract to play in the NHL," John says. "At the time, he was originally from a Syrian family, but he was Lebanese. Maybe in the old country and the Middle East there's conflict, but here there's no conflict between the Lebanese and Syrians."

"How did he feel about this card?" I ask.

"Didn't bother him at all. He was proud of his heritage. He was proud to have an NHL hockey card."

We jump into John's pickup and drive to George Street on the other side of the strip. As John pulls around a corner, he spots a man in beige slippers, gray shorts, a long-sleeved navy shirt, and a beaten-up cap sitting on the porch of an old house.

"This is perfect, guys," John says. "That's Kevin Morrison sitting on the step here."

We park and walk over.

"I've got a couple of gentlemen I wanna introduce you to," John says.

Clean-shaven and gray-haired, when I later researched Kevin's career and flipped through old photos of him, many were of a player who looked like he'd come straight out of the cult movie *Slap Shot*, with wild black hair, sideburns, and a menacing mustache.

"So I was telling them about how you went end-to-end and slid it to Wayne Gretzky for his first goal," John says.

"That's the way I remember it," Kevin says and laughs.

The story has morphed over time since it happened on October 20, 1978, shortly after Gretzky turned pro with the Indianapolis Racers of the World Hockey Association (WHA). Which version Kevin tells depends on who he's talking to. When a CBC reporter came by on the fortieth anniversary of Gretzky's first pro goal and asked Kevin how it went down, "I said, 'I picked the puck up behind the net and I went up and deked everybody out and I slid it out front and he top-shelved it,'" Kevin recalls. "Then after he shut the camera off, he asked, 'What really happened?' I said, 'I stepped out from behind our net, hit him at the red line, and he went in and scored. But my version sounds a lot better.'"

Dave Semenko is credited with keeping Gretzky safe in Edmonton during the NHL's goon era. But before Semenko, before Gretzky even made it to the NHL, a cadre of players with the Racers were tasked with protecting Gretzky in the WHA, at a time when fights were almost as frequent as goals and teenage superstars had a target on their back. Among Gretzky's security detail was Kevin, one of several rough and tough Lebanese players from Sydney who fought their way from the strip to the pros.

Although Gretzky's time in Indianapolis was short, no one did dare touch the scrawny seventeen-year-old, who was all of 160 pounds when he joined the team. Decades later, after both had long since retired from the game and lost touch, Kevin ran into his old Racers teammate at an autograph session in Newfoundland. Gretzky recognized him right away and thanked Kevin again for helping shepherd him safely to the Oilers.

"It was tough hockey back then, eh?" I ask.

"Oh yes, anybody that was suspended in any league was in our league," Kevin says and then points toward himself. "And guess who gets to fight them?"

"Yeah, you were Gretzky's first protector," Adrian says.

"Well, there was four of us on the line," Kevin says. "He'd go on the ice and there was me, I was 210 pounds, my defense partner, he was 240 pounds, and his two wingers were 230 pounds each. So he had about nine hundred pounds with him. He only lasted eight games with us, but he never forgot."

Although he could fight, Kevin had been no goon. His lone season in the NHL came at the end of a long career in the minor pro leagues and the WHA. Over his six years in the WHA, he played in several all-star games and was the first defenseman to get a hat trick and the first to score twenty goals in a season. He remains one of the highest-scoring defensemen in league history.

But the role of enforcer had taken its toll on Kevin. Now in his seventies, he's had both knees replaced and moves around slowly. The last time he got on the ice was for the inaugural Lebanese and Syrian Heritage Hockey Game, before the pandemic. It paid tribute to the community's connection to the game, and to players like Kevin who made it from a strip in small-town Sydney all the way to the NHL.

"I wouldn't trade it for a minute," Kevin says. "I'd do it over. Maybe a little bit better money."

Mark Pottie sits beside me as he recalls what little he remembers from that night. A dead ringer for the actor Billy Bob Thornton, with a black cap of his Detroit Red Wings tucked tightly over his eyes, his voice is barely audible over the din of the dressing room.

After making the five-hour drive to Halifax, Adrian and I have ended up at Centennial Arena in the city's Fairview neighborhood for a night of pickup hockey. While we get ready in the dressing room, we watch as, one after another, Mark's beer-league brothers come up to their longtime teammate, happy to see him but half in disbelief that he is still alive. It hasn't been but ten days since he almost died right there on the ice.

"How ya feeling?" one of the players asks.

"Ah, I feel great. No complaints," Mark replies. "Only that I can't come out and play hockey."

"Good thing you're alive, man," says another, who'd seen Mark interviewed on TV the night before. "I caught that yesterday. I said, 'Ah, I'll just check the news,' and I'm like, 'Oh, Pottie's in the news, that's wild.' And then I'm like, 'Oh, fuck.'"

"I know," Mark says. "I say, 'Oh, fuck' every day I'm vertical."

"I still get goosebumps every time I see you now, bud," says a third.

One by one, they keep coming, some looking like they've seen a man resurrected from the dead.

"You got a lot of friends here," I say to Mark when the handshake line finally ends.

"Oh, brother, you wouldn't believe it," he says. "When I woke up, by the time I got my phone there must've been a hundred messages on it. A lot of hockey. And they just kept rolling in all week."

Mark remembered little from that night, so others had to fill in the blanks. He'd just scored a goal and was skating up the side boards for the faceoff at center ice when he collapsed. It looked like he'd just caught an edge, but he didn't put his hands up in front of him to break his fall. He went down like a boxer knocked out cold before hitting the canvas.

He was unresponsive. So they called 911 while one of the players grabbed the arena's AED (defibrillator) machine.

They got to work, cutting Mark's jersey to get him out of his gear and putting him on a backboard so that he wouldn't get cold lying on the ice. By then, Mark had started going into convulsions, so they began doing compressions, two pairs of players doing thirty thrusts at a time.

By the time paramedics arrived, they'd gotten a heartbeat. On the way to the hospital, Mark had a heart attack in the ambulance, but he would wake up with no more than broken ribs.

"I died, but there was no light that I can remember, the Old Man wasn't waiting for me," he says. "I woke up, and if they wouldn't have told me, I wouldn't have known. I would've thought I got hit by a Mack truck, but that's about it."

According to Mark, it wasn't the dozen or so games a week he usually plays that caused his heart to fail that night but a congenital heart condition that happened to hit him when he was on the ice. Now fifty-one years old, he's long known his condition is genetic, a ticking time bomb of two blocked arteries: one that is completely shut and the other nearly three-quarters plugged. But the risk isn't enough to stop Mark from playing. Within a month, he tells me, he'll be back on the ice.

"Yeah, I got hockey problems."

In the morning, Adrian and I drive across the Narrows, through Halifax's sister city, Dartmouth, and over to the Black Cultural Centre for Nova Scotia. Outside, between two large concrete pillars, stands the center's large gray Freedom Stone, "dedicated to the memory of our ancestors and their quest for liberty." We walk into the lobby and meet RCMP Sgt. Craig Smith.

On top of his full-time post as site commander of the Lower Sackville detachment, Craig has a volunteer position running the African Nova Scotian Experience Workshop to help educate officers on how to better serve diverse communities. What began as a one-day workshop at local detachments had morphed into a five-day course that was taking him across the country. It will become his full-time job once he retires from his detachment in two years.

"Sometimes people don't know the history that exists within the country," Craig says as he leads us upstairs to the mezzanine. "As I go across the country speaking and doing presentations, people are always completely blown away. They say, 'Well, how long have Black people been in Nova Scotia?' And I say, 'Okay, my mom was descendent of the Black loyalists in 1873. My dad was a descendent of the Black refugees, and that was 1812, 1813.' They're always thinking like you're one or two generations as opposed to five or six. And that's in our own country, let alone south of the border. They got no clue whatsoever."

Craig spent the previous five years as president of the center and has written six books on African Nova Scotian history and culture. "Chronicling firsts and Black firsts in history is the passion," he says as we reach the Black Ice Hockey and Sports Hall of Fame exhibit, tucked into a corner under the sloping roof, brightly lit under the buzzing of a fluorescent light.

Among those firsts was the Colored Hockey League of the Maritimes (CHLM), formed in Halifax in 1895 by a group of preachers and lawyers who were sons and grandsons of escaped slaves. Lasting for thirty years, at its height the CHLM had about a hundred players and a dozen teams spread throughout the Maritimes. The teams had names like the Jubilees, Stanleys, Eurekas, Sea-Sides, Rangers, Royals, and Victorias, each carrying a subliminal meaning, including the Moss Backs, an allusion to how runaway slaves found their way to Canada at night by following the moss that grew on the north side of dead trees.

"The one good thing about newspapers in those days, because you had no TV, they really made it vivid to what you were reading," Craig says. "A lot of stuff talks about how exciting the style of play was in that league as opposed to the White leagues. You hear them talk about large crowds, about the play on the ice and it being so much different than the White leagues, more acrobatic and more sensationalized."

The CHLM was rooted in Nova Scotia's Black Baptist churches. One of the league's main recruiting hubs was the old Cornwallis Street Baptist

Church, which iced two teams, the Halifax Eurekas and the Halifax Stanleys, drawing players from the tenements along nearby Gottingen Street. Since renamed New Horizons Baptist Church, the old church was the hub of Black hockey and the organizational center of the CHLM. The league gave birth to stars like Henry Sylvester Williams, James Johnston, and James Kinney, as well as Eddie Martin, the first player to take a slapshot, and Henry "Braces" Franklyn, the first goalie to drop to his knees to stop a shot, a precursor to the butterfly style that dominates goaltending today.

The CHLM paved the way for other Black players to follow, many of whom we find on display at the center, including Herb Carnegie, a trailblazing player from the forties and fifties who received three offers to play for the New York Rangers. He turned them all down to stay with the Quebec Aces of the Quebec Senior Hockey League, where he played with Jean Béliveau and earned more money than the Rangers offered him.

"Of course, Herb Carnegie is the guy who Conn Smythe made the comment that he'd give ten thousand dollars to anybody who could turn him White," Craig says.

Craig continues as we inch our way through the exhibit. There is Manny McIntyre, part of the first all-Black line in pro hockey, alongside the Carnegie brothers, Herb and Ossie. Art Dorrington, the first Black player to sign an NHL contract, after being drafted by the New York Rangers. And Percy Paris, Bob Dawson, and Darrell Maxwell, the first all-Black line in Canadian university hockey. Several others aren't yet on display but surely will be when the center gets more space: people like John Paris Jr., the first Black coach and general manager in pro hockey, who was born in nearby Windsor, as well as Bill Riley, who was the first of several Black Nova Scotians to play in the NHL.

Craig begins to list some of them off. "Guys like Darren Beals, Craig Martin . . ."

"Pokey Reddick," Adrian chimes in, mentioning the Halifax-born goalie who had a long and successful pro career, some of it in the NHL.

"Exactly," Craig says. "You think of those who came after the fact, this is what laid the foundation for all of that. My wife's from North Preston, and so she talks about growing up with her brothers and uncles playing hockey on the ponds and the lakes up there. My mom is from New Glasgow. Same thing. She said, 'We could skate before we could swim.' Because you go out on the ponds and on the lakes, and what do we have in Nova Scotia? A whole lotta lakes and ponds. So they knew how to play."

The NHL came into existence just as the CHLM began to decline during World War I. When the No. 2 Construction Battalion, the first all-Black battalion in Canadian history, was formed, many of the unit's soldiers were men who'd either played or were involved in the CHLM. Those who made it home to Nova Scotia tried to find jobs and restart their lives, including resurrecting the league. But little had changed for them, despite having gone to war for their country. The CHLM eventually folded and its history was ignored. The Hockey Hall of Fame has not a single artifact of the league on display.

"I think you make the country better," Craig says, "if we talk about everybody's story."

Attempting to pin down hockey's origins is a mug's game. Many places claim the genesis of the game: Ottawa, Montreal, Kingston, Pictou, Deline, Dartmouth, Halifax. But the boldest claim of all comes from Windsor, Nova Scotia. The renowned Society for International Hockey Research long ago rejected it, but that hasn't deterred Windsor from keeping it alive. In 2017, town council even applied to have Highway 101 between Halifax and Windsor renamed Hockey Way.

It takes about an hour for Adrian and me to drive up the highway to Windsor, twinned with Cooperstown, New York, where baseball is said to have been born. If Windsor's claim is to be believed, hockey as we know it began on a pond in back of a pumpkin farm on the outskirts of town.

Skeptics might note that this claim rests on author Thomas Haliburton's fictional writings about Long Pond in the early 1800s. Still, so hallowed is the pond that *Sports Illustrated* named it one of the seven wonders of the hockey world.

The pond sits back of the Dill family farm, which is almost as old as hockey itself. From the parking lot, the gravel walkway, lined with tiny pumpkins, leads past a large pumpkin costumed as a rooster up to the sales office and souvenir shop. Two large autumn trees flanking the building nearly match the big bright-orange pumpkin out front. Above it, a large sign reads:

LONG POND

BIRTHPLACE

OF HOCKEY

Windsor, N.S.

c. 1800

Property of HOWARD DILL

"Pumpkins and hockey," says Danny Dill as he walks out from the family farmhouse to greet us. They've been the two main constants in Danny's life, just as they were for his late father, Howard, whose email address Danny still uses to communicate. For five generations, the farm has been part of the Dill family, and with it the legendary Long Pond.

Adrian and I follow Danny into the souvenir shop, his tall, sinewy frame barely filling out his blue jeans and light-gray Birthplace of Hockey hoodie. Shelves, tables, walls, everything is covered in team and player photos, newspaper clippings, sticks, mini-sticks, banners, mugs, caps, bobbleheads, hockey cards, and bottle caps with NHL team logos. There is an original set of skates made around the mid-1800s, a seat from the fabled Forum in Montreal (Section 311, Row A, Seat 3), a signed black-and-white photo of Bobby Orr soaring through the air after scoring the most famous goal in NHL history, and a set of Russian hockey cards that Adrian buys for $20. On the table, a pumpkin-shaped orange sticky note reminds visitors, "Nice To Handle. Nice To Hold. If You Break It. Consider It Sold."

Down on one of the lower shelves, Adrian catches sight of a board game, a Monopoly knock-off called Pond Hockey-Opoly.

"I found it in a local store in town," Danny says. "I looked at and said, 'Well, geez, we're there too.' They had all the stops. Probably some of these places you're going to."

Adrian and I look over the locations.

Long Pond, Roulston Lake, Parry Sound, even Gretzky's backyard rink in Brantford. They all check.

Danny points to a shelf. "They're a bunch of old pucks that came out of the pond," he says. In various states of decay, some have inscriptions carved into them, like "1919 KCS," for King's College School, which borders the farm, while others bear names of students. Many are more than a hundred years old.

"God knows how many are back there still buried," he says.

Danny leads us back outside and points the way to Long Pond. His life in the game is inseparable from his life as a pumpkin farmer. Named after the legendary broadcaster Danny Gallivan, with whom he shares the same birthday, he's been working on the family farm his entire life. As Adrian and I begin walking toward the pond, we see the pairing everywhere. A ten-foot-high hockey stick propped up against a barn sits beside a giant 1,187-pound green pumpkin resting on a pallet. Along the path behind the barn, a Canadiens goalie made out of plywood directs visitors to the pond. Flanked by pumpkin fields, the path is lined with "Didja Know?" signs, relaying hockey lore about the game's precursors:

The boys from King's College School founded in 1788 were playing "hurley on the long pond" and "ball o'er the ice" between 1800–1836.

As we near Long Pond, we come to more signage. One is a blue-toned rendering of a pond hockey game going on in the dead of winter, another a drawing of an unnamed Maple Leaf. A third, a sketch of hockey's first superstar, Frank McGee from the legendary Silver Seven, greets us in front of the pond, where a weatherworn wooden bench, half surrounded by trees, reflects off the water.

On the hill to our right is the school. Since the 1700s, students have been walking down the hill through the woods to play on Long Pond. The water has stories from four centuries to tell. Many more pucks are buried in the bottom, perhaps a stick or two, maybe even a set of skates. Part of me is wistful for winter, filled with regret for not being able to skate on the pond. But I knew I couldn't cram the entire road trip into winter, so some of the stops would have to come in fall and spring. Instead, Adrian and I walk through the long grass to dip our hands in the holy water of Long Pond, seeking a blessing as we continue on our way through the Maritimes.

Back to the souvenir shop, Danny is waiting for us with Adrian's purchase in hand. Adrian asks Danny if he can get a photo with him.

"Back here, have hockey in the background," Danny says, making sure to stand in front of the packed shelves. "You're not here for pumpkins, you're here for hockey."

Long before the Confederation Bridge was built, a daily steamer shuttled people across the Northumberland Strait between Nova Scotia and Prince Edward Island. It ran year-round, stopping only in winter if the ice became difficult to navigate. When it did, an iceboat would be the only way across.

During hockey season, it was not uncommon for teams in the Colored Hockey League of the Maritimes to take an iceboat across the strait. Charlottetown's West End Rangers once had to endure a seven-hour ride to catch the train for a game in Halifax against the Eurekas. In March 1907, a local team called the Abbies was nearing the end of a five-day trip home from St. John's, when an ice floe trapped their ship for a month as it was crossing the strait. It wasn't until April that the ice relented and allowed the team to return home.

Once on Prince Edward Island, Adrian and I drive north on a series of two-lane potholed highways up the eastern part of the province. When we arrive in the town of Montague, Cornelius Van Ewyk greets us at his home, all pink-faced, white-haired, black-shirted, and smiling warmly as his harmless dog, Benny, yaps at our heels. He then leads us to a room off the front hallway. Inside, framed photos hang from the off-yellow walls above three glass-topped, handcrafted, wooden cabinets. The thin drawers within contain shelf after shelf after shelf of hockey cards, all of one player.

Cornelius was only eleven years old when his family emigrated from the Netherlands in the 1950s. Even though he's lived in Canada most of his life, he'd never been much of a hockey fan until he married his second wife, Lorna, in 2004. It was shortly after their wedding that her younger cousin, Brad Richards, from nearby Murray Harbour, came home to Prince Edward Island that summer with the Stanley Cup after winning it with the Tampa Bay Lightning.

"That's when I started this collection," Cornelius says.

"Did you ever play hockey?" Adrian asks.

Cornelius had never played. "I grew up on a farm, and all you do is farm," he tells us. For him, collecting cards of his famous cousin-in-law was his way of getting into the game. When Cornelius started his collection, Richards had played only four years in the NHL, all with the Lightning, so it didn't take Cornelius long to catch up. Then he began working backward into Richards's teenage years with the Rimouski Océanic of the Quebec Maritimes Junior Hockey League. But then Richards started changing uniforms as his NHL career continued, jumping to the Dallas Stars, then to the New York Rangers, Chicago Blackhawks, and Detroit Red Wings, winning the Stanley Cup once more and becoming the best player ever from Prince Edward Island. His hockey cards proliferated in step, and Cornelius found it harder and harder to find them all. There were also several outliers to hunt down, like one of Richards in the red, white, and green jersey of Ak Bars Kazan, his name spelled out in Cyrillic, from his short stint in Russia's Kontinental Hockey League. Cornelius put each card in its own protective case and, a carpenter by trade, built the cabinets himself to house them all.

"What does Brad think of all this?" I ask.

"I have no idea," Cornelius replies.

I do a double take and then ask, "Has he ever seen it?"

"He's never seen the collection itself."

I look over Cornelius' shoulder at Adrian and shrug. I ask again just to make sure I haven't been misheard.

"He's never been to see the collection?"

"He's never been in here to see it."

"He should," Adrian says.

"Yup, it's quite a collection," Cornelius says. "His grandfather has been here, and pretty much his whole family was here."

About to turn eighty years old, Cornelius estimates he's spent more than $30,000 collecting a thousand-plus cards of Richards. So many companies produce so many cards that it is difficult for him to know how close he is to having them all. To the best of his knowledge, he is missing just one. It comes from one of two sets (one blue, one white) of eight cards that spell out "RICHARDS" in all caps from his days with the Rangers. Cornelius has the blue set complete and framed, but one letter from the white set has proved elusive. Even normally reliable eBay, where he finds most of his cards, has turned up empty.

"I'm still searching for that 'D,'" Cornelius says. "I'd love to have that one together and then I'll get it framed the same."

"If you could find that card, how happy would you be?" I ask.

"To go with that? It would be lovely to have them two together. That would make my day."

Six months later, while I was driving through the Northwest Territories, I received an email from Cornelius: "Ronnie a miracle happened." He'd found the missing 'D.' "Arrived two days ago. I am extremely excited to have it complete, thought I would never get it. Now will frame it like I done with my blue one."

While driving through New Brunswick, after returning to the mainland from Prince Edward Island, Adrian and I pass a hitchhiker on the other side of the road thumbing for a ride in the opposite direction. He has a backpack over his shoulders, a duffle bag at his feet, and a hockey helmet on his head. *Only in Canada*, I think to myself as I drive by.

When we get to Miramichi, we meet up with Carl Watters, a fellow traveling hockey player and Maple Leafs fan. He treats us to lunch in town and dinner at home and has arranged for us to sleep in a friend's empty trailer after getting us on the ice tonight. Hockey as hospitality.

After dinner, we follow Carl to Lord Beaverbrook Arena. The dank old barn stands next to a white silo advertising Miramichi as "Canada's Irish Capital" in green lettering. But inside the arena, all is English. A plaque commemorates the "munificence" of Lord Beaverbrook, a British-Canadian newspaper publisher, for giving the people of Miramichi the arena. Below it is an inscription from the poem "A Song in Storm" by the English poet Rudyard Kipling:

> *The game is more than the player of the game. And the ship is more than*
> *the crew.*

We follow Carl into the dressing room, taking in the mix of chirping, reminiscing, profanity, and self-deprecation that are the hallmarks of pickup hockey as we get ready for the game. After suiting up, I wait outside the room with the rest of the players until the Zamboni leaves the ice.

That first step onto a clean sheet of ice never gets old. Sometimes it is a soft step for some shinny or an easy glide before a practice. Other times, it is a launch through the gates. But every time there is a vigor to it, a vitality that shoots up from the ice, conducted by the blades into the body.

One by one, the players file onto the ice. When it is my turn, I charge up the ramp and leap through the gate. The ice is fast, the chill of the barn invigorating, the friendliness of Carl's crew warming. No puck hogs or ice hogs, no cliques or hierarchies, no dressing room drama. Just darks and lights of all skill levels and ages, playing a friendly game of pickup hockey in a 1950s-era, character-filled arena built and christened by Englishmen in an Irish-Canadian town.

There is a certain smell that comes with playing hockey. Roses to players, a stench to non-players, it is a beer-league brew of sweat fermented in the refrigerated air of the rink, the pressure cooker of the hockey bag, and the humidity of the dressing room. In the tiny old concrete rooms of Lord Beaverbrook Arena, after the game, the smell is pungent, the air thick, heavy, and damp with sweaty bodies and sweat-soaked equipment. But no one complains. Players linger in the dressing room after the game, bantering and bullshitting over beers, while steam coils in from the showers, mixing with the sweat evaporating from our sodden equipment. Some shower and change. Others sit sweaty and half dressed, the game's minotaur: half shielded hockey player, half frail human.

On our way out, Carl shows us around the arena, pointing out photos and jerseys honoring players and teams from around Miramichi. A touch of nostalgia comes into his voice as he talks about the kids he coaches.

"I always tell them to enjoy it while it lasts," he says. "Because fifty, sixty years down the road, we all end up at a cold, lonely rink like this playing shinny with other older guys and girls and maybe enjoying a beer or a pop after the game."

Instead of continuing west, Adrian and I detour south down Highway 126, to a motel just off the Trans-Canada. It is out of the way, near Moncton, but in a country full of roadside kitsch, the motel is just too Canadian to pass up.

It isn't a luxurious spot. The motel's musty carpets are dirtier than the floors of the ferry from Port aux Basques, and there are meth heads doing laps around the parking lot. What has drawn us here are the themed suites. A little over a decade ago, management came up with the idea of redesigning some of its old rooms into jungle, ocean space, and Lego suites. And an old office on the second floor was converted into a family-sized hockey room. It takes Adrian and I a few frustrating minutes to find it. For whatever reason, the motel has numbered the suite 200, even though it is beside rooms 215 and 216, with rooms 201 and 202 at the other end of the hall.

Judging by the decor, the suite was designed right around the time when Sidney Crosby won his first Stanley Cup. There were posters of Crosby and the 2009 champion Pittsburgh Penguins, a photo of the 2008–09 Boston Bruins, a T-shirt from the New York Islanders' 2008–09 training camp, and framed autographed jerseys from the Moncton Wildcats and the University of Moncton Blue Eagles. Whoever designed the suite had tried to think of every last detail to cover every part of the room. Below a *Hockey Night in Canada* jersey, there is a net set up in the long entranceway, with mock rink boards running along the walls. The bathroom boasts a Stanley Cup curtain, while a framed collage of Crosby hangs over the queen-sized bed in the main room. The bedding on the adjacent bunk beds features the logos of Canada's NHL teams. Photos of Crosby, Carey Price, Alex Ovechkin, and other NHL superstars—past and present—hang throughout the room.

With New Brunswick being Canadiens country, it is surprising to see so much Maple Leafs paraphernalia. Just inside the door is a photo of Hall of Fame defenseman Borje Salming, while over the desk hangs a kid-sized pink Leafs jersey and on the same wall a poster commemorating the franchise's 1967 Stanley Cup. But looking a little closer, I think maybe a Canadiens fan has designed it, after all. The door closes on Salming, and the kids' jersey could be a baby metaphor to describe Leafs Nation, while the poster of the '67 champs might be a playful troll for just how long it's been since the Leafs have won the Stanley Cup.

Retracing our route from Moncton up to Highway 108, Adrian and I carry on through the deep woods of New Brunswick, the forest crowding the road as we navigate the patchworked pavement. Although still in logging country, we're fast approaching New Brunswick's potato fields, where farmers produce spuds for McCain, the main employer in this part of the province. After two hours of this, Adrian and I come to Plaster Rock.

In the 1990s, the local arena had fallen into deep disrepair and there was no money to build a new one. The cost to renovate it would've been higher than building a new one. The town managed to squeeze five more years out of the old place, but with no rink to play in and no money, Plaster Rock had come to a crossroads.

One night at a hotel bar, Danny Braun and the hotel's owner came up with an idea. Within minutes they had the concept, the rules, and just about everything else figured out. It came together so quickly they almost laughed the whole thing off.

The first World Pond Hockey Championship was born, featuring forty teams from across New Brunswick, Nova Scotia, Prince Edward Island, and Maine. Games took place on the Tobique River, which cuts through the middle of town, with nearby Roulston Lake reserved for the championship game. The second year, the games were split. Since then, it's been all Roulston Lake.

More than twenty years on, the number of teams has surpassed one hundred and the number of participants six hundred, and they come from much farther afield than the Maritimes and Maine. Teams show up from almost every province and territory in Canada and as many as half the American states. Others fly in from Singapore, Brazil, Switzerland, China, England, Poland, Czechia, Egypt, Puerto Rico, and the Cayman Islands. Some teams bring their own accommodations, parking RVs near the lake. One team, the Montreal Lagers, even bought a house across from Roulston Lake to guarantee it has a place to stay. Most players commute to and from games from Grand Falls and Perth-Andover, about half an hour away, thanks to a shuttle service of seven vans that runs twenty-four hours a day during the tournament.

Hockey Day in Canada has broadcast from the tournament, and both *Sports Illustrated* and *The New York Times* have covered it, bringing little Plaster Rock and its eleven hundred people worldwide annual acclaim. Wayne Gretzky and former prime minister Stephen Harper have attended the tournament, and former NHLers have played in it, as well as a slew of players from various North American and European leagues. The tournament has had to battle snowstorms and rain to carry on, but it's never finished behind schedule. Only the pandemic could overpower the event. "This'll be our twentieth anniversary," Danny says. "It just took us twenty-three years to get here."

Danny takes us first to the new tourist information center, a large wooden lodge that was built for the town, along with the nearby arena and open-air pavilion, using revenues from the tournament. The lodge holds a glass cabinet of keepsakes, including promotional material from the first few incarnations of the tournament as well as the championship trophy, the Goodwill Cup, a heavy wooden chalice designed by a local man who worked at the mill. The cabinet also contains a copy of a promo poster for the tournament's fifteenth anniversary, the year Budweiser whisked Gretzky to Plaster Rock.

"They brought him over here and he did his thing," Danny says. "Couple interviews, we went out and dropped the puck, and away he went. He made two hundred grand, and he was here for like four or five hours. But he signed everything that anybody put in front of him. He was great. Didn't miss a person."

We follow Danny to the new arena behind the lodge. The ice hasn't been put in yet. The plywood boards are covered in plastic, and the bare concrete floor looks like an empty room stripped of its carpeting.

Adrian lets out a long sigh. "Oh, this is the saddest sight," he says. "No ice. Makes me wanna cry."

Around the rink are framed jerseys of teams that have come to the tournament over the years: the Barley Kings from Beaver, Manitoba; the Hockey Hobos from Grimsby, Ontario; the London Capitals from England; and the Annapolis Valley Pacemakers from Nova Scotia;

as well as the Has Been All-Stars, Puckweisers, and Wallbangers from Massachusetts. Some even come with an explanation. The YANKS are "Your Average No-talent Knuckleheads from the South," while the Cayman Breakaway describe themselves as "the Caribbean 'ice hockey' version of the Jamaican bobsled team" whose "only ice in their country 'is in our drinks.'" The Narco Rangers are named for a group of detectives in the NYPD's Narcotics Division, while the Scandic Vikings from Smidstrup, Denmark, are "a local favorite due to the connections to our fellow countrymen living close by in New Denmark, New Brunswick."

We leave the rink and walk to the log pavilion at the edge of Roulston Lake. All three of us pause to look upon its waters. Only nine feet deep and half a mile around, on the surface there is nothing special about it. It could be any one of Canada's two million lakes, give or take a hundred thousand. But for four days every February, when Plaster Rock's population swells to three times its normal size, Roulston Lake becomes Canada's holiest body of water.

"There's something about the location in winter," Danny says. "There's some romanticism to it, too, for the hockey purists. It takes them back to their childhood a bit. We've had guys as old as eighty participate in it. Guy from Alberta, he came and his wife passed away when he was here. She was the one that made him come. He wasn't going to come. We've got an award named after him now that we give out annually to the oldest player. John Chadwick was his name. I think he's gone now."

It is only mid-October when Adrian and I arrive, but Danny has already wrapped up his first meetings for next year's tournament. More will follow. Then on New Year's Day, volunteers will start clearing the lake, right to the shoreline, after each snowfall, to make it easier to handle any potential rain and to keep the ice smooth for the potato farmers in the area, the region's ice gurus, who transform Roulston Lake every year.

In the early years of the tournament, volunteers plowed the lake with pickup trucks and used measuring tape to mark the rinks. Now the plowing is done with a mix of skid steer loaders, snow blowers, and other equipment, while organizers use a GPS system to outline the two dozen rinks, created in the same spots every year, with the championship rink kept pure for the final.

We all pause again as we stare at the lake. We can almost see what it will look like come winter.

"It's just a body of water like any other lake in this country," I say. "And yet there's something about . . ."

"What it transforms into," Danny says.

What Plaster Rock has figured out that every spot that claims hockey's origins hasn't is that no one outside of the game's high societies cares *where* hockey was first played. It is *how* it was first played that they care about. It's the nostalgia for hockey played at its purest.

"The teams, when they first get here, they go register and then they walk right down to look at it, every year," Danny says. "We've seen older guys with tears in their eyes. They say it reminds them of when they were a kid. If you're just out there and listen when games are going on, it's just skates and sticks and pucks. That's what you hear, and guys laughing."

We linger at the pavilion for a while, talking hockey. The plastic owls in the rafters are doing a lousy job keeping away the pigeons, who've shat all over the concrete floor in the carpet-bombing manner of their urban kin. Players used to be able to come directly off the ice and skate right up to the bar to buy a beer, but now they walk in on mats. Every year, a couple of days before the tournament starts, when the rinks are fully groomed and ready to go, Danny comes out and just stands at the edge of the shore.

"That sight never gets old," he says. "All those rinks, and there's nobody out there at that point. But you could stand here and just close your eyes and listen and you know what's going on."

Danny walks us back to the lodge, hands us some swag, and wishes us safe travels for our drive to Quebec. Adrian heads back to our room, while I take a slow stroll around Roulston Lake. The trail is a mix of gravel, dirt, mulch, and mud. Except for the area around the pavilion, the forest has grown right up to the shoreline, and the water, as still as the ice it will transform into for the tournament, mirrors the multicolored leaves around it. Only the lily pads on its surface break up the lake's reflected water-painting of the world around it. There are benches at the water's edge. I sit down at one of them.

If hockey is religion in Canada, places like Roulston Lake are sacred. From frozen ponds to frozen arenas, hockey evolved as naturally as the Trans-Canada followed the first paths across the country. Yet just like the Trans-Canada, hockey has become commercialized and kitschy, a type of pornography in which more and more Canadians prefer to watch professionals play onscreen than do it themselves. Pond hockey strips all this away. Where the original Pond of Eden is, no one knows. It is enough that places like Roulston Lake still hold their transcendent power over the game, enough for a small town to afford a new rink from the simple act of people playing pond hockey every year.

Quebec: What Is a Canadian?

No longer am I merely a fan, cheering from the sidelines for the great Canadian game and the great Canadian players. I am one of "us": a hockey player, and therefore (I can't help feeling) a Canadian, fully fledged at last. —Marsha Mildon, "Number 33"

THE PARKING LOT at the Colisée de Laval is a minefield of potholes. Nicknamed the "House of Pain," the old arena has been home to a slew of junior, semipro, and minor pro teams since opening in 1954. In the lobby, large panels celebrate the three years that Adrian's favorite player, Mario Lemieux, played his junior hockey here for the Laval Voisins in the early 1980s before heading to the NHL with the Pittsburgh Penguins.

From Plaster Rock, Adrian and I took the Trans-Canada over and around Maine. We followed it along the St. Lawrence as it hugged the river and then carried on to Laval for a pickup game at Lemieux's old haunt.

In much of hockey, the dressing room has a lot to answer for. The stories of hazing rituals in junior hockey are juvenile at best, criminal at worst. But the beer-league dressing room is different. Everyone here is a failed NHL dream. Even when Guy Who Still Thinks He Can Make the

NHL makes an appearance, the rest of the room quickly cuts him down. There is no hierarchy. Doctors are just organic mechanics, lawyers are professional paper pushers, financial executives are glorified money butlers, and writers are failed fast-food workers. No one cares where anyone comes from, how much money they make, what god they worship, who they sleep with, or what language they speak. Whether you know anybody or not, if you have a hockey bag, you're welcome without warrant.

Which also means you are fair game for chirping.

"So, what do you think of your new king?" one of the players asks us as we get dressed for the game.

His name is Didier Leroux. At first, I have no idea what he's talking about. My king? Then I remember. Queen Elizabeth II just died. But I hadn't watched her funeral or even considered the coming coronation of King Charles III. Caught off guard, I fumble the response.

"Uh, I dunno. Not much, I guess. Never thought about it, to be honest."

"What? But you're Canadian!"

It feels good to get chirped right away. It makes us feel part of the group. An art form unto itself, chirping is a game within the game, unique to hockey and distinct from insults and trash talking. It is an oral tradition of verbal gamesmanship, passed down from generation to generation, in which tried-and-true chirps are retold like old dad jokes:

"I've seen better hands on a clock."
"You couldn't check a coat."
"Does your coach know you're out here?"
"If you want more ice time, I hear they're hiring a Zamboni driver."

These and a legion of other time-tested chirps are always at the ready, but the best, like Didier's, are original. Only amateurs resort to profanity and personal attacks. The masters need neither. They use context for creativity. In a country where the hockey rink often mirrors the political arena, Didier has tapped into Quebec's long-standing separatist sentiment to chirp a couple of Canadian recruits.

An hour and a half and a 6–5 loss later, I am back in the dressing room getting chirped again, this time by Christian "Bill" Allard, a big burly man with a wild mat of dark brown hair and an impressive playoff beard for a pickup game in late October. An avid hunter and carnivore, Bill finds out I am vegetarian.

"Oh yeah?" he says as he wipes the sweat from his forehead. "I always say that the day I eat tofu is the day I can hunt it." Chirped again.

As Didier and Bill begin talking in French, Adrian angles into view from his perch next to me to get their attention and then picks up where we left off before the game. Everyplace we've been on the road trip, everywhere we've played, every player we've played with or against, we've wanted to know how their passport fits into their identity. Labradorians, Newfoundlanders, Cape Bretoners, Nova Scotians, Prince Edward Islanders, New Brunswickers, Acadians, they all, to a person, consider themselves Canadians second, if at all.

"So, for you guys, do you say you're from Quebec or from Canada?" Adrian asks.

Didier leans his wiry body against the dressing room wall. He thinks about it for a moment, then pulls himself forward and turns toward us.

"I am Québécois," he says. "I am Québécois because of my language. I will never, ever call myself Canadian."

Bill, still in full gear except for his helmet and gloves, is more explanatory.

"I'm a huge history buff," he says. "I love reading about history. What many people don't know is just how much of North America used to be French and how much of the continent was explored and discovered by the French. Even in the West, in the United States, there's a place called Butte in Montana. It's a French name. Before the English defeated the French, there were French people everywhere. Illinois, Missouri . . ."

"Louisiana," Adrian adds.

In a musty old dressing room in a rundown arena, the air damp with sweat but the atmosphere still light and playful, four men who've known each other for all of two hours begin talking separatism and Canada, half chirping and half conversational, all because of a game.

Didier then turns to us.

"I have a question for you, now," he says. "What . . . is . . . a . . . Canadian?"

Didier holds our gaze steady. It is a chirp, but it is also an honest question, one to which I have no answer, because I've never thought about it before. I mean, really, what is a Canadian?

Stumped for an answer, I think about it for a moment. The first thing that comes to mind is the irony of the sovereignty movement. If it were ever to leave Canada, Quebec, the country, would look nothing like Quebec, the province. In northern Quebec, where Adrian and I are headed next, the Cree in Eeyou Istchee, a great big swath of land about the size of Germany, would never go with Quebec, nor would the Inuit in the semiautonomous territory of Nunavik, about the size of Spain. Quebec would be left with a territory about half of what it is now and would lose most of its natural resources. But there would be one big benefit. It would instantly turn the Maple Leafs–Canadiens rivalry into an international showdown. Imagine the insanity.

I look around, searching for an answer. I am in a hockey dressing room, sitting in my hockey gear, with a bunch of other hockey players, after playing an hour and a half of hockey in a hockey rink. Although I can't say what a Canadian is, I at least know I am a Canadian. So I brush off my philosophy degree and put my Rene Descartes readings to good use.

Hockey ludo, ergo Canadian sum.

"I play hockey, therefore I am Canadian."

As it does across many parts of the country, the Trans-Canada splits apart in Montreal. The southern route runs west to Ottawa, while the less-traveled northern branch, Route 117, runs up through Val d'Or. As the towns thin out, and the services become fewer and farther between, it's tempting to call this part of the highway remote, but in truth, it goes only a quarter of the way up Quebec.

We bypass Val d'Or and carry on north up Route 113. At some place called Lebel-sur-Quévillon, we leave the paved highway for Chemin du Moulin, which turns into Route 1000, which turns into Route 1055. All just one long potholed tire trap. Skidoo trails crisscross the gravel road, all boasting mini ARRÊT signs that snowmobilers probably pay little attention to. Who would drive this road?

It is late the afternoon when we finally roll into Matagami, a tiny mining community about a day's drive from Laval. On the way to our motel, a sign catches Adrian's eye. "ARENA" is all it says.

"I wonder if there's hockey tonight," Adrian says.

The arena is small but looks new. In a corner of the lobby is a photo of a player in a Maple Leafs jersey, Lorne Stamler. I look him up. He played parts of four seasons in the NHL in the 1970s, including one with the Leafs. What brought him to Matagami in the summer of 2017, I have no idea, but he saw fit to leave behind a message: "Dreams do come true."

In another corner, we find the arena schedule. Rec hockey, eight o'clock.

We leave the arena and check into Motel le Caribou, the only motel left in Matagami after the other burned down earlier in the year. The lobby reeks of smoke, and the wood-panel walls, dinky TV, fake wood vinyl floor, and windowless bathroom of our tiny room give it the feel of a low-budget horror movie. With no restaurants in town, we dine on what fare we have in supply, take a pregame nap, watch the first period of an NHL game on TV, then head back to the arena.

Eight other players show up as well as two other goalies, neither of whom seems happy to have to rotate with Adrian. During a break in the game, the players tell us that Matagami used to have a thriving beer league with four full teams. But then the local mine went to seven days on, seven days off shifts. Miners stopped buying houses in town and started commuting from elsewhere. The players here this night, including a couple who canoodle during breaks in play, are all that is left of the league.

When we get back to the motel, I go inside and find the late game on TV, while Adrian stays out for an evening joint. I am already half asleep when he comes in.

"I just saw a couple come out of the bushes and go into the room next door," he says.

Neither of us thinks anything of it, until around midnight, long after I've passed out to the sound of the Calgary Flames beating the Pittsburgh Penguins. The walls turn out to be paper thin as the man and woman go from fornicating to arguing, and then to all-out hellfire raging, followed by screams of "Do you love me?" from the man punctuated with bouts of heavy sobbing. Then comes a guttural barrage of "WHY? WHY? WHY?" as the man slams his hands against our adjoining wall.

I shoot out of bed. The Flames are up by three goals late in the third period. Adrian is lying on his side wide awake.

"I'm expecting one of them to burst through the wall like those old Kool-Aid commercials," he says.

This goes on for another two or three hours. Fornicating to fighting, interspersed with shouts of "Don't you love me?" and "Ouch, you cut me!" and more wall slamming.

"Should we go over?" Adrian asks. "It sounds like someone might get killed."

Not long afterward, someone pounds on their door. We hear the loud voice of another man in muffled French. Whether it is the motel owner or one of the construction workers in the room on the other side, we can't tell, but it calms the couple for a little while. When it starts up again, Adrian and I consider jumping into Gumpy and getting out of there before we end up in a newspaper headline. But I am exhausted, so I just put in my earplugs, leave the game on, and lay down again.

"Let's just get through it and leave at first light," I say, and then fall asleep.

When I wake up in the morning, Adrian is lying on the edge of his bed flipping through his phone. He hasn't slept a wink.

"They left sometime during the night," he says.

We toss our bags and backpacks into Gumpy, stop for gas, water, and supplies at the service station, and leave Matagami without looking back.

A little way out of town, we stop at the southern entrance to the Billy Diamond Highway. Originally known as the James Bay Road, in 2020 it was renamed after the former grand chief of the Grand Council of the Crees. It was Billy Diamond who fought Quebec's plan to build the world's largest hydroelectric project around James Bay. In the end, the project went ahead, but Diamond unified all the Cree bands in Eeyou Istchee, "the People's Land," and became the main Cree negotiator for the landmark James Bay and Northern Quebec Agreement, widely recognized as Canada's first modern First Nations treaty.

The highway, 620 kilometers (385 miles) in length, was built as an access route for all the hydroelectric stations constructed in the James Bay region. The only waystation is Relais Routier du Km 381, which is open all day every day. That 381-kilometer (236-mile) gap between gas stations represents the longest stretch of road in Canada without services. We stop there for the night and get set to carry on the next day.

After an overnight snowfall, the morning dawns with the first winter weather of the road trip. In honor of its renaming, the Billy Diamond Highway has been repaved, so driving it feels like skating on a fresh sheet of ice. With no towns for its entire length, it is as though we've left everything behind, like we've snuck behind the defense and broken away from the pack, skating on an asphalt river through boreal forest and timeless taiga, with nothing between us and the goal, Chisasibi, at the end of the highway.

Several access roads branch off the Billy Diamond Highway, reaching the hockey towns of Nemaska, Waskaganish, Eastmain, and Wemindji. But the only one that is paved is the one to Chisasibi. When we arrive, we check into our hotel and head over to Job's Memorial Garden Arena. Signs leading to the ice forbid bullying and spitting sunflower seeds. Center ice features the bear, goose, and fish crest of the Cree Nation of Chisasibi. From one end to the other, flags and banners hang from the beams overhead, including Canada's and Chisasibi's, and one bearing the logo for the local men's team, a carbon copy of the Chicago Blackhawks' logo.

Poking our heads inside the arena office, we ask for Roy Neacappo, whom I've been in touch with for the better part of a year.

"You're looking for Roy?" the man there asks. "Just walk around the arena and look for the handsomest guy you see. That's Roy."

I like Roy right away. Only in his mid-fifties, he already has fourteen grandchildren from his five children. He fidgets with his keys as he speaks, and often aspirates "hhhockey," giving the word a weight I've never heard before.

The Billy Diamond Highway is to Chisasibi, and the other ten Cree communities in Eeyou Istchee, what the Trans-Labrador Highway is to Labrador. It allows goods to be trucked instead of flown or shipped in once a year on container ships that sail around Labrador and into Hudson Bay and James Bay. For the people of Chisasibi, the road is a lifeline. For players in Chisasibi, it is a weekend road trip.

Before the highway, teams from Chisasibi would have to fly to play games elsewhere in Eeyou Istchee. Even after it was finished in 1974, the only access to the other Cree communities was winter ice roads. Often it was quicker just to go overland.

"Some of the players would take their skidoos," Roy says. "They'd get there faster than going by truck. But now it's much easier. The road is better, it's safer, so they drive. It was an adventure, too, for some of the guys. 'Let's go by skidoo!'"

"So bad weather, bad roads, nothing stopped you guys," Adrian says. "That was it. You guys love hockey."

"We love hockey. We did all of that stuff because of hockey."

Roy has lived here all his life, before the community voted to move from the island of Fort George in 1980 and relocate inland, where Chisasibi has since grown to about six thousand people. The two are still connected, by ice road in winter and ferry the rest of the year. After the move, some stayed behind, while others would go back on weekends. Many are now returning, building small cabins on the island and bringing life back to

Fort George, where hockey in the community was born. Roy has offered to take us on a tour the next day.

"Is Chisasibi the biggest Cree community in Eeyou Istchee?" I ask.

Roy nods. "And they have the most handsomest people, starting with me. You can quote me on that."

When the community was still on Fort George, there used to be two rinks on the island, both outdoors, one each at the Catholic and Anglican residential schools. The rinks were made of plywood, cleared with shovels, flooded with a hose, and lit with light bulbs so that people could play at night, which they often did. Before the community had access to proper equipment, people would go into the bush, chop down trees to make sticks, and cut pucks out of firewood. Fans would watch the games from the snowbanks piled up around the boards.

"That is the one bright spot," Roy says. "It was the residential schools that introduced hockey to us. I think that was the only positive thing."

Just then, a young man walks in. Drop-in hockey is on the docket tonight.

"Registering?" Roy asks. "Nine o'clock skate tonight, free."

Roy then turns and gestures to us. We'll be playing, too.

"You get to hit these guys!"

"I'm a goalie, so you just hit me with pucks," Adrian says.

In the morning, Roy picks us up at our hotel and drives over to Fort George. All I know about the tiny island is one small but key piece of hockey lore: Bill Barilko and Henry Hudson landed here to unload some of their gear on their way home to Timmins, Ontario, after their fishing trip up to Seal River, Quebec, just north of Chisasibi. While on the short ferry ride across, I ask Roy where their floatplane would've landed back in 1951. He points to a spot near the dock on the other side.

"The water used to be orange," he says, "from the fuel of the planes."

When we get to Fort George, Roy drives slowly through the island along a bumpy, unmaintained dirt road. By its side are small cabins of various colors, in states of either renovation or disrepair. Many have flags of NHL teams fluttering in the sharp wind coming off the water.

"These are weekend getaway cabins for people," Roy says.

"Cottages?" Adrian asks.

"Something like that. They started building them just to get away from everything."

We drive through a small forested area and stop outside an empty cabin at the edge of the Grande River. When the community was still on Fort George, it hauled rocks across the water and piled them at the water's edge to stop the erosion that would eventually force people to move inland. It's still working here. But farther down, the edge of island has eroded away where the old dump used to be, strewing bags of garbage across the brown sand beach below.

Roy points to a tall grassy area topped with a wooden cross.

"This was the Anglican residential school," he says. "See that hill? That's where they covered it. I think that's why there's a cross there."

Roy parks and we all get out. The wind is blowing strong off the water. Piles of bear scat are scattered around the area.

"There's nothing left," I say.

"Right behind there was the rink," Roy says. "I don't know if we can get through here. This was the residential school, and over there was the rink. It used to be clear, but there's been a lot of growth. Forty years."

Nearby is the old Anglican church, across from the church cemetery. Some of the small stained-glass windows are broken, but it otherwise looks in good shape. The white walls and green trim have barely faded or peeled. Trees have grown tall on one side, and on the other is brown grass and multicolored moss, a favorite of what remains of the decimated caribou herds in the region.

We continue on and drive by an old boarded-up Hudson's Bay Company storage building from 1832, then on past a closed-up summer chip stand with a Coke sign, an overgrown baseball diamond, and the site of the old hospital, which was razed after the move. Across a creek, we come to another grassy area, this one less overgrown.

"This is where the Catholic residential school was," Roy says. "They had the school here, and right next to it there was the hockey rink."

There is nothing left of it, either. No boards, no foundation, nothing.

"When they tore down the residential school, the priest didn't leave the site," Roy says. "He was just there watching, overseeing what was going on, the men were saying, as if he was afraid they might find something."

The spots where Barilko and Hudson refueled, the locations of the residential schools, the empty cabins, the boarded-up old Hudson's Bay storehouses, the eroded dump, and then, a little way inland, a grounded ghost ship—it all gives Fort George a feeling of permanent transition. Once full of life, touched with trauma, then deserted, it's now slowly being reconnected to Chisasibi through all the cabins being built or restored and the horrors being healed.

"We just started having a residential school gathering here, these past couple of years," Roy says. "People from other communities come in, who came to school here. It's like healing for them. It's closure, sort of, for them. That's what we want to do. Even though I didn't go to a residential school, we still feel its effect, the intergenerational effects of what happened to our people."

There is a quote in the Hockey Hall of Fame that has always stuck with me. It is from an exhibit that honors Indigenous hockey. It comes from William Littlechild, commissioner of the Truth and Reconciliation Commission and a residential school survivor himself: "Hockey was the one bright light of a positive experience for many students." Littlechild, who spent fourteen years at the Ermineskin Indian Residential School, once said, "I owe my survival to hockey."

"Hockey was the only thing good about residential schools," Roy says as we drive back to the dock. "It was an escape."

During our first of two nights of shinny in Chisasibi, Adrian and I were taking a break at the bench when a player came over and asked us where we were from and what we were doing here. Adrian gave him the spiel: Toronto, the Travelling Goalie, the road trip.

"Where are you going next?" he asked.

"Waskaganish," we replied.

"Waskaganish, eh?" He paused for a moment, took a swig of water, and turned to go back on the ice. "Make sure you lock your doors so your car doesn't get stolen. It's pretty ghetto there."

It wasn't a warning. The player was just messing with us, having a laugh at our expense while letting us in on some of the friendly chirping that goes on among the Cree communities in Eeyou Istchee. Most of it takes place online in the lead-up to the weekend tournaments for the region's Class A teams, the class of Cree hockey.

From Chisasibi, Adrian and I begin retracing our route south down the Billy Diamond Highway. After about five hours, we turn onto the gravel access road west to Waskaganish, where we meet Charles Hester at the Rupert River Sports Complex, named for the waterway above town that empties into James Bay. With eight children and nine grandchildren, Charles has earned the right to wear the blue "Dad Jokes All Day" T-shirt he has on underneath his black jacket. He just got back late the night before from a tournament in Eastmain, 322 kilometers (200 miles) away, where one of his eight sons, all hockey players, was competing.

"You could have your own a team bus," Adrian says.

Charles laughs. "I used to have a van, a big van."

Hockey has been a way of life for Charles for as long as he can remember. It was his great-grandfather, George Gilpin, who introduced hockey to the Cree in Eeyou Istchee after seeing the game being played in Kingston, Ontario, where he was being treated for tuberculosis. Five generations later, hockey has become one with the Hesters, Waskaganish's original hockey family.

Charles leads us into the lobby, brightly lit with floor-to-ceiling windows. On one of the walls is a photo of a team with three of his sons. One of the players is holding an envelope.

"What's in the envelope?" Adrian asks. "Money?"

"Yup. Usually they don't give you the money right up front. You have to go pick it up at the office."

While players south of Trans-Canada chase the NHL dream, the Cree in Eeyou Istchee have carved out their own high-level hockey league. There are no cameras or color analysts, no first-class flights or five-star hotels, just the two-lane Billy Diamond Highway and the adventurous gravel access roads that run off of it to the eleven towns in the region.

"Hockey is the national sport of the Cree nation," Charles says.

Formerly Rupert House, Waskaganish is where the first Hudson's Bay Company outpost was established, in 1668. It is also where Billy Diamond was born and raised. Much is known about Diamond's fight against the Quebec government. Little is known about his contribution to Cree hockey.

In 1976, less than a year after negotiating the James Bay and Northern Quebec Agreement, Diamond and his friend Walter Hester Jr. established the Waskaganish Wings, named and modeled after their favorite NHL team, the Detroit Red Wings. Along with the Chisasibi Hunters, Wemindji Wolves, and Eastmain Trappers, the Wings were part of the Original Four, a quartet of teams that gave the Cree here a hockey identity all their own apart from residential schools. Not quite a league, but more like a roving rotation of tournaments that shifts from one remote town to another in and around Eeyou Istchee, the Class A circuit is competitive, high-stakes hockey. Prize money for each tournament can hit as high as $30,000, frequently paid out in cold hard cash after the final game. One season, the Wings took home more than $250,000.

"There was talk about reducing the cash prizes," Charles says. "I think it stems from this team here. And then I tell them, 'Hey, there's fishing derbies that people win fifty-thousand dollars. What about those?' At least this is a sport. We play hockey. Traditionally fishing has never been a sport for our people. It's a way of life."

"Is hockey becoming a way of life for the Cree, like hunting, fishing, trapping?" I ask.

"Hockey, in a sense, has replaced what the powwow was," Charles replies. "We have a lot of hockey tournaments, and that's when the nation comes together. You're bringing fifteen, twenty guys from each community, and of course they're going to bring their spouses, they're going to bring their fans. Events like that are important for us in the Cree nation. Getting together as one nation under one roof, it creates a bond with the other communities too. It really solidifies our nation."

During the long winters, hockey is the biggest thing to the towns along the Billy Diamond Highway, and the Class A tournaments are the biggest draw, particularly the Rupert River Cup in Waskaganish, the largest tournament in all of Eeyou Istchee. Even teams from Cree communities in Northern Ontario, along the southern shores of James Bay, make the trek, some by skidoo over the frozen waters of the bay.

"Some of the guys, they're really seen as local heroes," Charles says. "They have a following. Especially the kids, they really look up to them. Maybe that's why they don't wanna go play in a beer league down south or a semipro league, because they get appreciated here. They get to play in front of their fans, in front of their family."

"You feel like a pro," Adrian says.

"Yeah, you do. You go there, it's loud and the stands are packed. It's a hockey town. People like hockey here."

But getting to Waskaganish, or anywhere else in Eeyou Istchee, is not easy. Were it not for the Billy Diamond Highway and the Route du Nord, a 407-kilometer (253-mile) gravel road that runs east from it to the Cree communities inland, none of the teams would exist beyond their own town. Even then, from Chisasibi on the coast in the west to Mistissini inland in the east is a sixteen-hour drive.

"I think it's safe to say in all the world, no other team is going to travel six hours there and six hours back just to play a couple of games, that's unheard of," Charles says. "My son has played teams down south in the Montreal area for summer hockey, and for some of the parents traveling half an hour to go to the rink is even too much for them. This is the most vast, in terms of territory, expanse that we have to travel just to get to a game or two."

From the lobby, Charles leads us past the dressing rooms to the rink. On one side are the stands, on the other the benches, with the logos of every Class A team arrayed above them. We walk out to center ice and stand below the score clock suspended from the beams of the wooden ceiling. Underneath hangs the town's flag, a flying goose set against the sun. When Waskaganish hosts a Class A tournament, the score clock goes pretty much non-stop. With too many teams to follow a normal schedule, games are often played well after midnight. Some teams even ask to play late to accommodate the long drives and players' work schedules.

"You gotta be crazy about hockey to travel all that distance with your teams and to schedule games at three in the morning," Charles says. "It's very unique. I don't know how it happens anywhere else."

Former prime minister Pierre Elliott Trudeau once described Canada as "a country whose main exports are hockey players and cold fronts." Like its cold fronts, Canada sends hockey players to all corners of the globe. Canadians make up more than forty percent of players in the NHL, as well as the majority of those in the American Hockey League and East Coast Hockey League, the top two minor pro leagues in North America. Many players export themselves to Russia's Kontinental Hockey League and other pro leagues across Europe in search of bigger paychecks. Canadians are also found in lesser-known semipro circuits like the Asian Ice Hockey League, the Australian Ice Hockey League, and the Turkish Ice Hockey Super League. Others like Adil El Farj, Ralph Metki, and Qais Hafsi are imports who fall for the game in their adopted country and then export it back to their ancestral homelands.

It is Halloween when Adrian and I get back to Montreal. We meet Adil at his house and drive to a local poutinerie to feast on Montreal fare and drink beer and meet his friends and fellow Canadiens fans, Ralph and Qais. They all met through hockey: Adil as the former coach and now director of player development for the Royal Moroccan Ice Hockey Federation, Ralph as the co-founder of Hockey Lebanon and president of a Lebanese expat club team called the Flying Cedars, and Qais as the secretary-general for Hockey Algeria and a player for the men's national team.

Adil came late to the game. He was already sixteen years old when his family emigrated from Morocco in the late 1980s. After finishing high school, he had to take a mandatory sports class at CEGEP. On a whim, he went with hockey. He learned how to skate and then a few years later was asked to play goal. He would never play out again. Eventually, he caught on as a goalie with the Moroccan national team.

"It's funny because you had players who'd never been to Canada or seen a pro game," he says, "and they're talking about Raymond Bourque and Patrick Roy."

Born in Lebanon and raised in Canada, Ralph learned to skate at Raymond Bourque Arena in Montreal's west end. When he first told his father he wanted to play hockey, his dad bought him a table hockey game. "No, no, no, I wanna play hockey, on the ice," Ralph told him. And he did, even though it had only been a year since the family had fled the war in Lebanon and landed in Canada to start a new life.

"I don't know how he did it," Ralph says. "It's an expensive sport."

Like Ralph, Qais has been in Canada since he was six years old. He is a full-blown Montrealer, with a tattoo of the city crest to prove it. Born in the United States to an Algerian father and a French mother, Qais calls himself "a citizen of the world," and with American, Canadian, French, and Algerian citizenships, he can back it up. He's also been in the game all his life, as a player and jersey collector, and now as a player and organizer for Algeria.

"I always joke that I learned to skate before I learned to walk," he says.

When we meet at the poutinerie, Adil is only days away from flying to Kuwait for the women's Development Cup, an International Ice Hockey Federation sanctioned tournament for non-traditional hockey countries where the climate is antithetical to ice. Ralph has been busy preparing for an exhibition game in Laval between players from the Lebanese and Armenian national teams, many of whom live in Canada. The two of them have been working with Qais to put on exhibition games in Montreal between their three federations.

"On the ice, we're foes, we're enemies," Adil says. "But we collaborate a lot."

"Has hockey brought you closer to your roots?" I ask them.

"It has for me," Qais says. "It's been a way for me to get closer to Algeria."

"It did for me, too," adds Ralph, who goes back to Lebanon at least once a year. "With the whole federation thing, it increased our trips to Lebanon, it increased our interest in it. And we have to be thankful for Canada, because we learned the game."

"Definitely, yes," Adil says. "When I tasted hockey, it was like 'I tasted this good play, let's bring it back to all the Morocco kids and everything.' And then I find out they already know and watch Patrick Kane and they try to mimic his moves they see on YouTube. And I'm like, 'What the fuck is going on?'"

Here we are. A Moroccan-Canadian, a Lebanese-Canadian, a French-Algerian-American-Canadian, a Maltese-Canadian goaltender, and whatever you want to call a writer of Welsh and Danish descent born in Canada. Hockey has brought us together, speaking a mixture of English and French. We talk until we lose track of time and are the only ones left in the restaurant.

"Do you wanna go see the Canadiens' practice facility?" Ralph asks.

"It's on the program," Adil replies.

Adrian wants to visit Cimetière Notre-Dame-des-Neiges, where Maurice Richard is buried. "It's Halloween!" Adrian says. "We'll go say a prayer for the Rocket."

We never do go pay our respects to Richard, at least not at his gravesite. Instead, we go to the practice facility of his NHL alma mater. There we grab seats at an empty wooden table in the bar, from which we can see games going on at the rinks on either side of us. The players are beer-leaguers, no different from us, skating under the white banners listing the Canadiens' Stanley Cups and red banners displaying their retired jersey numbers. Although Adrian and I are behind enemy lines, in both city and team, we still belong, as foils. Toronto and Montreal, the Maple Leafs and the Canadiens, each is unthinkable without the other. The two cities and their citizens have long respectfully disliked one another, mirroring on the municipal level the mutual disdain between their hockey clubs. Torontonians look at Montreal and see a city of European lassitude and lax morals, with a fashion sense that falls somewhere between hipster and homeless, while Montrealers regard Toronto as the third-largest city in the United States, filled with stuck-up suits and anal urban tree-huggers.

But the rivalry between Toronto and Montreal pales in comparison to the bilious hatred between Montreal and Quebec City, which spilled onto the ice for sixteen years between the Canadiens and the Nordiques. Or "les Merdiques," as Adil and other Habs fans like to call their old provincial rival.

"Ninety percent of decisions for Montreal are made in Quebec City," Qais says. "It sucks. We can't even build one bridge when we need fucking ten bridges in Montreal. I don't wanna give anything to Quebec City because they're our rival city. I hate them as much as I hate Toronto, if not more, because they're a local rivalry. Quebec has always been a rival for Montreal. No doubts about it, it's always been about that. We always hated Quebec City. We hated them more when they had the Nordiques."

"I feel what Qais is saying about Montreal compared to the rest of Quebec," Adil adds. "When I go outside Quebec, I'm proud to be Canadian. But when I speak to other French people, like from Switzerland, they say, 'Oh, okay, you're from Quebec.' And I say, 'No, no, no, I'm a Montrealer from Quebec.' 'Okay, well, what's the difference?' Well, there's a big difference. You're gonna see in Quebec City, it's a different mentality. We call it 'the big village.'"

Just outside downtown Quebec City, the future of NHL hockey in the provincial capital looms large over its past. The Centre Vidéotron, which opened in 2015, dwarfs the Colisée Pepsi, which closed the same year. The former seats more than eighteen thousand and is home to the Quebec Remparts, the local junior team. The latter, which looks about half its size, somehow crammed in 15,176 fans back when it was the Colisée de Québec, the home of the long-lost and much-mourned Quebec Nordiques.

"How the hell did they manage to play NHL games in this thing?" I say as we pull up to the old arena and venture around back.

Instead of demolishing the building, the city opted to renovate it. Drab and gray, the color of dirty snow, it looks like a discarded kitchen sink sitting beside the giant washing machine opposite it. But the Colisée Pepsi has one significant thing on its successor. It had seen the NHL, and it was glorious.

In Canada, and very likely the world, no city self-identifies with a sports team that no longer exists more than Quebec City. The city has spent more time without the Nordiques than the twenty-three years the team was there, and it's still waiting for its beloved Nords to return.

When the Nordiques were set to join the NHL in 1979, after seven seasons in the World Hockey Association (WHA), the Canadiens vetoed the move, citing infringement on their territory. It took a nationwide boycott of Molson, the owner of the Canadiens, for it to relent. Then, after sixteen years without so much as sniffing a Stanley Cup, the Nordiques up and left for Colorado, just as the team had become a championship contender. A few months after the move, the Canadiens traded goalie Patrick Roy, who was born in Quebec City and had already won two Stanley Cups, to the newly renamed Colorado Avalanche, a trade they never would've made had the Nordiques remained in Quebec City. It was Roy who put Colorado over the top. The Avalanche went on to win the Stanley Cup in their first season, less than a year after leaving Quebec City. Since the Nordiques left, the NHL has passed over Quebec City nine times in welcoming six expansion franchises and relocating three more.

Quebec City will never be complete until the Nordiques return. What makes a hockey team, especially one that no longer exists, so synonymous with a city? In Canada, it is difficult to divorce hockey from politics. The Nordiques were born in the midst of political turmoil in Quebec. They entered the WHA in 1972, just two years after the October Crisis, and their tenure in the NHL covered the tensest fifteen years of Quebec's push for independence from Canada, bookended by a pair of referendums on sovereignty: one in 1980, during the Nordiques' first season, and the second in 1995, the year the team left for Colorado. When the Nordiques were brought into the NHL, Quebec media began to challenge the Canadiens' hold over the hearts and minds of Québécois. The Nordiques fleur-de-lis logo became symbolic of the sovereignty movement, while the CH of the Canadiens symbolized a team out of touch with the contemporary political climate in Quebec. Winning the Stanley Cup in 1993 helped the Canadiens, but it wasn't until the Nordiques left for Colorado and the 1995 referendum narrowly rejected sovereignty that the Canadiens reclaimed their place as the sole NHL representative for Québécois hockey.

We walk around the arena, looking for a way in, but it's sealed tight. Adrian presses his face to the glass doors and cups his eyes.

"See anything?" I ask.

"Nah, just some old posters and stuff."

If there is a story that typifies what the Nordiques meant, and still mean, to Quebec City, it comes from Paul Stewart, who played twenty-one games in the NHL, all with the Nordiques. Stewart retired from playing in the early 1980s, then spent seventeen years in the NHL as a referee. In 2009, after he retired from officiating, he was asked to referee an NHL Legends Game at the Colisée Pepsi.

Stewart was to be introduced after Mark Messier and Mario Lemieux. Tough gig. While standing in the runway before the game, he turned to them and said, "I'll bet you both that I get the biggest ovation."

Messier and Lemieux looked at each other and laughed.

"Yeah, 'Stewy,'" Lemieux said. "Whatever you say."

"No, I'm serious. Let's make a bet. If I win, you buy me dinner tonight. If I lose, it's my treat."

"You're on."

Messier was introduced first, to a huge cheer. Lemieux, who was born in Quebec, received a standing ovation that lasted two minutes. When it was Stewart's turn, the crowd was crickets.

Messier and Lemieux smirked and chuckled to themselves. Then Stewart told them both to wait. There, in front of a full house, Stewart pulled off his zebra stripes. Underneath was a Nordiques jersey with his old number 22 on it.

The crowd erupted. When he hammed it up and pointed to the Nordiques crest, they went wild.

Stewart skated by Lemieux.

"I think I'll have wine with that dinner."

Driving 100 kilometers (62 miles) due south of the capital, along the rolling pastoral backroads of southeastern Quebec, we arrive early at the arena on the edge of downtown Thetford Mines, an old asbestos mining town. It is cash only, with hands stamped for in-and-out privileges during intermissions. The arena has old-school wooden benches, arranged in a hierarchy of orange, blue, and red. The seats are only about half full, which isn't bad for a game in early November, but the suites are all packed, as is the makeshift press box. Standing room only is full, too. The sightlines are so good and so close to the ice that many fans choose to take in the game while standing and simultaneously eating, drinking, debating one other, and yelling at opposition players.

The Jonquière Marquis come out first, in their green road jerseys, to a chorus of boos. Then come the Thetford Mines Assurancia, in their white home wear, to the roar of the crowd. Everyone turns toward the Canadian flag for the national anthem, sung in French, and then back to the ice as the game operations crew spins "Eye of the Tiger" for the opening faceoff. As the players take their spots, number 23 for the Assurancia, Thomas Bellemare, and number 24 for the Marquis, Chris Cloutier, line up beside each other and begin an animated discourse at center ice. It is only the seventh game of the season for both teams, but Bellemare and Cloutier have already accumulated sixty-two minutes in penalties between them. Neither player has scored a goal, and they won't the entire season.

The fans cheer Bellemare and curse Cloutier as they seek their pound of flesh early. It looks like the two are going to give it to them right away: Bellemare and Cloutier turn to face each other. When the puck is dropped, Bellemare's gloves do, too, along with his stick. He lunges for Cloutier but finds only air. He's been duped. Cloutier has faked dropping his gloves and instead jumped onto the bench. The Marquis' first line leaps over the boards and onto the ice in a mismatch against the Assurancia's fourth line. As the boos rain down on Cloutier, I can see him smiling from the bench. He won't play another shift the rest of the game.

Unlike NHL rinks, which have the players' benches beside each other on the same side of the ice, in Thetford Mines the benches are on opposite sides. For good reason. Goals still win games in Quebec's oddly named Ligue Nord-Américaine de Hockey (LNAH), but in Thetford Mines, as well as a handful of other small towns in southern Quebec, fights are what sell tickets.

Since the league was founded in 1996, there have been two constants: fighting and Thetford Mines. The town is the only franchise that has managed to maintain a team the entire time. It has reached the final a league-record twelve times, with three championships to show for it. There is a reason why the team has managed to stay in Thetford Mines all this time, while every other team has come and gone. People here support their own. At just twenty-five thousand people, Thetford Mines isn't Montreal, Quebec City, or even Sherbrooke, but year after year, the town comes out to support its team. It makes many players want to come home to Quebec and play, long after the expiration of their pro careers.

During the first intermission, with the game tied 2–2, I take a walk around the rink. From the cluttered ice, to the covered boards, to the backs of the players' benches, to the tops of the wooden seating, to the massive white and maroon Pizzeria du Boulevard ad that runs the length of the rink, it is awash in advertising. Gaudy, it gives the arena the feel of a small-town newsletter packed with ads from local businesses. But the ads are what keep prices down for tickets ($17) and beer ($5.25) and keep the team in town. Like so many local arenas across Canada, Thetford Mines could've sold the naming rights to its old barn, which opened in 1964, but hometown hockey heroes mean something to a town of this size, especially former Quebec Nordiques goaltender Mario Gosselin, whose name graces the arena.

As the teams return to the ice, game operations throw on AC/DC's "Thunderstruck," that hard-rock staple used to turn hockey games into boxing matches. The theatrics from the first period carry over into the second. This time, the fans get into the act. A tall skinny man wearing a Canadiens T-shirt staggers down to the Marquis' bench. He must've already had at least $42 worth of beer, because he starts doing the chicken dance behind the bench, hurling at Cloutier the hard consonant swear words that make French profanity so visceral and violent sounding. He receives the third-loudest cheer from the crowd in a game full of them.

Later in the period, with the Marquis up two goals, Cloutier lifts his skates over the boards during a scrum on the ice, only to take a seat on top as the melee continues. One of the Assurancia players makes a beeline for him. He would've made it if one of the officials hadn't tackled him like a linebacker mere feet from the bench. Cloutier, cool as Carey Price in a playoff game, never flinches.

It is pro wrestling histrionics, and the fans love it. I must confess, it is great theater.

The period finishes with the Marquis up 5–4. The English soundtrack continues as the players head to their dressing rooms for the second intermission.

Not known for its literary flair, Wikipedia deadpans its description of the league and its players: "the LNAH is not known for its skill level." Yet dozens of ex-NHL players have come through here, most at the end of their careers, as well as hundreds who've played in Europe or minor pro leagues in North America. To play in the LNAH, players must've been born in Quebec or played in either the Quebec Maritimes Junior Hockey League (QMJHL) or at a Quebec university. For many of them, it is their last chance at pro hockey, and they use the league as a way to transition into life after the game.

The LNAH is a weekend league, with a work-hard, play-harder philosophy of hockey. Earning only a minimal stipend per game, each player has a day job. Only a couple of Assurancia skaters live in Thetford Mines. Most commute from Montreal, others as far away as Ontario. To make sure their players get to and from games safely and on time, the Assurancia have four team vans. The players finish work early on Friday, jump into one of the vans midafternoon, and are driven to wherever the game is that night.

When the Marquis and Assurancia return for the third period, they hit the ice to "Start Me Up" by the Rolling Stones. Cloutier continues trolling the Assurancia and their hostile fans. At a break in play, he makes a steroid gesture to one of the biggest players on the Assurancia, pumping an imaginary needle into his arm. During a TV timeout, Cloutier jumps onto the ice for a little skate, eliciting a deluge of boos, colorful metaphors, and shouts of "Assiez-toi!" and "CLOOOtiyaaay!"

With about seven minutes left in the third period, and the Marquis still up by a goal, a heavily tattooed waitress comes down to the Marquis' bench and hands the coach a pint of beer. He toasts the entire arena, takes a gulp, and sets it down on the bench. The crowd laps it up.

Yet with all the theatrics, and all the expectations of a fight night, a funny thing happens. A hockey game suddenly breaks out.

Without much time left on the clock, the Assurancia get a powerplay. Desperate to score, the team pulls its goalie. The crowd begins chanting: "Go ThetFORD Go! Go ThetFORD Go! Go ThetFORD Go!" Then it happens. A shot from a defenseman floats from the point, through a crowd of bodies, toward the net, and past the goalie. The Assurancia have tied the game with just 0:45.9 left to play. Centre Mario Gosselin shakes to its foundation.

Before the start of overtime, Cloutier goes out for another skate, but the fans don't care anymore. With momentum clearly on their side, it takes just thirty seconds for the Assurancia to complete the comeback.

The crowd is electric, the Assurancia players ecstatic. Cloutier is apoplectic. He tries to goad the Assurancia into postgame fisticuffs, but they are too busy taunting him with the scoreboard. The officials eventually force him off the ice as the Assurancia leave to Kool and the Gang's "Celebration."

After the game, Adrian and I wander down to the Assurancia's dressing room. We go up to the first staff member we see and ask if we can talk to the coach.

When we walk into Bobby Baril's small, windowless office, he gets up from his chair to shake hands and welcome us to Thetford Mines in his broken English, which is far more serviceable than my fractured French.

"What I can do for you guys?" he asks.

"That was my first LNAH game," I say. "It was a really good atmosphere. The fans were wild, the atmosphere was amazing, and there was a lot of energy in the building."

"For a game in November, it's nice," Bobby says. "Because, you know, in the league, in December, the caliber and the people in the stands jump. And after Christmas, jump again. And in the playoff, something else."

"So you get a packed house here?" Adrian asks.

"Tonight, we have eleven hundred, and last year in the playoff it was two thousand and more, every game. You see the atmosphere tonight? Put another thousand in that place, it's awesome."

Over the team's existence, several NHL players have come through Thetford Mines, including Mathieu Biron, Yves Racine, and Simon Gamache. The team has also dressed its fair share of pure pugilists, including Kevin Bolduc, who somehow racked up 493 penalty minutes in just 113 games over nine seasons with the team while not registering a single point.

"I know the league has a reputation for fighting," I say. "But there weren't any fights tonight."

"You saw the game," Bobby says. "They had one guy, with the beard."

"Yeah, Cloutier."

"He didn't want to go."

"Yeah, we saw the mind games," Adrian says.

"It's cheap to do that, you know? We don't do that. We're the tougher club in the league. We've got eight to ten guys that can go every time. We can dance a lot. We can dance long time."

Born nearby and raised in Thetford Mines, Bobby is now in his thirteenth year as coach and general manager of the Assurancia, all while living in Quebec City. He coached for seven years in the QMJHL, but with three kids he wanted to spend more time at home and less on the road. For him, it is the perfect setup. During the week, he works his day job at a car dealership in Quebec City. On weekends, he coaches his hometown team and drives back home to sleep in his own bed every night. After the team's win over the Marquis, Bobby has to get back to take his daughter to soccer early in the morning.

"One last question, though," Adrian says as we get up to leave. "As someone that's from Thetford Mines, are you a Nordiques fan?"

He isn't. Nor is he a Canadiens fan.

"My name's Bobby, and my father give me that name because of Bobby Orr long time ago," he says. "So my father bring me to the old Boston Garden to see the Bruins. Every year I go to Boston to see one games. I'm got a son who's twenty-six, and every year we go, me and him, to Boston, see a Bruins games, every year like my father did too with me when I was kid."

Adrian looks at me and grins. Thetford Mines is his last stop with me after six weeks on the road together. The next day, we'll be heading back to Toronto, Adrian to fly to the Middle East to add flags forty-four and forty-five to his stick bag from Oman and Bahrain, and me to continue the drive solo through Ontario.

"Hockey road trips," he says.

Ontario: Hockey's Heartland

Scratch a Canadian and you will get a hockey story. It may be the first atom game played on a subzero winter night or a hat trick in a beer league contest of forty-year-olds. —Bruce Dowbiggin, *The Meaning of Puck*

I T IS MIDMORNING as I walk through the hangar at Expedition Helicopters and outside to FODI (Foxtrot Oscar Delta India), a sleek, black-and-gray Eurocopter AS350 A-Star helicopter that has just returned from a diamond-drilling operation up north. I've driven up to Cochrane on assignment for *The Hockey News* to meet with Chad Calaiezzi, resident helicopter pilot and Maple Leafs fan. Aside from his blue Leafs cap and my black trapper hat, we're dressed about the same for our daytrip some 75 kilometers (47 miles) into the bush north of his hometown: waterproof boots, double socks, insulated pants, multiple upper layers, and gloves.

In his gravelly, yet friendly, voice, Chad gives me a thorough review of all emergency measures and runs through every emergency device. The briefing complete, he tells me to hop in and buckle up. He then fires up the blades and waits for FODI to warm up. Once the engine is roaring, he lifts us into the sky, makes a swooping right turn over the Trans-Canada, and points us north of his hometown, to the spot marked "BARILKO" on the screen in the cockpit.

It's been sixty years since Bill Barilko was found in 1962, and thirty years since The Tragically Hip resurrected his story in a song in 1992. In all that time, there have only been four known visits to the crash site where Barilko and Henry Hudson died in 1951, every one of them by air, and none since the plane was retrieved in 2011.

The lack of interest in the wreckage remains the most puzzling part of the Barilko story. The most important artifact from one of the most legendary events in Canadian history, and yet no one wanted it once it was pulled from the muskeg where it had lain for sixty years. Not in Toronto, where Barilko played, nor Timmins, where he was born and is buried. Nor anywhere in the rest of Canada.

In that way, the fate of the wreckage parallels the fate of the story. There is a conspicuous absence of anything honoring the man who scored the greatest goal in Leafs history and one of the most iconic of all-time. All there is of Barilko is the original banner hanging in Timmins' McIntyre Arena, a copy that hangs in Toronto's Scotiabank Arena, and a privately funded billboard, erected seventy years after his death, at the edge of Porcupine Lake, from where the plane departed and never returned.

This lack of recognition becomes even more puzzling when the story is put alongside its closest American analogy, the death of Buddy Holly. Yet despite checking off many of the same boxes—dapper young man, made a snap decision to fly, died in a 1950s plane crash in his early twenties at the height of his career—Barilko has never achieved the same mythic status in Canada as Holly has in America. There is no statue, monument, or plaque that honors him; no school, street, park, or arena named after him; no public exhibit, display, or exposition to remember him; no movie or full-length documentary that tells his story; just a couple of books and songs, a nine-minute mini-doc, and a screenplay from 2003 that never saw the light of day.

The sun is hiding behind the clouds as Chad continues north, but the gray-blue sky is clear at five hundred feet. We pass the brown Abitibi

River, "muddy like the Mississippi," Chad says over our headsets, and soon after we spot a pack of three bull moose and another of seven. As the houses thin out and the two-lane Trans-Canada gives way to concession roads, then logging trails, it doesn't take long for civilization to surrender to wilderness. The last vestige is the Island Falls hydroelectric line that cuts a swath through the forest all the way to the Detour Lake gold mine near the Ontario–Quebec border.

Barely five minutes into the flight and the forest is already growing denser. Flying above the trees, I now understand why it took so long to find the plane. All I can see, as far as the horizon, is black spruce, like a tightly woven greenish-black carpet sprinkled with winter white. They're packed so tightly that no one would've found the plane unless the sunlight hit the twisted metal at just the right angle to catch the eye of a passing pilot, as happened on May 31, 1962, when Gary Fields spotted the most famous plane wreck in Canadian history.

Half an hour later, Chad announces, "It's basically right underneath us."

He banks right to a snow-covered bog nearby, where the drainage is so poor that trees struggle to grow beyond the height of a human. He uses the blades' downthrust to clear a landing pad, then sets us down softly into the snow, like landing on a giant pillow, "nose down, tail up," he says, so that the tail rotor doesn't clip a tree.

"FODI down and clear."

Like so many Canadians under fifty years old, and still others more over that mark, I'd never heard of Barilko until The Tragically Hip released their album *Fully Completely* in 1992. The lyrics from "Fifty Mission Cap," plucked from the back of card 340 in the 1992 Pro Set Hockey series, brought the story to a generation of Canadians who hadn't been born when Barilko disappeared in 1951 or even when the wreckage was discovered in 1962. More than thirty years on, the song is still doing that. Whether it holds any special significance for The Hip, only the band can confirm. But the first time they headlined Maple Leaf Gardens, where Barilko scored his legendary overtime winner, The Hip saw fit to shine a spotlight on the 1951 Stanley Cup banner hanging in the rafters just as singer Gord Downie reached the line, "The last goal he ever scored won the Leafs the Cup." And for their final show ever, with Downie diagnosed with terminal brain cancer, the band chose to kick off their farewell concert with "Fifty Mission Cap."

"Fifty Mission Cap" is not really a hockey song, though. The repeated verse that gives the basics about Barilko (it mentions neither the plane nor the crash) is combined with a chorus about a hat that represents fifty successful wartime flights. The narrator keeps a hockey card of Barilko in his cap, which he wears to make himself look like a man of vast experience.

Perhaps it's fitting that it's not a hockey song, because the Barilko story is not really a hockey story. It is a Canadian story, one that hasn't received its due, and likely never will, because it happened in Canada.

Many Canadians know that Bill Barilko won four Stanley Cups in five seasons with the Leafs, scoring the cup-clinching overtime goal on April 21, 1951. That summer, on August 24, Barilko joined Hudson on his floatplane for a fishing trip up to Seal River, Quebec, not far from Chisasibi. After two days of fishing for Arctic char and brook trout, they left for Timmins on August 26, stopping in Fort George on their way back. They never made it home. Authorities searched for months in what remains the largest aviation search and rescue mission in Canadian history.

"If that story had happened in the United States, if Bill Barilko was a baseball player and he hit a grand slam home run and won the World Series and was killed a couple weeks later in a plane crash, we would know all about it," said bassist Gord Sinclair in an interview with the Canadian Press. "There would be movies about it, and Robert Redford would've played him. It took a hockey card and a goofy little band from Kingston to sort of resurrect that story, because we don't do our own stories very well. We don't build on our myths."

Once the blades stop turning, Chad and I hop out and get ready for the trek into the bush. Chad swaps his Leafs cap for a toque and then checks his GPS and compass, while I wander around to soak in our surroundings. It is only 1.3 kilometers (0.8 miles) to the crash site, but that is as the crow flies. In the Hudson Plain, there is no such thing as walking in a straight line, just a perpetual zigzag necessitated by constant choices between bad and worse options. It is a minefield of muskeg, marsh, and peat, covered in cotton grass, moss, and lichen, underneath a shrub layer of dwarf birch, willow, and northern Labrador tea, topped by a canopy of mostly black spruce with jack pine, birch, poplar, aspen, and tamarack mixed in. And all of it atop water, which makes it feel like walking on a wet sponge. To get through it all, you must pick your way around trees and past brush while trying not to fall into waterholes or lose your footwear to the suction of the muskeg.

"At one point, they actually flagged a trail in here," Chad says as we get going. "The first time they came."

The first people to reach the crash site did so on June 6, 1962, after Fields had returned to the area to find the plane again and mark it from the air with toilet paper, the best GPS of the time. That day, ground parties from the Department of Lands and Forests, the Ontario Provincial Police, and the Department of Transport all went in. There they found the plane nose deep in the muskeg, with what was left of Barilko and Hudson in their seats.

Consumed with the conspiracy theories that had surrounded the disappearance for eleven years, the police took an axe to the pontoons in search of gold that Hudson, a dentist who used it for fillings in his practice, was rumored to have been running. They found nothing. After retrieving the remains of Barilko and Hudson, the authorities picked the wreckage clean of mementos and took the parts with the plane's identification numbers on it, then left the rest of it to rust in the forest.

For forty-three years, the plane remained where it crashed. By then, the site had to be found all over again because the original coordinates had been logged incorrectly. So on May 20, 2005, after several flights to pinpoint the wreckage by air, Dr. John Shaw, who'd taken over Hudson's dental practice in Timmins, hiked in with a group from a lumber company licensed to harvest the area. There they marked the site again and replaced the original plaque put up in 1962, which made no mention of Barilko or Hudson:

WRECKAGE OF FAIRCHILD 24. CF-FXT
CRASHED 26 AUG. 1951.FOUND AND
INVESTIGATED JUNE 1962 BY ACCIDENT
INVESTIGATION DEPARTMENT
DEPARTMENT OF TRANSPORT
OTTAWA.

In its place, Shaw put up a sign with an image of a yellow Fairchild 24 model G and a simple inscription underneath:

At this location

August 26, 1951

Bill Barilko

and

Dentist

Henry Hudson

Lost their Lives

Rest in Peace

Later that year, Chad guided in some colleagues and friends on Christmas Eve. Six years after that, the wreckage would receive its fourth and final visit in the bush, when a group from Timmins decided it was time to bring it home.

On October 16, 2011, with the blessing of Barilko's and Hudson's families, sixteen people set out for the crash site on an expedition led by Shaw and financed by local businessman Bill Hughes. Among them were Timmins residents Kevin Vincent and Mike Mulryan, Barilko's cousin Sandra Cattarello, and eighty-six-year-old Archie Chenier, whom Barilko replaced on the fishing trip when Chenier had to cancel last minute. With mining and logging encroaching in the area, the worry was that parts of the plane would start ending up on eBay.

The group was helicoptered to around where Chad and I landed. When they reached the wreckage, Cattarello led them in prayer, after which Shaw read an A. E. Housman poem, "To an Athlete Dying Young." Then everyone got to work. Using nothing but axes, shovels, and their bare hands, they pulled what was left of the plane from the ground and netted it for Chad, who made three trips to airlift it all onto a flatbed truck. Before leaving, Mulryan nailed a Leafs puck underneath the sign Shaw had put up six years earlier.

With the plane safely stored in Timmins, the group began working on finding a permanent home for the wreckage. They reached out to the Hockey Hall of Fame, the Timmins Victor M. Power Airport, the Timmins Museum National Exhibition Centre, the Timmins Sports Hall of Fame, and the Canadian Bushplane Heritage Centre. There were no takers. There was a promising meeting with Maple Leaf Sports Entertainment about creating a traveling exhibit to crisscross the country. Then MLSE's president resigned, the email trail went cold, and no one from the organization has picked it up since.

After nearly ten years of trying, the only person to step up was a Leafs superfan, who picked up the wreckage from the shipping container it was sitting in back in Timmins and displayed it at home with the rest of his collection. Nearly seventy years after his disappearance, it was as if Barilko had been forgotten all over again.

"The people involved, they all had big plans for this," Chad says as we reach the halfway mark of the hike. "To me it should be in the Hockey Hall of Fame."

Slowly but surely, Chad and I make our way through the forest, moving around bushes and between trees, climbing over fallen trunks, pushing back branches while dodging recoiling ones, trudging through thigh-high snow, and stepping into waterholes. Every so often, we brush against a tree that plops cartoonish piles of snow onto our heads. Our waterproof boots turn out to be water-retaining boots, and we've already sweated through our base layers.

"Imagine walking in here back in 1962 with no GPS, looking for toilet paper," Chad says as he continues to lead us through the bush. "They'd be on the compass steady, trying to make sure they were walking straight."

"Just a mile, eh?"

"Oh, I'm sure we're going to walk three by the time we get there."

Chad stops and points to some underbrush and then to some tree roots to avoid.

"Thickest bush in North America," he says as we approach an area of alders that looks impassable. "It's starting to look like what I remember the crash site being. I remember a tree like this. I wondered if it had been damaged back when the plane came down in '51."

As we get closer to the crash site, Chad starts counting down in meters.

"Two hundred twenty-five meters . . . One hundred seventy . . . One sixty-five . . . One hundred . . ."

At the eighty-meter mark, we hit a wall of cedar. We have no choice but to plunge through it.

"The hockey gods are making it difficult for you to tell your story," Chad says.

"That's okay. As long as we have their blessing."

With fewer than fifty meters to go, the GPS starts to have directional dyslexia because of the density of the forest, leading us every which way.

"The arrow's still pointing ahead, but we're still the same distance away," Chad says. "I'm going to try to reset it. 'Head southwest to BARILKO,' it says. I think what we've been doing is walking around it.

"Twenty-nine meters . . . Twenty-five meters . . . Twenty meters . . .

"'Northeast to BARILKO.' We're definitely going right around it. We just went southwest and now it's telling us to go northeast.

"Six meters . . . Three meters . . . Two meters . . ."

We stop at a small clearing. To our left is a downed tree, to our right a wall of snow-laden spruce. We search for the sign Shaw put up in 2005 and the Leafs puck Mulryan nailed to the tree in 2011. We see neither. Chad suggests splitting up to look for them.

"We're at the location," he says. "Try to find the sign. If the sign fell off the tree, it's buried. All I can say is kind of wander around."

We walk in opposite directions. After half an hour of searching, still unsuccessful, I stop and take in the Northern Ontario bush. With Chad out of earshot, I hear nothing but silence. It's so quiet it's loud. I think about Barilko and Hudson and wonder what it is that has brought me here. It isn't morbid curiosity or dark tourism, for there is no wreckage to see. It isn't to see the sign or the puck, because I know the tree they're nailed to could've fallen down and been covered by the snow. I've come to pay my respects to Bill Barilko and Henry Hudson, who was my age when he died. I've come to honor their story.

According to a local tourist information center in Timmins, the places visitors most want to see in town are the Maple Leaf Tavern, where singers Stompin' Tom Connors and Shania Twain got their starts, and Barilko's headstone in Timmins Memorial Cemetery. Among those who've made the pilgrimage to his grave is Oliver Solaro, aka "Brokentooth," who rode his motorcycle from Toronto to Cochrane in the dead of winter in search of the crash site nearly ten years ago.

Barilko's disappearance in 1951 left a huge hole in the Leafs' defense. It was Tim Horton who eventually replaced him. After visiting Barilko's grave, I meet Oliver at one of Horton's pluralized eponymous franchises. It is easy to pick him out of the crowded coffee shop. Already six coffees deep when I walk in, he's wearing the same Scottish attire he had on in the documentary he made of his own trek in tribute to Barilko.

"It had to be the guy in the kilt," I say.

"How did you know, I'm trying so hard to blend in," Oliver says as he adjusts his clothes. "Sorry, my kilt is bunching up. It's disconcerting."

Oliver has just picked up a new motorcycle in preparation for shooting some footage for a pilot episode of an upcoming trip across the Arctic. It is the next in a long list of northern adventures that has branded him Canada's Ice Road Biker for his epic motorcycle rides through the North in the throes of winter. Given the moniker and the kilt he's wearing at this time of year, I assume Oliver is a fellow cold-weather junkie.

"Dude, I hate the cold," he says. "But I love what the cold shows me. I love what the cold peels back that you can't see at any other time of year. I'll put up with it for that, because of the beauty, the art, the magic, the wonderful assault on the eyes that you get in the wintertime when you go to places and see things that you can't see at any other time. It's worth losing a finger, it's worth freezing a cornea, it's worth cutting off your toes."

Oliver still has all his digits, although he did almost lose three toes to frostbite and has nerve damage in three of his fingers. He's also lost some vision in one eye after a cornea froze on one of his trips. In 2013, Oliver drove the world's longest ice road, the 752-kilometer (467-mile) Wapusk Trail, the first person ever to do so by motorcycle. In 2018, he converted a motorcycle into a snow bike to haul a sled filled with one thousand pounds of donated dog food to Churchill, Manitoba, to feed local mutts after the rail line to the town had been washed out. In between, Oliver set out to reach the Barilko crash site by land, something no one had ever done. Now in his mid-fifties, he was my age when he made the trip in 2014.

"Even if you're not a rabid hockey fan, the Barilko story is fucking brilliant," he says. "It's such an awesome story. It's a tragic, sad, dark ending, but the story itself, on its own, is brilliant. The world needs to know this story."

Oliver's pilgrimage started after a game at Mattamy Athletic Centre in Toronto. Formerly Maple Leaf Gardens, it now houses Toronto Metropolitan University's athletic facilities. Under the watchful eyes of suspicious security guards and lingering fans, he placed a loonie at center ice under the cathedral ceiling of the old arena, where Barilko scored the Stanley Cup-winning goal in 1951, and then put it back in his pocket to be placed at the crash site. The next day, Oliver rode his Kawasaki KLR, "Agatha," up to Expedition Helicopters, where Chad helped him choose the snowshoe-friendly route least likely to end in Oliver's demise.

"I thought, 'He's the one who's going to have to haul my frozen, half-eaten carcass out of the woods,'" Oliver says. "When the critters come to get me after I've fallen off a ridge and there's nothing but a satellite spot beacon sticking out of a steaming pile of bear scat—he's going to have to be the one who's going to have to fish out the beacon."

After spending the night in Cochrane, Oliver drove north to the end of an unmapped logging road that got him nearly 7 kilometers (4 miles) east of the crash site. There he left Agatha in a snowdrift and strapped on his snowshoes. He set off into the bush with his camping gear, an axe, a GPS, video equipment, the best $50 sleeping bag he could find, and a book of poetry by Robert Service.

It didn't take long or far for Oliver to get acquainted with the bush. Every ten steps or so, he would plunge through waist-high champagne powder snow, get caught in the tangled roots below, and wrestle and wriggle to wrench himself free. After a full day of this, he made it only a little over a mile before setting up camp, which meant making a tent out of the black spruce and sleeping underneath it. After more of the same the next day, Oliver hunkered down for another night of reading poetry in the minus-thirties. In the morning, after briefly flirting with the thought of carrying on, he decided to turn back, vowing to one day return.

"It was heart-wrenching," Oliver says. "I remember looking up at the sky and choking back tears for being so close and not being able to do it."

"So what was it that drew you to the site?" I ask.

"The most important thing was just literally standing on the spot," Oliver replies. "Not telling the world that I'd been there, but telling myself, and that was enough. If nothing came of it, if no one ever read anything about it, if no video was ever made, it would've been ten-thousand-fold worth it for me to just say to myself, 'I stood there, where Henry and Bill met their makers. They saw the end of the world right there.'"

After coming out of the bush, with the loonie still in his pocket, Oliver decided that if he couldn't lay it at the crash site, he would do so at Barilko's grave.

Oliver rode Agatha to Timmins Memorial Cemetery and found Barilko's headstone. He cleared away the snow and then stripped out of his motorcycle gear. Wearing nothing but a black sweater, winter boots, an Indiana Jones hat, and a kilt, he sat down in the snow, leaned against Barilko's headstone, and sipped some single malt Scotch as he scribbled in his journal. Before leaving, he pulled the loonie out of his pocket and laid it on the base of the headstone. In his short doc, *Blue Line*, Oliver narrates the scene:

Imagine for a minute you're William Barilko. You come from a poor family in a Northern Ontario mining town, and you're just twenty-four years old. Tonight, you're going to play in a Stanley Cup Final game against the great Montreal Canadiens. And you don't know this yet, but it's going to be you that they hoist up onto their battered shoulders. You. You're going to kiss the girl and drink from the cup as an entire nation celebrates you. Until the bony hand of fate plucks you from the sky.

On Good Friday, March 31, 1961, about five hundred people packed the Wellington Street Arena in Gananoque for the provincial bantam semifinal against Parry Sound. Gananoque won the first of the two-game total-goals playoff series on the road a week earlier. Parry Sound made the long road trip from the shores of Georgian Bay to this little town on the St. Lawrence for game two.

In the crowd that night were several NHL scouts, including a young Scotty Bowman from the Canadiens, as well as Wren Blair and legendary center Milt Schmidt from the Boston Bruins. Blair and Schmidt had made the drive to Gananoque to check out a pair of local players, Doug Higgins (number 8) and Rick Eaton (number 17), but by the end of the second period their eyes had become glued to a small skinny kid from Parry Sound wearing number 2. Five years later, Bobby Orr debuted for the Bruins.

Lost in the lore of Orr is how that game in Gananoque ended and what became of the two players the Bruins came to scout. Gananoque was a powerhouse in the 1960–61 season. Doug and Rick were the team's two superstars. Both knew that bird dogs from the Canadiens and Bruins were going to be scouting them that night. After Parry Sound jumped out to a 2–0 advantage in the first period, Gananoque tied it up 3–3 by the end of the second, with a goal from Rick and a pair of assists from Doug. Eventually, Gananoque took the lead. Orr managed to send the game into overtime, but it would not be his night, even if the game ended up charting his NHL career. Doug got his third assist as Gananoque won the game and the series in overtime.

I track down Doug at his home in Petawawa in eastern Ontario. All these years later, he can still recall, in detail, the night they beat Bobby Orr.

"Oh, it was a hell of a game," Doug says. "You better believe it."

"Did you know about Orr when you played him?" I ask.

"No, we didn't know about him. But he probably knew about Ricky and me by that time."

I like Doug's swagger. He had it as a kid, and he still has it into his seventies.

In the annals of Orr, Doug's story usually ends there. But after beating Parry Sound, Gananoque advanced to the best-of-five provincial final. There they played a team from Goderich, on the coast of Lake Huron. It was a tight series, but Gananoque won it in five games. Doug had four goals and one assist in the Saturday night final to give his hometown its first provincial championship.

"That was our Stanley Cup, winning that," he says.

The town feted the players like it was a Stanley Cup. When they returned home in the early hours of Sunday morning, just about all of Gananoque came out to meet them. The local fire engine siren blared and the players were brought up to the balcony of the old Provincial Inn in the heart of Gananoque, where the town often made announcements. As captain, Doug had to give a speech to the crowd.

"I looked down the street and it's rows of people welcoming us," Doug says. "They got us out of the car, put us on the firetruck, took us through the town, frickin' siren going, the streets lined with people. This old lady came running out in her nightcap, and she goes, 'Has the whole goddamn town gone crazy?' Everybody got behind it. That doesn't happen today, but that's what it was back then."

After that season, Doug went on to play junior hockey and college hockey in southeastern Ontario. Although he never made it to the NHL, he did end up signing a contract. Two, in fact.

One night, Doug came home from school and his father told him to sit down. Bowman had called. The Canadiens wanted to sign him.

"Well, Christ, that was my dream team as a kid," Doug says. "I stood up and literally was dizzy thinking about it. So he came and I signed a contract with Montreal. Still have it."

At the time, the NHL consisted of the Original Six teams. The other five quickly came calling. When it was Boston's turn, the Bruins phoned and asked if they could come over to talk with Doug. His father told them they were wasting their time.

"We'll be over tomorrow night," they said.

The next night, Blair and Schmidt arrived at the house. Doug's father told them again that his son had already signed with the Canadiens. Blair opened his briefcase.

"Well, Doug, Montreal actually can't sign you," he said. "I got your release here from the town of Gananoque."

In what was common practice at the time, before the NHL instituted a draft, the Bruins had been sponsoring Gananoque's hockey system under the table for years in return for being the first NHL team in line to snatch a prospect or two coming out of town. It was through this side deal that the Bruins got first dibs on Doug.

Doug was only a teenager, but the kid had moxie, and he wasn't afraid to negotiate, even with hockey's big guns. He'd already received new skates from the Canadiens, and the Chicago Black Hawks, who won the Stanley Cup that year, had sent him a stick autographed by the entire team. Doug knew he had leverage.

"I wasn't stupid at fourteen," he says. "I told them, 'You buy my parents a new car and I'll sign. The contract plus a new car.' They said, 'We don't have that authority. We'll have to speak to the owner of the Bruins. We'll give you a call in about five days.'"

They left the house at midnight. At seven o'clock the next morning, the phone rang.

"Have your parents order the car," Blair told Doug. "We'll be over tonight."

Doug never did play a game with the Bruins, but his parents got that car: a brand-new 1961 Ford.

Doug's place in the Orr story has followed him everywhere, including Petawawa, where he resettled with his high school sweetheart, raised their three daughters, and had a long career in the federal government. For his part, Orr never forgot that game in Gananoque. He sent Doug a large autographed framed photo of the goal Orr scored to win the 1970 Stanley Cup:

Doug,
Thanks For The Pass
From Parry Sound to Gananoque
Your Friend
Bobby Orr

"You can't believe how this story affected my work and how it opened doors for me," Doug says. "It was amazing the way it helped my career."

All these years later, people still ask Doug about Orr and reporters come calling. Some he'll talk to, others he won't. I didn't ask Doug why he agreed to talk with me. Maybe it was because I took the time to read the footnotes in the Great Book of Hockey History instead of just the chapter headings. Or maybe it was because he was a fellow road tripper. Since retiring, Doug had been making semiannual hockey road trips with a group of ten friends (five Canadians and five Americans) in an attempt to see a game in every NHL city. So far, they've checked off Montreal, Toronto, Buffalo, Chicago, Detroit, Philadelphia, Pittsburgh, Columbus, Washington, and New York.

"It's a road trip like you're doing," he says. "We meet the Americans there. Sometimes they fly, but we always drive. We have more fun in the van than anything. I think we might just do Ottawa this year. The Americans wanna come to Ottawa because they like skating on the canal. We took them curling one year, and they all came out on the ice with helmets on."

When I mention to Doug that I haven't been able to track down Rick, he tells me he's still living in Gananoque. As kids, they lived just a block away from each other and played every level of hockey together until they aged out and went to different teams. They were fast friends growing up, and still are. Doug calls his old running mate.

"You just got out of the hospital? A new heart valve? Oh, a pacemaker? Holy Christ, the way you used to skate around me you don't need a pacemaker. Okay, I'll put Ronnie on, Rick. I'll be in touch, buddy."

Instead of following the Trans-Canada down to Highway 401, I opt for the meandering backroads of eastern Ontario that bring me to Perth for the night and then down to Gananoque in the morning, backdooring me into town. I drive over to Rick's house just down the road from the Lou Jeffries Recreation Centre, which replaced the old Wellington Street Arena and where today a photo of Doug and Rick and the rest of the 1961 championship team hangs in the lobby.

When I meet Rick at his home, he's been one day out of hospital. He is wheezy and has difficulty breathing. He's still getting used to his pacemaker. But his memory is sharp, especially of that championship season.

"We were beating most teams we played, and then we came to Parry Sound," Rick says. "That was tough."

Rick recalls that game much as Doug described it, then offers an additional detail. After the game, players from both teams poured into Boston Café in Gananoque. Among the group were Doug, Rick, and Orr, sharing Cherry Cokes after their hard-fought series. Hockey historian Bill Fitsell was smart enough to snap a photo for posterity. Everyone is all smiles, even Orr.

"I don't know if we'd have went if we'd lost," Rick says. "But we didn't lose."

After that championship season, Rick played a few more years with junior teams across Ontario. He even played briefly with Orr in junior hockey during Orr's first season with the Oshawa Generals. Like Doug, Rick also signed with the Bruins, although he never made it to Boston. He did have an offer to play semipro in Australia but turned it down, giving up hockey for good and taking a job at a local medical company, where he worked until retirement.

"You know whether you've got the talent to do it or you don't, and I knew after a certain point I didn't," Rick says. "I realized what my capabilities were and got out of it."

Although he was born in British Columbia, Rick was raised in Gananoque and has spent almost his entire life here. Having left when he was young, Doug never had to deal with the small-town chatter.

"'You're not as good as Bobby Orr,' I would get that a lot," Rick says.

"Nobody was as good as Bobby Orr, except maybe Wayne Gretzky," I say.

"No, but that didn't matter to some of them."

The fact is that only about 5,500 Canadians have played in the NHL since its first season, 1917–18, and most of those got only a touch further than Doug and Rick did in signing NHL contracts.

For the most part, Rick has treated the Orr chapter in his life as a positive. "Did I enjoy it while I was doing it? I loved every minute of it," he says. "They were great times while they lasted."

"Welcome to the Chardis!" says Chad Dobbin as he greets me in his backyard. "This is where the magic happens. Usually, the hot tub's rockin' so I'd have a big entrance, and you'd walk in and it'd be open and bubbling, but my heater went. Come on in, have a seat, take your jacket off."

Chardis is a mash-up of Chad's name and the Tardis from *Dr. Who*. It is the name Chad has given to the renovated backyard shed behind his small bungalow on a quiet side street about ten minutes north of the Scarborough Bluffs. I've made a beeline for it on leaving Gananoque. Above a faux retro red gas pump and a fire pit, the Chardis bears a handcrafted sign:

12 & ½
Shed Life Pub
BLHHOF Studios

Inside, all is as it should be. No computers, cubicles, filing cabinets, swivel chairs, or fluorescent lighting. It is a beer-league spa filled with hockey knickknacks and bric-a-brac.

Underneath a skylight is a seating area with a big-screen TV, a glass fireplace, and the out-of-order hot tub. Above the door, upon which a plaque bears the words "Beer League 4 Life," Chad, whose girth is equal to his gregariousness, has put up a sign that reads, "We Don't Skinny Dip. We Chunky Dunk." In the next room is a fully stocked bar, a bar fridge, and a small stage with a spotlight. On the far wall is a bookcase chock full of hockey memorabilia, with a gold Elvis bust, some Star Wars swag, wrestling figurines, a vinyl collection, a pinball machine, a bowling pin, and a dartboard. Completing the decor are some old license plates, posters for beer and motor oil, a Maple Leafs logo, and a liberated arena sign reading, "City staff visit this rink 2 times a day to flood and scrape, weather permitting."

I've just finished the tour when Chad's part-time teammate and long-time friend Greg Majster walks in, drinks and psychedelics in hand. Both forty-something, lifelong beer-leaguers, Chad and Greg go by the nicknames "Chippy" and "Stro." As co-founders of the Beer League Hockey Hall of Fame, they wear the titles of prime minister (Stro) and vice-prime minister (Chippy).

"Because we're in Canada, kid," Chippy says when I ask why.

The seeds of the BLHHOF (that's Beer League Hockey Hall of Fame to the uninitiated) were originally planted during the 2004–05 NHL lockout, when the league's billionaires (owners) and multimillionaires (players) held fans hostage during negotiations for a new collective bargaining agreement. A glimmer of hope came last minute, when the players caved to the owners' demands for a salary cap, but the capitulation wasn't complete enough for Commissioner Gary Bettman and the owners.

So on February 16, 2005, Bettman stood before the hockey world and canceled the season. The only other year the Stanley Cup has never been awarded was in 1919 during the Spanish flu pandemic. Even two world wars and COVID-19 didn't kill the cup. Only money could.

"I was like, this is bullshit, the Stanley Cup is a challenge cup," Stro says. "Lord Stanley made this fucking cup so that teams could challenge for it, and anybody that could win it would win it."

"Look at you spittin' facts," Chippy says. "Reality."

On March 18, 1892, Governor General Lord Stanley of Preston donated a trophy as an annual award for the best amateur hockey team in Canada. It was first awarded in 1893 as the Dominion Hockey Challenge Cup, until it was later renamed after its donor. Back then, there was no NHL, no organized pro league. The Stanley Cup was more like a boxing title than a championship hockey trophy. Any team could challenge the reigning heavyweight hockey champ, and the winner kept the cup until they lost a title fight. It stayed that way until it became the official trophy of the NHL.

When the league failed to award the Stanley Cup in 2005, Stro decided it should return to its roots. He drew up a letter to the NHL and the NHL Players' Association, contesting their hold over the trophy, and challenged them to an old-school on-ice duel:

Dear NHL and NHLPA:

Please accept this letter as written notice that I am personally with my hockey team challenging for the Stanley Cup, this June 20th, 2004, in Toronto at 4:30 pm at John Booth Arena located at 40 Rossmore Road.

I hope to hear from you soon regarding this matter.

Sincerely,

Greg Majster

"He tried to fight the NHL to let them have the best men's league team play for the Stanley Cup," Chippy says. "He went to war with them."

"I was like, 'Fucking, let's go, I got a team,'" Stro says. "'Bring whoever. Last year's winner? I don't care.'"

"Tampa Bay Lightning," I say, referring to the last team to win the Stanley Cup before the canceled season.

"Bring 'em on!" Stro says. "All I needed was money for a lawyer. "

Stro made several dozen copies of the letter and sent them out to the league and various media outlets. No one responded. Nor did the Lightning show up to the game. Or maybe they did and Stro just wasn't there. John Booth Memorial Arena is at 230 Gosford Boulevard. William H. Bolton Arena is the rink on Rossmore Road.

Undeterred, Stro wasn't done there. He went shopping in vintage shops and found something that resembled a championship trophy for $50. A scenic carpenter by trade, Chippy built a base for it, and they christened it the Spirit Cup, the new challenge cup of Canadian hockey.

That is when Chippy and Stro started talking about creating a hall of fame for beer-leaguers like themselves. Both were playing in the Adult Safe Hockey League (ASHL) in Toronto, the highest level of beer league in the country.

"We were a good hockey team and we were playing great hockey and shit, and Chippy was talking about his stats and how he keeps all his stats," Stro says. "I'm like, 'We should be in the Hockey Hall of Fame for this shit. We're no different than the NHL. We need our own hall of fame.'"

For more than ten years, Chippy and Stro let the idea percolate until they finally got to work. With the website, logo, and a small plaque in place, they hosted their inaugural induction ceremony in 2019. Nominations are open. They come from all over the world. Once a nomination is accepted, Stro calls the nominee to deliver the news, just like the Hockey Hall of Fame does, and Chippy sends them their paperwork. Inductees receive a certificate, a plaque, and some swag, including a BLHHOF T-shirt. They're even allowed to have their day with the plaque, like NHL players do with the Stanley Cup. For the lesser lights of the hockey world, induction is the crowning glory of their beer-league careers. In 2022, Michael Lalonde, the ASHL's all-time leading scorer in the nearby Oakville league, showed up to the ceremony with his entire team. "Fifteen guys in a stretched Hummer, loaded," Chippy says. "Everyone who ever gets inducted just goes all out."

Chippy and Stro are too Canadian to nominate themselves for induction. But in time they should go in. Stro has long dominated the ASHL as "the beer-league Lidström," as he likes to say, referring to the legendary Detroit Red Wings defenseman, while Chippy has been keeping track of his stats since he was fifteen years old. Game after game, season after season, he's kept handwritten rolling totals that cover more than one thousand games played and show more than five hundred goals, one thousand assists, and fifteen hundred points—hall-of-fame numbers for any player.

"When I started playing men's league and keeping stats for myself, I was always like, 'Why can't a guy, who doesn't play in the NHL, go get a thousand games and five hundred goals, and why shouldn't it mean as much to him?'" Chippy says. "I said I was gonna keep track from day one in men's league, and that's what I did. I have every single thing I've done, and I celebrate all the things along the way."

"It's one puck, one game, the spirit of hockey," Stro adds. "That's what it's about. It's about playing the game, not about anything else. To me, that's where I feel comfortable, that's my therapy. The metaphor for life is in the game of hockey in a way. That's the spirit of the Spirit Cup and why we did the Beer League Hockey Hall of Fame."

Peter Austin smiles and waves as I walk across the lobby of the Central Recreation Centre, not far from the Burlington Skyway, which extends over the western corner of Lake Ontario. Ahead of their game tonight against the Red Wings, the one I'm crashing, he's chatting away with some of his teammates on the Maple Leafs, one of six NHL-named teams in the gold division, the lowest and oldest in the Burlington Oldtimers Hockey

Club. On a roster full of players in their fifties, sixties, and seventies, Peter is the team's eldest statesman. But he wears his eighty years of wisdom well, with a mop of gray hair and a squinty-eyed smile that rarely leaves his face.

"You know how you can tell when the gold division's playing?" Peter says. "The handicap spots are full, there are more nitro bottles on the bench than water bottles, and every team has their own doctor."

I follow Peter into the dressing room, where he carves out a spot beside him. Leafs jerseys are hanging all around the room.

"How many of you are Leaf fans?" I ask his teammates.

"Unfortunately too many of the damn things," says Peter, a lifelong Canadiens fan born in Montreal.

"The thing about this room is there's actually people that can remember the Leafs winning the Stanley Cup," says one of the players.

"I actually watched it on TV," Peter says.

The bodies are older, the equipment more worn, but it is like any other beer-league dressing room. Age hasn't changed the dynamics despite all the talk of soreness and tightness. There is the same banter and bullshitting, the same chirping and teasing, the same profanity, and even a pregame pep talk from one of the players.

"Guys, let's get on the forecheck out there 'cause we don't wanna fall behind, so let's get the first goal," he says. "Just stick on them, forecheck, and everybody back hard, block some shots and away we go."

I hope I'm still playing when I'm eighty. Peter still plays twice a week and could be playing for decades more. His grandfather cross-country skied until he was 109 and was recognized as the oldest person in the world for two months before he died at 111.

As I finish getting dressed, Peter pulls out a jersey for me.

"There you go," he says. "Ceremonial handover of the sweater."

The guys play hard against the Red Wings, even if it looks like slow-motion replay out on the ice. A few accidental bodychecks are thrown. Peter didn't register me for the game, so I have to stay under the radar. I take a stride or two, then glide and look for a teammate to pass to.

On my last shift, I decide to hotdog a bit, ragging the puck as I dangle around the Red Wings' net, trying to find an open teammate. Eventually, some player in his seventies strips me of the puck. We lose the game 5–1.

Founded in 1975, the Burlington Oldtimers Hockey Club is the largest old-timers club in Canada, with forty-eight teams and more than one thousand members.

"We did a survey a while back: you want to be a league or be a club?" Peter tells me over beers at Hector's, the club's after-game haunt in another part of town. "And the answer was a club."

Club members sit at banquet tables and seats under an office-style ceiling. The place is packed. Four TVs show a mix of football, poker, and hockey. At the bar, a ZZ Top lookalike pours pitchers and pints and twists off bottle caps for members. On one wall are framed Leafs jerseys of Andy Bathgate and Curtis Joseph. There is even one for Wayne Gretzky, in the Leafs jersey he never got to wear because former team owner Steve Stavro decided having the Great One play in Toronto would cost too much money. On the opposite wall, four jerseys, each featuring a letter, spell out the club's abbreviation, BOHC.

"When we first started the league, we had letters on the back of the sweaters instead of numbers," Peter says. "I don't know why. Originally, when they assigned the letters, they didn't assign any vowels so you couldn't spell a dirty word."

Peter pulls out a hockey card from his induction into the 80+ Hockey Hall of Fame a couple of months ago. On the front is Peter, posing in a Canadiens jersey, stick on the ice, same contagious smile, his name written vertically, and his number 3 in the top left corner. On the back, in both English and French, are his details: place of birth, birthdate, position, wife, children, grandchildren, education, career, hobbies, motto, mentor. His famous saying catches my eye. It is in German, picked up during the fifteen years Peter lived in Munich.

Prost, dass die Gurgl nicht verrost. Cheers, so your throat doesn't get rusty. We toast the game and Peter's recent induction.

"It's a fantastic thing for a lot of guys because it gives you a reason to keep trying," he says. "As you get older, and you start to slow down, you start to fade, and you shouldn't do that."

It is important to celebrate life's little victories, at any age. In a culture that ritually casts aside the old for the young, here is a hall of fame dedicated to honoring anyone who continues to play the game into their golden years.

There are only two criteria for eligibility: players have to be eighty years old and registered in a league. At an induction ceremony with their peers, inductees are knighted with an old hockey stick from the 1930s and the words: "As a person active in the game of hockey as an eighty-year-old and recommended by your team, the 80+ Hockey Hall of Fame is proud to knight you as a new inductee member. Congratulations." Players receive a uniform, a medal, and fifty hockey cards, and their names go on a plaque kept at the organization's headquarters in Ottawa. For the past four years, the organization has also put on an international octogenarian game between Canada and the United States. Peter pulls out his phone to show me a photo of a group of fans at the game holding a sign that reads, "Break a Leg Not a Hip!"

"Here comes one of the reprobates now," Peter says as a man walks through the door. "Grab a chair and come on over. Ronnie, this is Bill Leithead. He's one of our inductees. He's a whole month older than me. Did you win?"

"Yup, 2–1. You won't believe it, but the two over-eighty guys scored the goals."

Bill was inducted alongside Peter. He had a heart attack when he was sixty, but that hasn't stopped him from playing. Nor has a quadruple bypass. His cardiologist told him, "'No more hockey. It's the worst sport you can play,'" Bill recalls. Twenty years later, he is still at it.

"What keeps us going is hockey, if you're lucky enough to survive," Bill says. "I don't run, I don't go on a treadmill, but I do play hockey. It's the one thing that keeps me going."

"It's true," Peter adds. "It's what keeps us alive. At our age, you say to yourself, 'It's gonna happen sometime, so just keep going.' I don't worry about getting a heart attack. I worry more about tripping and falling into the boards and breaking a shoulder or hip, because that's something you can't afford to do. You're gonna go sometime anyway, so if I go on the ice, I got no problem with it."

For all its monuments to Alexander Graham Bell, inventor of the telephone, and Joseph Brant, the city's founder, Brantford is the city the Gretzky's built. The truth, of course, is that Wayne Gretzky long ago outgrew Brantford, but Brantford has never outgrown Wayne Gretzky. It is a city synonymous with someone who hasn't lived there since he left town as a teenaged phenom, a place that cannot get out from under everything it has erected and named after him and his father. Wayne Gretzky Parkway cuts through the heart of the city, while in the city's north end the Wayne Gretzky Sports Centre, on Walter Gretzky Boulevard, is fronted by a twelve-foot bronze statue of the Great One. The arena, statue, and boulevard are all within walking distance of the family home at 42 Varadi Avenue, otherwise known as Gretzky Street, where tourists take drive-by selfies. There is also Walter Gretzky Municipal Golf Course and Walter Gretzky Elementary School, named after Wayne's father.

From Burlington, I get onto Highway 403 bound for Brantford, about half an hour away. On the outskirts of town, I stop at a coffee shop, not far from the local Zamboni factory, the company's first international plant. There I find Jimmy MacNeil sitting quietly in front of an electric fireplace.

"You're lucky to get me today because my wife and I were Christmas shopping," he says. "I asked her, 'Can you drop me off for an hour or so?' Then she went on to continue shopping. I don't know if that's a good thing or a bad thing because she's got the credit card."

Jimmy has a soft chuckle that would sound sinister coming from a larger man. But he looks boyish in his beige Zamboni cap and black fleece Zamboni jacket overtop a gray hoodie, and he speaks in a high-pitched tone that makes him sound much younger. All that gives away his age is his reddish-gray beard.

There are no highways or arenas in Brantford named after Jimmy, and no boulevards, schools, or golf courses named after his father. No statues of him have been erected, and no one stops in front of his childhood home to snap a photo. The same age as Gretzky, Jimmy is the kind of behind-the-scenes blue-collar worker in hockey that only a country like Canada could turn into celebrity for a time.

Jimmy was born in Brantford and into Zambonis. His father was once the only authorized Zamboni repairman for all of Canada. Some machines he would repair at his shop on the family farm; others he would travel to fix onsite, across Ontario and even into upper New York State. Each of his eight kids helped him at one time or another.

"I was basically his assistant," Jimmy says. "I was never smart enough to be as good of a mechanic as he was, but I could change oil and I could do the little things that could be done just to help him out."

Jimmy's first job was at an arena in St. George, north of Brantford, where he learned to drive and make ice with an Olympia, Zamboni's main competitor. When he moved on to the old Civic Centre in the city, Jimmy began to make a name for himself, goofing around with the fans and hamming it up for the crowd. During one game, with the World Cup going on, he put the Olympia in gear and let it run down the ice while he climbed out of his seat, stood on the snow tank, and kicked soccer balls into the stands.

"Of course, that brought the crowd to their feet and brought my boss back to visit me, too," Jimmy says. "And it was just never done again."

In the 1990s, the Civic Centre was home to a semipro team called the Brantford Smoke in the now-defunct Colonial Hockey League. When new owners took over the team, they went for a wholesale rebranding, right down to their eccentric Olympia driver. They had a jersey made up for Jimmy and put a nickname on the nameplate: Iceman.

"I now have to explain to people it's because I made ice, not because

I'm associated with the mob," Jimmy says. "Gotta be careful and clarify. I don't wanna get whacked someday just for using the wrong term."

In 1999, the year Gretzky retired from the NHL, Jimmy was nominated for Zamboni Driver of the Year in honor of the fiftieth anniversary of the machine's invention. He went up against drivers from the NHL and around the world. But nominees didn't have to be professional Zamboni drivers. Anyone who'd ever driven a Zamboni in a movie or even for a promotion at an arena was on the list. That little loophole added musicians, actors, and athletes into the mix. Garth Brooks, Matthew McConaughey, former basketball star John Stockton—Jimmy beat them all.

After becoming the world's most famous Zamboni driver, Jimmy was handpicked for a cross-country road trip two years later in support of the 2002 Olympics in Salt Lake City. At the time, Canada hadn't finished first in Olympic hockey since 1952, so the road trip was dubbed the Drive for Gold.

From September 30, 2001, to January 24, 2002, Jimmy drove a Zamboni in a series of stops across Canada, from St. John's to Victoria. Two transport trailers shuttled the Zamboni and a backup from place to place, while a tour bus carried the crew of sixteen, including Jimmy and his brother. At each stop, with a police escort, the crew would start at first light on the outskirts of the city or town, unload the Zamboni, and then Jimmy and his brother would take turns driving until mid-afternoon, topping out at about 5.5 kilometers (3.5 miles) per hour. People could buy a ride at $20.02 for 1 kilometer, sitting in special seats added to the Zamboni, equipped with a mock steering wheel for kids.

In all, Jimmy made sixty-nine stops, many of them in the hometowns of players on the men's and women's Olympic hockey teams. On average, he hit one town every other day. Travel one day, drive through a town the next. No flat tires, no breakdowns, just a couple of oil changes and a hiccup in Newfoundland when they ran out of gas (the Zambonis had been converted to gasoline to prevent the propane lines from freezing up). They never did need the backup.

"Was it Andy Warhol who said we all get fifteen minutes of fame?" Jimmy says. "I've gotten at least that. Sometimes I think I'm into overtime, and then somebody like you contacts me. I can talk all day."

We talk for about two hours until Jimmy gets a text from his wife, who's waiting in the parking lot. We walk outside, shake hands, and drive away in our respective rides, me alone to Cambridge in Gumpy, and Jimmy home with his wife in their Ford Escape with its "NICE ICE" license plates.

Drive north on Shade Street in Cambridge and Galt Arena sneaks up on the left, past the Fairway Café golf cart dealer on one side and Werner's Auto Sales & Service on the other. But approach it going south on Shade Street off Dundas Street North, through Soper Park, and Galt Arena announces itself with a grandeur befitting its history. As the longest continuously operating arena in the world, it has seen it all. Lacrosse, roller skating, boxing, wrestling, school graduations, home shows, cat shows, concerts, even the local public school skating races that have been running since 1930. And it has seen more hockey greats than the Hockey Hall of Fame: Terry Sawchuk, Bobby Hull, Syl Apps, Gordie Howe. If the walls could talk.

When I walk in, after the half-hour drive up from Brantford, I find Dean Bevan in the office engaging in some midday banter with his long-time crew, including his lead hand, Ed.

"If you're gonna do a book on arena guys, you can start with him," Dean says. "That's all you'll need to do. This is what it entails right here: drinking coffee and lipping the boss off. Thirty-three years of it, oh my god."

"And you haven't caught up to me yet," Ed says.

"This is the first I've seen him without shorts on, in pants," Dean says.

"You like the cold?" I ask.

"Work in a rink."

"He's just not that bright," Dean says.

Built on an old bottle dump, Galt Arena has not ceased operations since opening on January 20, 1922, not even during the massive renovations in the 1990s after town council came within one vote of turning it into a parking lot. Its current capacity is about two thousand, down from thirty-five hundred in the arena's heyday, when the whole place would shake as fans stomped their feet on the wooden floors after every Galt goal. Yet much of the arena, more cathedral than rink, is just as it was when first built. The original steel doors and art deco brickwork facade remain, as does the arched red Douglas fir roof. The old vapor barrier has been removed. Skylights, which had been blocked to keep the sunlight out, now bathe the ice in an ecclesiastical glow.

"All the rooms that were on this side of the ice were underneath the stands, and every time you stood up you hit your head," Dean says. "When you'd be in the dressing room and someone would score, people would stomp their feet and there'd be like dust falling down on you while you're trying to get dressed."

Dean leads me to the display case in the lobby, where jerseys, team photos, newspaper clippings, and an original program from the grand opening in 1922 reveal what has gone on inside these century-old walls. Much of it chronicles the town's senior and junior teams before and after Galt's amalgamation into Cambridge: the Terriers, the Pups, the Red Wings, the Rockets, the Black Hawks, the Hornets, the Winterhawks, and now the Redhawks.

I follow Dean up the stairs, into the warmth of Alumni Hall, where murals and memorabilia honor town and team, and then out into the chill of the rink. Before the renovations, the guts of the building were all wood, including the concessions, dressing rooms, and stands. When construction crews ripped out the floorboards, they found piles of empty liquor bottles fans had discarded through cracks in the old wooden flooring.

"Whoever was in Section R, Row 3 sure liked his whiskey," Dean says. "There were ten, twelve liquor bottles down there."

As we walk around the outer rim of the rink, public skating is going on below. On the east wall hangs a picture of Queen Elizabeth II. When the queen died, etiquette called for a black curtain to be put over her. But Dean's crew had already put the ice in, so he would've had to bring in a lift and drop the safety netting to get at her. Dean decided to leave her up for another year and put King Charles up after his coronation.

"If you get closer, she's got some puck holes in her," Dean says. "In my opinion, I think she should stay up, and the king go beside her."

Before the renovations, the queen used to take in games from the west wall, but she was moved to make room for a huge glass-covered mural of fans celebrating Cambridge's Allan Cup victory in 1983. A couple of hundred people feature in the mural, commissioned to honor those who've been part of the history of the building. The artist who painted it has been tasked to add a few dozen more, including Dean and his son. When they're all added, the mural will feature a mix of fedoras, baseball caps, flash-bulb cameras, and iPhones.

Next to the mural is a ten-foot-tall painting of Cambridge's favorite son, Kirk Maltby, and beside him hangs another of the town's favorite adopted son, Gordie Howe. Maltby brought the Stanley Cup home to Cambridge four times as a member of the Detroit Red Wings. As a teenager, Howe spent one season with the Galt Jr. A Red Wings in the days when NHL teams sponsored junior hockey clubs. He practiced and played exhibition games, suiting up for just one regular season game, though it was stricken from the record after the opposing team folded. Soon afterward, Howe was suspended because Galt had two import players from Western Canada, one of whom was Howe. The rules allowed only one.

"He didn't officially play a season here, he just practiced with them," Dean says. "But when he came back to visit, Gordie remembered everything."

Dean leads me into the bowels of the arena. The original trapdoors are still here. Before its first refrigeration system was installed in 1936, the arena had a sand floor. Crews would smooth the sand as flat as they could, and when the weather got cold enough they would open the trapdoors and let the air in to freeze the sand solid. Then they would start flooding and build the ice.

As we walk back to the front of the arena, Dean talks about ice-making. Ice is his element and Galt Arena his second home. Whatever rink he is in, Dean has a sixth sense for when the ice is off, how it needs fixing, and when it is just right.

"As soon as I walk into an arena, I know right away what kind of ice it is," he says. "I can just feel it. I can either feel it's damp and it's gonna be shitty ice, or it's cold and it's gonna be fast. Before they even touch the ice, I tell my team all the time, 'Boys, it's gonna be fast out there, so move your feet.' And they're like, 'How do you know that?' 'Because I've spent my whole life in a friggin' arena.'"

On October 19, 2001, the London Knights were at home to face the Belleville Bulls. Rick Nash left the dressing room and headed for the ice, a short walk he'd made many times before. But before stepping onto the ice, he did something unusual. He stopped, pivoted on the rubber mat, and gingerly walked out backward.

In the second period, with game tied 0–0, Nash scored, ending a goalless run that had stretched over seven games. As he made his way to the bench to touch gloves with his teammates, Nash saw trainer Don Brankley chewing his gum and grinning widely. It'd been Brankley who suggested he walk onto the ice backward as a way of breaking his jinx. Brankley would pass along that piece of superstitious advice just one other time in his thirty-eight years with the Knights, the longest tenure in the history of the Ontario Hockey League (OHL).

From Cambridge, I take the windy backroads through the rolling hills of Mennonite country and on into London, where they like to name their downtown arena after watered-down beers. When it opened in 2002, it was the John Labatt Centre, better known as the JLC. Brankley worked there. And lived there, quite under the radar. It became Budweiser Gardens in 2012, four years after Brankley retired.

On the third level of the arena, between sections 309 and 310, stands the Don Brankley London Knights Hall of Fame, named after their late star trainer. The hall opened two years after Brankley passed from respiratory complications in 2017. It features Knights of note from back to 1965, when the franchise was founded. Many of the inductees starred in London under the guidance of the hall's namesake, who for all but two of London's first forty years as the Knights (they were the Nationals for their first three years) was the guiding hand for hundreds of players funneled through the organization.

I walk into the bowl and look out over the rink, where the Knights held a celebration of life for Brankley at center ice after he died. I haven't been here since March 28, 2008, in what turned out to be Brankley's final game as trainer of the Knights. London was at home down three games to one to the Guelph Storm in the first round of the playoffs. Late in the third period, during a stoppage in play, with the Storm up 5–0 and 1:02 remaining in the game, the announcer asked the crowd to thank Brankley for his decades of service to the organization. The standing ovation lasted over a minute, forcing the linesman to put the puck down on the faceoff dot and wait for the applause to abate. Embarrassed, Brankley waved to the crowd. It was the kind of ovation reserved for hall of fame players, not a sixty-year-old trainer. But such is the legend of the original water boy.

The last time I spoke with "Branks," as he was known in London and throughout the OHL, was a couple of weeks before that game, over the final weekend of the 2007–08 regular season, his last with the Knights. He invited me on a tour of the unofficial Knights hall of fame he'd set up in the team's dressing room, long before the organization would bestow his name on its official shrine in 2019.

The weekend featured three games in three days. For the first of them, on Thursday, March 13, the Knights drove west to Windsor along Highway 401. It was the last time they would face the Spitfires that season and the last game they would ever play at the old Windsor Arena, built in 1925 and better known as "the Barn" or "the Madhouse on McDougall" Street. The Spitfires would move into a new arena the following season. It was also Branks's final visit to the fans who'd taunted him for more than thirty years, and whom Branks had shown his appreciation for with the old one-finger salute.

Before the game, Branks had to do newspaper and radio interviews, as well as tape a segment to be aired during the second intermission on a local sportscast. The players noticed their trainer working faster than normal, but he still got everything done as usual. When they arrived at the rink, their base layers under their gear were hanging clean and dry in their stalls. If they'd been playing at the JLC in London, they would've found them fresh out of the dryer, timed so that they were still soft and warm before they put on their equipment. As the players dressed, Branks taped any aching shoulders, knees, elbows, hands, or ankles that needed support. Then he began his rounds: first water and Gatorade, then Rolaids for anyone battling pregame nerves, followed by ginseng and chewable vitamin C tablets. The players knew instinctively which cups to take, without ever forgetting a "Thanks" or a "Thanks, Branks." If one did, Branks would stop, stare, and wait until the player remembered the drill. Players came in as boys and departed as men. Branks considered it part of his job to make sure they left as gentlemen, whether for the working world or the sporting world. He was just as proud of his players who went on to be doctors, lawyers, businessmen, or garbage men as he was of those who became NHL stars, like Dino Ciccarelli, Brendan Shanahan, and Rick Nash.

Branks took a rare break before the game, which would see the Knights get shellacked 9–5. He'd had an even longer day than the eighteen hours he routinely put in, so he slipped outside for his "mental health," as he called it, and pulled out his Player's Filter. Six years earlier, he'd been working through three packs a day. He was now down to one. As Branks lit up, Nash appeared around the corner. After two years in London, Nash had made it to the NHL with the Columbus Blue Jackets. With a day off between games, he decided to make the three-hour drive from Columbus to Windsor just to be at the pregame ceremony.

"Holy crap! I didn't know you guys were playing in Detroit," Branks said, thinking the Blue Jackets were playing just across the border.

"We're not," Nash said.

"What the hell are you doing here, then?"

"I came to be here for you."

Long before the age of social media, a chant that started at the Barn went viral around the OHL. In 1975, Branks and the Knights were in Windsor for a game against their archrival. Games in Windsor, especially in the 1970s, were raucous and often fight-filled. Back then, there was an old adage around the league for players coming to play in Windsor: better bring a bucket to the Barn so you can take your head home in it.

Fans were right on top of the players' benches then, well within punching, kicking, and spitting distance. There was no glass around the benches and nothing to protect visiting players going to and from the dressing room. Knights players, coaches, and especially their trainer would be lucky if all the fans hurled at them were insults. Popcorn, nachos and cheese, beverages, and even spittle would rain down on them if the game got out of control. For a stretch, Branks needed a police escort.

"Four would surround me and take me to the bench," Branks told me. "Two would stay by the bench during the period. The other two would walk around the building, and in the last minute those guys would come back and take me to the dressing room. I was like a big rock star."

Branks played the heel well whenever the Knights were in Windsor. He would yell at the Spitfires' goalie, goad their players, insult the referees, bang on the boards, and even taunt the fans. Whenever he had to tend to an injured Knight on the ice, his walk back to the bench would often slow to a crawl, as the derisive chant rained down from the stands, to which Branks would slyly clear his eyes with his longest finger. On one such walk, he doffed his jacket to reveal a Spitfires jersey with "Save the Windsor Arena" across the back, drawing a deafening roar from the fans. In the 1980s, he periodically wore a shirt while on the bench that read, "I Hate Windsor" on the front.

For his last game ever at the Barn, the Spitfires were set to pay tribute to the man Windsor's rabid fan base loved to hate. A red carpet led from the boards to center ice. Branks was dressed in the same black golf shirt, cargo pants, and white sneakers he wore every game. A white towel hung from his belt, and a first aid pouch fell across his right hip. As his stubby fingers gripped the microphone, a wry smile snuck across his tawny, furrowed face. Below his dyed, light-brown hair, his sky-blue eyes, so youthful despite the luggage of late nights underneath them, darted around the arena.

"WA-TER-BOY! WA-TER-BOY! WA-TER-BOY!" rang throughout the wooden acoustics of the arena. Under a standing ovation, Branks waved the microphone around to whoop up the crowd.

"Am I in the right city?" he began, raising the decibel level in the rickety old building. "Well, let's see, all kinds of memories come flooding back. I've been sweared at, spit on, and punched here. I remember the time our bus was broken into and the night our tires were slashed. I'm happy for the people of Windsor that they're finally getting a new arena. It's not like it wasn't time. But they'll have to work at capturing the same kind of atmosphere that was in this place. Bring the craziness to your new building, and I'm going to wave goodbye to you now. And you'll notice I'm using all of my fingers this time."

Friday, March 14, 2008. After getting whipped by Windsor, the Knights returned to London to face the Erie Otters in the second game of their back-to-back-to-back stretch to end the 2007–08 regular season. Branks stayed up late to prepare the Knights' bench, as he did every night ahead of a game. Before going to bed, he strolled down to York Street for the last of the dozen coffees he drank every day, always black with four sugars and always from Tim Hortons. As usual, he picked some up for the night watchmen at the JLC, who kept his secret safe from municipal officials: Branks lived in the Knights' dressing room, sleeping on a cot in the laundry room under sheets in the team's green and gold color scheme.

Branks's first gig as a trainer came during his last two years of high school. A couple of friends on the Garson City/Falcon Bridge Combines, near his hometown of Capreol, asked him to help out with the team and party with the players. Branks did, although he didn't get paid for it. He then went to the Chelmsford Canadiens for one season before being accepted to Laurentian University in Sudbury with the intention of studying history. He was all set to go when he received a call from the Knights, offering him the position of trainer. He'd applied two months earlier without giving the job much thought.

One year into his career with the Knights, Branks received a job offer from the Boston Bruins to jump to the NHL. He turned them down. In the early 1980s, Edmonton tried twice to lure him out west, just before Wayne Gretzky and the Oilers went on to win four Stanley Cups in five years. But Branks would not leave London.

"People always asked me, 'Why didn't you go?' Because I got small fingers and those big rings would've been hokey."

In all his years with the Knights, Branks never married, what with the crazy hours and all the time spent on the road. He did come close once with a woman named Betty, with whom he had a daughter. It ended when she asked him to leave his job and take steady factory work.

Early in his career, Branks put in so many hours at work that he just ended up living in the dressing room. Despite having the entire building to himself, he never went for a skate. "Would a postman go for a walk on his day off?" he quipped whenever asked why not. Over the years, he saved photos, memorabilia, and notes from Knights who'd come through the organization, some on their way to the NHL, and put it all up over the dressing room. When the team moved from the Ice House to the JLC, it took him two months to pack it all and put it back up in the new dressing room.

To Branks, Thanks for being not only the best trainer but a best friend as well. All the best, Rick Nash

To Branks, Still the best trainer I've ever seen. Brendan Shanahan

To Branks, Thanks for all the help over the years. Your pal, Jason Allison

Branks, I couldn't have made it this far without your friendship. Thanks for everything. Always, Louie [DeBrusk]

To Buddy Branks, Go Knights! I'm proud to be in the London Knights and Branks hall of fame. All the best, Grapes [Don Cherry]

In the weight room hung a large photo of Shanahan from the 1987 NHL draft, when he was selected first overall by the New Jersey Devils. Shanahan was so anxious that day that Branks helped him pick out something to wear and went with him to help calm his nerves. Encased in glass about ten feet away was a Detroit Red Wings jersey from Ciccarelli. In his second-last year with the Knights, Ciccarelli broke the femur in his right leg in half, shattering in the eyes of his doctors any chance to play hockey again, much less in the NHL. Branks was one of the few who told Ciccarelli he would. The signed jersey was the one Ciccarelli wore when he scored his 545th goal to pass Maurice Richard on the NHL's all-time goals list.

To Branks, This goal's for you

In the middle of the dressing room, sitting on the Knights logo in the carpet, was a full-size Ping-Pong table, where the players played one another using the personalized paddles Branks bought each of them for Christmas. Equipment hung throughout the room. Nameplates above the stalls listed the Knights players, including leading scorer Pat Maroon. At the back of each stall were the nameplates of every Knight who'd ever sat there, a tradition Branks started and the organization has continued.

"Guys come in with their sons and say, 'This is where Dad used to sit,'" Branks said. "All this stuff means a lot to them."

Many of those players had returned to London to be at the pregame ceremony for Branks ahead of the Knights' game against the Otters. After all the speeches were finished, Branks was handed the microphone. Unlike in Windsor the night before, he hadn't prepared a speech. He didn't know what he was going to say and didn't know where to look when the camera settled on him as he stood on the red carpet extending from the Zamboni bay. By the time he finished talking, he'd received two standing ovations. The Knights went on to beat the Otters 7–0.

Saturday, March 15, 2008. The Knights were in Owen Sound to play the Attack in the last of their three games in three days to finish the 2007–08 regular season. With the playoffs approaching, Maroon was stuck in a six-game scoring drought. Before the game, Branks pulled the Knights' star forward aside.

"I'll tell you what I told Rick Nash . . ."

In the second period, Maroon scored.

The farther north I drive, the further south the mercury drops, until Celsius meets Fahrenheit at the southern checkpoint of the Wetum Road. When I pull up, a man comes out of the tiny cabin wearing a T-shirt and holding a clipboard.

"Name?"

"Ronnie Shuker."

"Destination?"

"Moose Factory."

"Business or leisure?"

"Both."

As he walks behind Gumpy to grab my license plate number, a fox darts out the forest and sits in front of the hut.

"Alright, you're good to go. Have a safe trip."

I jump back into Gumpy while the man scampers back into the warmth of his cabin. As I pull away, a donut flies out the window and drops at the feet of the fox, who snatches it and disappears into the trees.

I am on my way.

From Toronto to Smooth Rock Falls, which lies on the northern route of the Trans-Canada, to the Abitibi Canyon Generating Station at the end of Highway 634 up from Fraserdale, and then another 48 kilometers (30 miles) along Otter Rapids Road, Northern Ontario's northern roads have led me here, to the Wetum Road, a 177-kilometer (110-mile) ice road that runs atop the muskeg of the Hudson Plain. Rebuilt every winter, it stretches from the hydro outpost of Otter Rapids north to Moose Factory, at the southern edge of James Bay. I start out slowly from the checkpoint, not knowing what to expect. At first, the road dips and dives through the forest, but eventually it grows straighter and flatter as the forest loses its thickness and the trees dwindle in size until they look like scraggly straw cleaners. Occasionally, I come up to what I take to be chunks of dirty snow in the middle of the road, only to watch as a flock of ptarmigans fly away at the last minute or stand their ground and force me to drive around them. Empty snow-clearing machines are left running, even with no one around, because if stopped, they may not start again. The snowbanks, formed from plowing the road, function as guardrails. The drive takes longer than it should've, only because I can't resist the urge to stop and stand in the middle of the road and listen to the silence. That and pull out my hockey stick to flick bits of ice over the banks. If only there were enough players for some ice road hockey.

When I arrive at the northern checkpoint, another man jumps out, checks off my name, and welcomes me to Moose Factory. I don't know if he is a Cheechoo, but it is a name heard often around these parts. Within five minutes of walking into the Thomas Cheechoo Jr. Memorial Complex, on Jonathan Cheechoo Drive, I meet three Cheechoos. Tanner hands me off to Darcy, who calls his father, Charlie, who is over within minutes.

"Charlie Cheechoo," he says, extending his hand. "Mr. Hockey in Moose Factory."

Intermixed with snorts and sniffles, after walking over to the rink in the minus-whatever weather, Charlie speaks in a kind of fragmented hurriedness. He is easy to like. Underneath his snowmobile jacket, his black T-shirt reads, "I'm the nicest asshole you'll ever meet." A former deputy chief of the Moose Cree First Nation, Charlie loves to have a good laugh and to weave a clever yarn.

On one wall of the lobby is the black Great White of the San Jose

Sharks' crest. On another, "Home of Jonathan Cheechoo," the only player from Moose Factory to make it to the NHL, is written in shaded stencil. In 1992, the year the arena opened, Cheechoo called his shot at twelve years old when he wrote a letter for a class assignment about what he would be doing in ten years. He said he would be playing in the NHL and that he would be doing it more than 3,000 kilometers (1,864 miles) away in California. Ten years later, on October 10, 2002, Cheechoo debuted for the Sharks.

In the display cases, jerseys chronicle hockey in Moose Factory and Moosonee, twin towns separated by a thin ribbon of the Moose River. There are the North Stars, Black Hawks, and Hitmen from Moose Factory, and the Bombardiers from Moosonee, but one sticks out from all the others. It is white with a thick blue stripe around the bottom and along the length of the sleeves. On the front is a similar-looking Maple Leafs crest but in a lighter shade of blue with the word "Scrappers" scrawled within it.

"Everybody thinks 'Scrappers' comes from the phrase 'scrapping,'" Charlie says. "But far from it. It came from 'scraps.'"

In 1974, a group of misfits failed to make the cut for the Moose Factory Flyers, the town's powerhouse Class A team at the time. Too young, too old, too slow, too soft, they were the detritus of local men's hockey. With no team to play for, they decided to form their own team of outcasts to take on the Flyers. Discarded like a heap of hockey trash, they called themselves the Scraps.

"The Flyers kicked the shit out of us the first year we put the team together," Charlie recalls.

Charlie wasn't on that first team, but he was on the second. After finishing high school in Barrie, Ontario, he came home to Moose Factory, along with several others, looking to get back on the ice. Flush with new players, several of whom were Cheechoos, the Scraps took on the Flyers again. Not only did they beat them, they beat them up.

"You do some of the things we did back then and you'd go to jail," Charlie says. "Brawls. Not regularly, but people who watched our team play were gonna see three, four, five fights a game."

Scraps no more, the team needed a new name as the kings of men's hockey in Moose Factory. But they'd grown fond of their name. Knowing they all could fight as well as they could score, one of the Scraps suggested extending their name to Scrappers. A new era of hockey in Moose Factory had begun.

"People always ask me how the 1976 Scrappers would compete with the 2023 Scrappers," Charlie says. "Oh, they'd whip us, but they'd be all sore. We'd beat the shit outta them. We'd make them pay for it. I don't think they'd wanna go in the corner with us."

Nearly fifty years since the Scrappers were born, teams at every level of hockey in Moose Factory now bear their name, and the men's team itself is still a powerhouse. In fact, the Scrappers were the reigning champions of the Rupert River Cup Tournament across the bay in Waskaganish.

In March 2020, just days before the pandemic hit, the Scrappers beat the Waskaganish Wings in the final to win the tournament and take home the $30,000 in prize money. Instead of going around James Bay and then up the Billy Diamond Highway, as Adrian and I had done, ten of the Scrappers decided to go across it. They'd made it from Moose Factory to Waskaganish without problem, but on the return trip, with the Rupert River Cup strapped to one of their snowmobiles, they met high winds and blowing snow. At some point on the journey, the trophy fell into the snow. They tried looking for it, but it would spend the night under the stars above James Bay. The next morning, they retraced their route and found the trophy, which otherwise would have sunk to the bottom of the bay come spring.

After giving me a history lesson on hockey in Moose Factory, Charlie offers to take me on a tour of the town. Among the wood-frame houses, NHL logos are abundant, something rarely seen in cities, suburbs, and even small towns south of the Trans-Canada anymore. Some of the logos are on flags, posters, and decals; others have been hand-carved from wood. The Leafs and Canadiens dominate, but the Sharks, Boston Bruins, and Chicago Blackhawks are also on display.

We stop at two identical beige houses, each displaying a large Leafs logo, one white and the other blue, hanging from the eavestrough above the doorway. One of the homes belongs to another Cheechoo, Bradley, although everybody calls him "Beuf."

"He's the superfan of superfans in Moose Factory," Charlie says. "No one comes close."

I follow Charlie downstairs to the basement and into Beuf's mancave. Flanking the hallway is a pair of Leafs flags, and above the entranceway hangs a miniature Leafs jersey bearing five lines in place of the crest:

We Play Together,
We Win Together,
We Lose Together,
We Stay Together,
Stoodis!

"What does Stoodis mean?" I ask.

"It's how we say, 'Let's do this! Stoodis!'" Charlie replies. "It's Cringlish. It's like 'Sgodan! Let's go then!'"

Beuf had slipped on the ice and broke his ankle. We find him sitting on a sofa with his crutches lying next to him across a Leafs pillow. Around the room hang several Leafs jerseys. Beside one for captain John Tavares are the words, "Hockey is where we live. Life is just a place we spend in between games."

There are fans, superfans, and then there's Beuf. I've met professional Leafs fans, been in their basements, sat in their mancaves, seen their multimillion-dollar collections. They like to say they "bleed blue and white," but I've never met any who've named their own blood after the blue and white.

"All my kids, they have all the initials, they're all TML," Beuf says. "My son's name is Theoren Memphis Lawrence, my daughter is Treasure Miley Liberty, and my other daughter is Temperance Marley Legacy."

I sit down on one of the sofas and take a long look around the room as Charlie and Beuf fall into conversation about Don Cherry. There is a

Scrappers jersey and a Sharks Cheechoo jersey, but most of the room is covered in Leafs trinkets, including a parking sign for "Maple Leafs fans only" and a street sign for "Maple Leafs Lane."

"So what do you think about Don Cherry getting the boot for saying, 'You people'?" Charlie asks me.

They were the two words that got Cherry fired from *Hockey Night in Canada* broadcasts three years ago, ending the popular *Coach's Corner* segment.

"I dunno. That's so long ago now."

"Actually, I do agree with him," Charlie says. "You come to Canada, there's a tradition of wearing a poppy, and some people don't wear it because they're not Canadians. You know why some of us think like that? For both World War I and World War II, Moose Factory had the highest volunteers per capita. I'll take you to the church."

"If you go to look at the monument he's talking about over there and think about our population here, imagine what it was back in the war," Beuf adds. "You're going to see all the names there."

In Canada, hockey is more than just a game. It is a segue. Carry on a conversation long enough and it will soon leave the ice and show up elsewhere, especially when it comes to war.

For just about its entire existence, and more than any other sport, hockey has bound itself to the military. War words litter the hockey lexicon. Most are harmless: "battle," "attack," "trenches," "fire," "blast," "howitzer," "cannon," "rocket," "sniper," "bullet." A few, like "shot" and "shoot," are even necessary, while others, like "warriors," are thrown around as carelessly as clichés in postgame interviews. Equipment is likened to armor, and players, when fully dressed, are sometimes referred to as gladiators. We even come fully armed. Sticks are looked upon as weapons, both to score and to scar, and are now made from the stuff of modern warfare, like titanium and even Kevlar.

From Beuf's basement to the old Anglican church on the other side of town, via Charlie's pickup, we arrive at a large black plinth, perhaps ten feet high, on the edge of town honoring the First Nation veterans of James

Bay from Moose Factory, Moosonee, Fort Albany, and Attawapiskat. The monument is split between World Wars I and II, with almost the same number of names for each one. I count 154 in total, five of whom are Cheechoos. Among the names are one of Beuf's grandfathers and three of his great-granduncles and two of Charlie's granduncles and great-granduncles. For a region that would've numbered in the hundreds at the time, it is a lot of people.

"You take away that number of men, and most of them were married and had kids, what happened in Moose Factory? Who looked after the families?" Charlie says. "The community came together and helped with that."

For almost its entire length across Ontario, the Trans-Canada is two roads. Tourists take Highway 17, the southern route around Lake Superior, while truckers take the old lumber route, Highway 11, an underappreciated drive that arcs across Northern Ontario, past the flying saucer in Moonbeam, the unmissable Claude Giroux welcome sign in Hearst, a giant snowman in Beardmore, and on down to Nipigon, where the two routes converge before splitting up again in Thunder Bay.

Judging by the dozen or so times I've stayed in town, Thunder Bay must have the highest percentage of fleabag motels in Canada. It's also produced the most NHL players per capita, roughly one per fifteen thousand residents. Since the NHL was founded in 1917, there's been at least one player from Thunder Bay in the league every season, something no other Canadian city of its size can claim.

Of the ninety-seven players Thunder Bay has sent to the NHL, twenty have won the Stanley Cup, thirty times in total. That doesn't include the seven times Jack Adams won the cup as coach and/or general manager of the Detroit Red Wings, or the three times Winnipeg-born but Thunder Bay–raised Patrick Sharp won the cup with the Chicago Blackhawks, or the three times Joe Szura and John Schella brought home the Avco Cup from the World Hockey Association championship in the 1970s.

Born in Karijoki, Finland, Pentti Lund isn't counted among Thunder Bay's NHL players, but he should be. He played in the 1940s, back when Thunder Bay was still the twin towns of Fort William and Port Arthur. Although he never won the Stanley Cup, Lund earned the Calder Trophy as rookie of the year in 1949 and was the first Finnish-born player to score a goal in the NHL. He spent five years in the league before returning to Thunder Bay, where he became the longtime sports editor for the *Chronicle-Journal*. Ten years after his death, Lund's success is still a point of pride for the city's Finnish diaspora, the largest outside of Finland.

As the main mechanic within the local Finnish community, Jussi Kuokkanen used to fix Lund's car, as he did just about every other Finn's mode of transportation in town. Along with all the other Finnish tradesmen in Thunder Bay, Jussi volunteered his talents to help build the Hilldale Lutheran Church, financed entirely by the Finnish community and constructed by the descendants of all the carpenters, plumbers, electricians, loggers, and construction workers who came over from Finland after World War II and settled in Thunder Bay. He is also the architect of Thunder Bay's longtime local Finnish team, formed in 1987 and still going all these years later.

In 2021, the Finnish community lost its longtime haunt, the old Finlandia Club, built in 1910, when the downtown building burned down, taking the well-known Hoito restaurant with it. Since then, they've been making do with the cafeteria at the church, where I meet Jussi for coffee along with about two dozen other Finnish men on a cold Monday morning in early February. Although everyone speaks English, Finnish is still their first language, Finnish food their preferred diet, Finnish culture their way of life, and Finland their hockey allegiance.

I grab a coffee and a slice of *pulla*, a Finnish coffee bread, and sit down with Jussi and Kenny Luhtala. A thin, soft-spoken man of seventy-three, Jussi is wearing a shirt of the famed Jokerit hockey club in Helsinki. The team, previously Russian-owned, left the top pro league in Finland in 2014 to become part of Russia's Kontinental Hockey League. But when Russia invaded Ukraine, the team left the league and has been trying to return to its old Finnish grouping ever since.

"The people are kind of up in arms," Jussi says. "'Since you left, too bad.' People are kind of cranky because the Russians own the rink in Helsinki, and they had lots to do with that team."

"Hockey and politics," I say. "They mix a lot."

"It's all politics," Kenny says.

Another man comes and sits down at our table.

"Here's a guy that likes talking," Jussi says. "You can talk to him."

His name is Kari Jämsä, and he has this endearing habit of saying "okay" to start and end a sentence.

"Okay, I'll start from the beginning, okay?" he says. "Just stop me when somebody else wants to say something. Okay, so why Finlanders came to Thunder Bay."

The first Finnish immigrants came in the 1870s. Many settled in Thunder Bay and elsewhere in Northern Ontario, founding Finnish communities like Alppila, Tarmola, Intola, Upsala, Nolalu, and Suomi. Many of the men worked as miners and loggers.

"The Finnish *sisu*," Kari says. "You know the word *sisu*?"

I do. Pronounced *see-soo*, it is one of the few Finnish words I know besides "sauna."

"It means something like 'guts,' right?"

"Guts and never give up attitude, okay," Kari says. "When Russia came and tried to take over Finland, there was a bunch of stubborn Finlanders over there. They were outnumbered on the frontlines ten to one, okay. If they don't have *sisu*, Russia would control Finland. But those stubborn old Finlanders, they said, 'This is our land. You don't come here. Period.'"

When the Soviet Union invaded Finland during the early part of World War II, the Finns lost territory but managed to keep the Soviets out. The war nevertheless left the country devastated, so a second wave of Finns immigrated to Canada in the early 1950s looking for work. Jussi and Kari came over with their families, as did Kenny's parents.

Aarno Peura, who joins our growing circle, was twenty-five when he came to Thunder Bay. He managed the Finlandia Club and the Hoito restaurant for many years. Although Aarno still returns to Finland every other year, Jussi has only been back to Finland five times and Kenny just once, while Kari has only just started going back more frequently.

"I am a Canadian, but as I get older, I am like a salmon, okay," Kari says. "You know how salmon go up the river where they were born? So I am like a salmon, I like to go to visit my birthplace, okay."

All of them, to a man, say they are Finnish first, although they are no less Canadian for it. Finnish is their first language, each has a sauna at home, as everyone does back in Finland, and all continue to dine on Finnish food, including Finnish pancakes, called *lettu*, and *suola kala*, a sandwich made with salmon or speckled trout rubbed with salt and brown sugar, then cured and pressed for up to twenty-four hours, and placed on thin slices of rye bread and topped with onions.

"When I have hockey parties for the guys, they all demand that I make it," Jussi says. "There's a few that are leery about, because when they hear that it's only salt cured they think it's raw fish."

I ask the group what it is that brought their families to Thunder Bay and kept them here.

"Because it's like home," Jussi says. "It's just like Finland."

"And it's the same four seasons," Aarno says. "Same type of winters."

Same type of hockey, too. There is an argument to be made that, population-for-population, there is no more rabid hockey country in the world than Finland. Consider that Finland's population is less than the six million living in the Greater Toronto Area. Yet year after year, the country hangs with hockey's heavyweights in international competition and sends a disproportionate number of players to the NHL.

"There's so many descendants of Finns that play hockey in Thunder Bay," Kari says. "But their names have changed."

One of those players is Hall of Famer Chris Pronger, who was born and played in Dryden, just west of Thunder Bay. His grandparents were Finnish, and his mother was born in Finland. Pronger's grandmother still lives in Thunder Bay. When his grandfather passed away earlier in the year, Pronger came back for the funeral at the church.

"I got a video where he talked about going to play in Finland," Jussi says. "He said, 'Well, I'm almost at home because my mother's from Finland, and I got all kinds of relatives here.'"

Kari looks at me and grins. "Salmon returning up the river."

Jussi didn't start playing hockey until he was twenty-three, well after he'd come to Canada. His first skates were cross-country ski boots with blades bolted onto them. Yet in 1987, Jussi was the one who started up Reipas Finlandia, an all-Finnish men's team in Thunder Bay that traveled to Finnish cultural tournaments across Ontario where other Finnish families had settled after the war. About thirty guys showed up at the outdoor rink for tryouts, and it was Jussi's job to cut that number down.

"I got some enemies even out of that, because I had to pick twenty out of the thirty," Jussi says.

"I don't think I made the twenty," Aarno says.

"We weren't great players or nothing," Jussi continues. "None of the cities had superstars. We were just ordinary hockey players. It was just to get together, party a little bit."

After coffee, Jussi takes me to his garage, where he still does a little repair work from time to time even though he's long retired. He flips on the heat and shows me his humble hockey shrine. A bookcase shelves an array of photos, plaques, pucks, and collectibles. Around it, Jussi has hung flags for Finland and Canada alongside banners for the NHL's Edmonton Oilers and Winnipeg Jets, as well as the Seattle Thunderbirds of the Western Hockey League, where his son played with Patrick Marleau, who would go to become the NHL's all-time games played leader. Another wall bears a decal of his hometown, Liperi, a map of Finland, and a couple of posters of the most famous Finnish player ever, Teemu Selanne. Jussi has also saved several of his old helmets, each featuring a decal of the blue-and-white Finnish flag on the back.

Jussi shows me some of the pucks from tournaments Reipas Finlandia had played around Ontario and then a photo of the current team.

"I don't think the new players even know about what we had in the olden days," he says. "They're called the Finn Kings, even though there's only one Finn on the team."

Before I leave, Jussi checks the pressure on Gumpy's tires. After hitting −49°C in Northern Ontario, I decide to warm up Finnish style before heading to the Prairies. So to end the road trip through Eastern Canada, I head downtown to one of Jussi's old hockey haunts, Kangas Sauna Restaurant, for some Finnish comfort food followed by a sauna.

"I haven't been there since our hockey days when we used to go after the games," Jussi says. "I just don't stay out that late anymore. We played hockey late as it was, and we'd stay late. Two o'clock in the morning. Those were the crazy old wild days."

The Prairies:
Big Game Country

The arena does not create the fans; the fans adopt and sanctify the arena. —Howard Shubert, *Architecture on Ice*

TOURISTS AREN'T MUCH for the Prairies. Too long, too flat, too boring, nothing to see, or so they say. But free from the claustrophobia of either British Columbia or Ontario, the open landscape and great big sky makes driving through the Prairies feel like skating on a giant open slough. It is just one long breakaway, from Winnipeg all the way to Edmonton and Calgary.

From Thunder Bay, I continue west along the Trans-Canada, driving through Ignace, Dryden, Vermillion Bay, and Kenora, finally passing the longitudinal Centre of Canada landmark east of Winnipeg. I bypass the Winnipeg bypass and continue on the Trans-Canada into downtown, slowing down to navigate the city's trademark potholed and pockmarked roads to a shop on a side street at the edge of the Red River.

The store is awash in memorabilia of every sport, but most of it is hockey-related and much of that is Winnipeg Jets–related. Jerseys in the polar night blue of the current Jets hang along the walls from the ceiling, setting off one with the blue-red-white color scheme of the second Jets, bearing the nameplate of the greatest Jet of all-time, (Dale) Hawerchuk. At the front of the store are three more jerseys, in a slightly different shade from the others and without a plane in the crest. They are for three players from the often-forgotten original Winnipeg Jets: (Bobby) Hull, (Ab) McDonald, and the shop's owner, (Joe) Daley.

"What the Jets mean to Winnipeg is way beyond just being able to go to the game and cheer them on," Joe says.

More than anyone in Winnipeg, Joe understands, as a player, a businessman, and a fan, what the Jets mean to the city. Just days from turning eighty, Joe's life has revolved around the Jets for the better part of fifty years, playing for the first incarnation, watching the second leave, and enjoying the third since their return.

Born in Winnipeg's East Kildonan, Joe spent years bussing along the interstate highways of the United States in various minor pro leagues before making it into the NHL. In 1972, after four seasons, just as he'd started making a name for himself, he received an offer to come home to Winnipeg to play for a new pro team in a new pro league. It was the best contract he'd ever been offered. More money and a longer term for a hometown boy on his hometown team.

"I said yes immediately, without even thinking of the repercussions," Joe says.

Joe played for all seven years of the World Hockey Association's (WHA) existence, every one of them for the original Jets, reaching the league final five times and winning three Avco Cups. His initial three-year contract gave him his first experience of financial security, and his subsequent four-year deal took him to retirement, after which he later opened the memorabilia store he runs with his son, Travis. When the WHA merged with the NHL in 1979, Joe left the game a champion in his final year and retired as the league's all-time leader in wins for a goalie.

When I meet Joe in early February 2023, it's been fifty years since the WHA took on the NHL in the 1972–73 season. The anniversary has been met with little fanfare. The NHL, which resists any attempts to recognize the WHA as its equal or integrate its statistics into its own, did nothing to honor the league. (If the NHL were ever to incorporate WHA statistics, it would have to rewrite its record book and Gordie Howe would surpass Wayne Gretzky as the all-time leading goal scorer with 975.) The Jets, too, underplayed the anniversary, which is a little surprising. If it weren't for Joe and the other players on the original Jets, especially Bobby Hull, Winnipeg would not have an NHL team today.

"I look back now, and what Bobby meant to the league, to this city, for hockey and everything, if we're not in the WHA we're probably not talking about a Jets NHL team today," Joe says. "There's no way that the NHL is gonna come to small-market Winnipeg and say, 'You guys deserve a franchise.'"

When Hull switched leagues and signed with the Jets on June 27, 1972, it changed the course of history in Winnipeg and momentarily made its major intersection the most famous in hockey. Even Canadians who've never been to Winnipeg have heard of Portage and Main, where Hull signed his multimillion-dollar contract, the largest deal in hockey history to that time. Portage and Main is also where Hawerchuk signed his deal on August 13, 1981, where Winnipeggers held Save the Jets rallies, mourned the loss of the team after its last game on April 28, 1996, and welcomed it back on May 31, 2011. It now hosts whiteout parties to cheer the Jets during the playoffs.

"I loved playing at home, I really did," Joe says. "And yet today, there's a lot of guys who don't wanna play in Winnipeg, even if they're from here. I don't know, but in the seven years I played in Winnipeg, not one person ever came up to me and said, 'Joe, I can hardly wait to get the hell out of here.'"

In a poll by ESPN, more than forty percent of NHL players listed Winnipeg as the last city they would want to play in. Perhaps it is the cold, or the small market, or the city's notoriously bad roads, but attracting players to Winnipeg has been a perennial problem for both the team and the city. A month ago, a former NHL-player-turned-TV-analyst took to social media to list his first-world problems with a hotel near Portage and Main: "Worst hotel in the NHL. The Fairmont in Winnipeg. Paper thin walls, very loud door, bedsheets that zap you upon entry, shit weather, almost no nearby restaurants, tough scene. Call me a prima-donna, I don't care."

"Unfortunately, he wasn't wrong on some points," Travis says from behind the counter.

"About the Fairmont or about Winnipeg?" I ask him.

"More the Fairmont. But he was wrong about the restaurants. There's a gazillion restaurants downtown."

"Any time your hometown gets slammed you're not gonna sit back and say, 'Oh yeah, I guess that's true,'" Joe says. "It's fine if I say, 'Ah, geez, our roads suck,' and they do, but that's okay because I live here and I was born here. I can say that."

The odd thing about the Trans-Canada is that for more than half its length, it is not a single highway. National in name only, it is a haphazard network of provincial highways strung together. Depending on the province, the Trans-Canada could be Highway 1, 2, 7, 11, 12, 16, 17, 20, 40, 66, 69, 71, 85, 104, 105, 106, 117, 185, 400, or 417. It splits in several places, mostly in Eastern Canada, forcing drivers to choose between alternate routes. Although it is one of the longest national highways in the world, all that really holds the Trans-Canada together as one long highway are its little green signs, each with a sad-looking maple leaf and the road's respective provincial owner stamped upon it.

About half an hour west of Winnipeg, the Trans-Canada splits apart once more, never to come together again. I continue along the southern route, about 110 kilometers (68 miles) west of Winnipeg, to the tiny town of Treherne. There I turn north, taking a series of turns through farming country to the edge of the Manitoba Escarpment and a colorful billboard that stands out against the snow. "Baker Community," it reads overtop a pastoral sketch of children playing in fruit trees along a path bordered by blue grass.

Gumpy lumbers along the private road, passing a sign with arrows showing the way to Baker's communal kitchen and community center, bookshop, and school, as well as its Better Air manufacturing plant, where the community builds ventilation systems for the agriculture industry. I follow the road to the right, past the plant, the carpentry shop, the car garage, around the rows of houses in the middle, past the kitchen and dining hall, and then over to the print shop. There, next to the outdoor rink, Chris Maendel and Nolan Waldner are waiting for me.

There are about fifty thousand Hutterites spread across about five hundred colonies throughout Western Canada and the northwestern United States. About 120 live in Baker, most of them Maendels and Waldners, sharing roughly five thousand acres of undulating prairie farm country. German is the main language, although everyone speaks English. There is one bank account for the whole community. Meals are taken together. People vote for their leadership, called "management," which is responsible for the larger organization of the community. In values and principles, Christian life among the Hutterites follows that of their sixteenth-century Anabaptist ancestors in central Europe.

I leave Gumpy unlocked outside the print shop and follow Chris and Nolan to the rink. Chris is in his thirties, married with children, thoughtful, well spoken, and deliberate with his words. Nolan still looks a teenager, with reddish-brown hair streaked with blond, a sparse beard along his jawline, and a cheerful grin that never leaves his face. We walk around the rink to the dressing rooms in a converted greenhouse, the glass replaced with pine that still looks new five years on. The rink itself is about five feet shorter than a regulation rink and narrower. The boards are all white, and the ice is clear, except for a couple of blobs where Nolan tried putting in logos for Better Air and the Baker Storm. The small manual score clock resting on the side boards looks like a miniature of the Fenway Park scoreboard.

I follow Chris and Nolan into the dressing rooms. There is a kids room first, a sign that reads "Crosschecking, it's how I hug," and the adults' room, filled with the unmistakable smell of sodden equipment despite floor fans working hard to disperse the stench. Both home and road Baker Storm jerseys hang along every wall. Chris and Nolan sit in a couple of stalls, while I pull up a folding chair between them.

Although kids can play with the adults, so long as they can keep up, most players on the Storm are at least fifteen years old, the age when a Hutterite child becomes an adult. There are only enough players to form two teams, so most games are intra-colony, although the Storm will sometimes play another Hutterite community or face a team from one of Better Air's business partners.

"Some refer to our league as the HHL, the Hutterite Hockey League, but there's nothing really in stone," Chris says. "There's no schedule. It's just a bunch of guys, buddies, calling each other up, 'Hey, let's have a hockey game.'"

Just like the origins of hockey itself, Chris and Nolan can't say with certainty when or where the game got started in Baker, but they do know it wasn't always accepted. When Chris's grandfather was growing up, cameras and radios weren't allowed, much less hockey. He and his friends would find discarded skates and equipment at the local dump, look in the woods for branches in the shape of a stick, and then go skating on nearby ponds and the Assiniboine River just south of the colony. They played games in secret at a nearby arena.

"Always under this cloud of it being forbidden by the local rules and management," Chris says.

By the time Chris was about ten years old, time and turnover in management had allowed hockey to be played and a rink to be built. The tipping point came when those who grew up wanting to play hockey became managers themselves. Hockey went from shinny with bare bones equipment to full-on games in complete gear with jerseys of their own design against teams outside the colony.

The next step, of course, is having a formal league and a schedule with games and tournaments against teams from other colonies and nearby towns. Another step is an indoor arena. Still, hockey has come a long way in Baker. Some of the Storm wear GoPros or strap them onto the caging behind the net to record games. Other colonies are live-streaming games.

The Hutterites see hockey as a character builder, Chris says. "We're using hockey as a vehicle to get to where we want to go, almost from a spiritual or moral standpoint and seeing hockey as having that ability of creating better human beings."

Eventually, the three of us slip into hockey talk, about the Jets, about the possibility of Jonathan Toews coming back to play in his hometown of Winnipeg, about the Jets not re-signing captain Blake Wheeler in the offseason, about general manager Kevin Cheveldayoff needing to make a big splash at the trade deadline. Soon it is dinnertime, with hockey for dessert.

"It's what you do after supper," Chris says.

"Come here, skate, have fun," Nolan adds.

When we get to the kitchen and dining area, Nolan pokes his head through a doorway into a room full of children.

"Do you want to play hockey tonight?" Nolan asks them.

"Yes!"

"Okay, be there after supper. I'll flood."

On the wall outside the room hang several aerial photos of the colony, in chronological order. The oldest is from 1978, five years after Baker was established. It jumps to a 1992 photo, with no rink, then to a 2004 photo, with a rink, built sometime around 1997.

I point to some of the ponds in the earlier photos.

"So would this have been where people played hockey before the rink was built?" I ask.

"Skating, for sure," Chris replies. "I remember as a kid skating on there."

"I think it was your dad who told me a story of a couple miles back in the bush," Nolan says to Chris and then turns to me. "They found a pond and built themselves a small wooden shack with a heater in there. They shoveled it off and that was their rink. They left their skates, everything back there. That's where they played hockey."

"Was it a secret?" I ask.

"Yeah, probably," Chris replies.

A buzzer starts going off. Dinnertime. I go into the kitchen, where several women are busy preparing plates of hearty German fare: meat pies, cheese bread, coleslaw, Caesar salad, carrots, cucumbers, and bacon and sausage soup. All grown or made right on the colony. I pick mine up, thank the cooks, and follow Chris and Nolan into the adults' dining room. Chris pours me some homemade ginger beer. Grace is said in German.

As we get down to eat, a man sits down next to me. Chris introduces him as Philip Waldner.

"You got my boys excited," Philip says.

"To play hockey?" I ask.

"According to them, you're working for the Winnipeg Jets."

This brings a good chuckle throughout the table.

"Well, I've interviewed some Jets before, but I don't work for them."

"That's all they need to know."

More men come to our table. Most are quiet, quick eaters.

"Have you ever been to a Hutterite community?" Philip asks.

"This is my first time."

"Well, you picked the best one in Manitoba."

There is stirring at the back of the room.

"I guess we're singing a song now," Nolan says. "Can you read German?"

I brush off my university German and do my best to follow along as Nolan pulls the lyrics up on his cellphone. When the song finishes, an English hymn, "Evening Star," follows. Finally, a prayer.

Nolan leaves to flood the ice while Chris and I finish our dinner. After Philip leaves, Tirzah (pronounced "Teer-zah") Maendel sits down with us. She has on a long colorful skirt with a baby blue Under Armour hoodie and a black hair covering. She is the Hayley Wickenheiser of Hutterite hockey.

Tirzah was eight years old when she got on the ice for the first time, after her father brought a box of skates to the school for Christmas that year. The community didn't have a rink and didn't allow hockey at the time. It was her dad who stood up and said, "'This is a waste. Why can't we tap into this?'" Tirzah recalls. "'I want my kids to be able to play.'"

With hockey allowed, Tirzah found her element. As she got older, she got better, and the restrictions on the game began loosening up. Before she was a teenager, not only was she allowed to play, she was playing with the men and hanging with the best of them.

"I was good enough to skate with the men, and I could do it," Tirzah says. "What is the saying? 'Hard work can beat talent if talent doesn't work hard.' I worked hard every day."

"So the women can play with the men?" I ask.

"I did," Tirzah replies.

"It's all about ability," Chris says. "If you have the ability, if you're twelve or thirteen or a woman or whatever, you play."

Chris and I finish off our meals, and the three of us head for the rink. I grab my skates, gloves, and stick out of Gumpy and get ready. The kids, some wearing Jets jerseys, Canada jerseys, Storm jerseys, and toques from various NHL teams, have gathered by the boards, hooting and hollering every time Nolan drives by on the Zamboni and champing at the bit for him to finish. When he gives them the all-clear, they shoot out of the gate, like an unleashed pack of dogs, Tirzah right behind them.

It is a free-for-all with about two dozen kids on the ice at the same time. I have trouble figuring out who is on my team. With numbers on their side, the kids instinctively play swarm defense. It works. None of the adults are able to get around them and score.

The evening is perfect, a touch below freezing, no wind, just a light snowfall that sparkles under the lights around the rink.

At one point, I go off to chat with Chris. Soon after, Tirzah follows.

"Old and slow," she says.

"Me too," I say. "Oh, well, it's nice just to feel the breeze, the crisp air."

"It doesn't get old."

There is something about an outdoor rink that neither a pond nor an arena quite captures. A hybrid of the two, it is a connection between where hockey came from and where the game is now, a bridge between the natural and the human worlds, an exemplar of how human artifice can harness the elements and create a place of play. Free from the confines of an enclosed space, hockey's smells and sounds evaporate into the cold air that invigorates your body even as it numbs your nose, eyes, fingers, and toes. Closer in spirit to a golf course, a baseball diamond, or a soccer pitch, an outdoor rink takes nature's gifts and gives them back in the form of a winter spectacle.

After getting on the ice, Chris and Nolan give me a tour of the Better Air shop, which employs most of the workforce on the colony and is as high tech as any Amazon warehouse. We then walk over to the carpentry shop nearby, where two men are busy making an ice shack.

"The heart and soul, the heartbeat of our culture and our way of life is to share everything," Chris says. "It doesn't matter if you're the CEO of Better Air or if you sweep the floors, you get fed, you get a house, a warm house when it's minus-twenty or thirty outside. You're taken care of, you're not homeless, you're not jobless. There's always work to do, and so we have virtually no unemployment, we have no homelessness."

"And all the homes are more or less than same?" I ask. "Nobody has a mansion?"

"More or less."

Next door is the garage. Most of the vehicles are pickups.

"So all these vehicles . . ." Chris says.

"They're basically shared," Nolan says. "Nobody owns them."

"We have about a hundred and twenty people, and with transportation and everything, we get by with twelve vehicles," Chris continues. "That power of sharing, sharing all that we have, really makes us very efficient."

We walk back to the print shop where Tirzah works. In 2011, she and two other women from Baker were at an arena in the nearby town of MacGregor, where a women's tournament was going on. They saw a local team play, felt they could compete, and asked for an exhibition game.

A date was set for the MacGregor Iron Maidens versus the Baker Storm.

"We were so nervous that first game," Tirzah recalls. "I think even spectator-wise it was mostly just family members that were there, like husbands, and kids running around . . . but it kept growing."

Word spread about a team of women playing hockey in colorful skirts that grazed the ice. As the years went on, the crowds got bigger, enough to turn the game into an annual charity event, until the Storm felt it had run its course after ten years.

"I read that your record against the Maidens was pretty good," I say.

"Eight and two," Tirzah says.

At first, the game was treated as a novelty: women in skirts versus women in hockey pants. But it was more than that. Hockey had opened a window to a world within the country that few people see and fewer understand.

"People tend to look at us and they see something rigid or stern," Tirzah says. "I think the beauty of what we did, it normalized us. Yes, we live a little bit differently, we dress a little bit differently, but we play hockey just like normal Canadians."

Here, as at so many other stops on my road trip, hockey is the bridge that takes me down some new avenue of Canadian culture. Everywhere I've been, we start with hockey and end up somewhere else.

"I think it was a positive way to share our culture," Tirzah says, "in that we're not stuck-up, backward . . ."

"Ultraconservative," Chris says.

"But even that, it's important to share that we're not a monolith," Tirzah says. "I think with the hockey that was also part of it. We're not just what you might think we are."

Tirzah shows me a few framed photos of the Storm hanging in the print shop, including a large collage with a photo of the players wearing white Canadiens practice jerseys. In the middle is a quote from the American author Mitch Albom: "Devote yourself to your community around you. Devote yourself to creating something that gives you purpose and meaning." The women are all smiling.

We follow Tirzah downstairs to the bookstore and look for books about hockey.

"I don't think Hutterite books would have any mention of hockey," Tirzah says.

I scan some of the titles. *My Hutterite Life, The Forgotten People, I Met Jesus at the Gym.*

"How about this one?" I ask.

Playing like Timothy. Against a yellow backdrop is an illustration of a Hutterite boy in goalie gear wearing a red plaid shirt and suspenders standing beside a much taller Hutterite woman, who's holding a stick with the blade toward the sky.

"Yup, that's about hockey," Nolan says. "Tirzah, we found one."

"Oh, right. I forgot about that. He's from here."

"What's this one?" Chris asks.

Chris passes the book to Tirzah, who scans the index for a hockey reference and then reads from it: "For all those that were guilty for allowing skating rinks and not countering them, which it shouldn't surprise many were guilty of, must all repent to the Great Assembly and they must remove this vice and evil and never allow it again in the future."

The four of us chuckle.

Tirzah closes the book, puts it down, and continues to rummage through the piles.

"And that's the bit that think we should be at home reading our Bibles," she says. "Which is a little bit what outsiders might think of us."

It is a cold Valentine Day's night when I roll into Lumsden. On my way into town, a board in the middle of the street advertises the first game of the Qu'Appelle Valley Highway Hockey League playoffs between the Lumsden Monarchs and Odessa Bruins and directs traffic to the Lumsden Sports Centre around the corner. From the icy parking lot full of pickups, I expect a fair-sized crowd, but when I walk in only a hundred or so fans mill about the lobby and the stands, some with 50/50 tickets in hand, others hoping to win a raffle for one of three jerseys: Maple Leafs' Mitch

Marner, Edmonton Oilers' Leon Draisaitl, and Lumsden native Peter MacDougall, who made it to the NHL as a referee.

At the other end of the lobby, by the concession stand, three men in Monarchs paraphernalia are talking casually while an NHL game plays on the TV behind them. As I cross the floor, pucks ring off the plexiglass of the lobby, which doubles as the end of the rink, startling the nervous systems, including mine, of those inside. President Chris Fisher, vice-president Verne Barber, and manager Randy Kuntz are doing their best to rep the team, each wearing some combination of a blue Monarchs cap, a red Monarchs jacket, and a gray Monarchs hoodie. Verne was born in Lumsden, and Randy raised his family here. Chris has spent nearly half his life here, too.

I try introducing myself, but the pucks are drowning me out. I can't hear a damn thing, so Verne suggests meeting up after the first period. I find a seat behind the net and wait for the game to start. The players turn to face the flag at the other end of the rink underneath the old-school bulb scoreboard as a recorded version of the national anthem plays over the sound system. The Monarchs aren't pros, but their jerseys look the part, a sleek mix of style and colors from the Canadiens, Washington Capitals, and New York Rangers, with "MONARCHS" stretching down diagonally from right to left.

In Canada, senior hockey occupies an odd space in the game. It used to be but a half-step below the bigtime, during the days of the Original Six, a de facto farm system for the NHL before it began expanding in 1967. Since then, senior hockey has shriveled up into a half-amateur, half-semipro purgatory, the last stop before the beer leagues for many former pros and university and college players, as well as those who age out of junior hockey. The best players get small stipends, but most play for free around their day jobs. In Lumsden and elsewhere throughout rural Saskatchewan, many are farmers.

In its heyday, senior hockey was the biggest draw in small prairie towns like Lumsden. Rinks were routinely filled to capacity, and players could scratch out a modest living. But by the 1990s, most of the leagues had disappeared. Somehow, the Monarchs managed to survive this mass extinction. They are the only team left from the original Number 20 Highway Hockey League, named for the highway that terminates in Lumsden. Since then, twenty-four teams have come and gone through various permutations of the Highway Hockey League, all victims of Saskatchewan's senior hockey shakedown.

I meet up with Verne during the first intermission, just as the jersey raffle is about to take place. As Verne leads me to the Monarchs' storage room, Randy is on the ice drilling holes for the net pegs ahead of the second period. A rack on the far wall of the small windowless room holds current Monarchs jerseys, while boxes on the floor are full of old ones. On either side of the door, steel shelving units hold everything from helmets and skates to promotional materials and trophies.

"Is this the current cup?" I ask, pointing at one. "It says 2018-19."

"That's the last time the Highway Hockey League championship was given out, because now it's a new league, and now we've got a new cup," Verne replies. "So because we were the last champs, this is gonna be its resting place."

Busted and battered, the trophy has been held together with duct tape and hockey tape. Senior hockey in Saskatchewan by analogy.

"It's been broken god knows how many times," Verne says. "And who knows what's been drank out of it."

As the second period gets underway, we walk back to the lobby and continue our conversation, punctuated with announcements from the scorekeeper and league president Gerry Tompkins.

"Six-fifteen mark of the second period, Monarchs' penalty number nine, Braeden Raiwet, two minutes cross-checking."

The Monarchs go back to the 1930s, when a lumber chain in Saskatchewan called Monarch Lumber sponsored the team. Back then, the Monarchs jumped from league to league before the formation of the Highway Hockey League. Most of the games they played were straight up Highway 11 between Regina and Saskatoon, hitting up small towns like Bethune, Holdfast, and Craik along the way.

"There's a lot of challenges to operating a senior hockey team in Saskatchewan, and it's the reason why there aren't anywhere near as many as there used to be," Verne says. "You could've gone up and down the roads here in the sixties and seventies and turned into a town and they would've had a senior hockey team. Now there's a limited number."

"Monarchs' goal scored by number seventeen, Riley Riddell, assists to number twenty-five, Tanner McKechnie, and to number twenty, Damian Bentz. Time of the goal, nineteen-oh-three."

Before becoming a teacher, Verne had played for the Monarchs from 1973 to 1981, during the halcyon days of senior hockey, and won three championships. As the two-time defending champions, if the Monarchs advance past the first round, the fans will start to come back, perhaps several hundred, but never fill the arena to the rafters like they used to.

"I hate to say this, but it's dying," Verne says. "I don't know how long this will be able to be maintained. It's expensive. It requires a bit of commitment on the part of the players. Even though it's basically weekend games, it's still a big commitment."

The buzzer sounds to end the second period.

"Get your fifty-fifty ready. Zero, five, five, two, three, five. That's zero, five, five, two, three, five, you're tonight's lucky fifty-fifty winner. One hundred and ten dollars, come down here and let Brian know."

I leave Verne to his volunteer duties and arrange to meet up with him again after the game. I grab some artery-constricting arena food and wander around the lobby. Opposite the concession stand are several glass display cases with Monarchs team photos. On the wall above the entrance is the Monarchs Wall of Fame. Of the eighteen numbers on it, only three are retired: number 1 for David Nugent, a goalie who died in a car accident, number 6 for Kim MacDougall, who played one game in the NHL with the Minnesota North Stars, and number 19 for Wayne Wagner, who died from brain cancer shortly after he retired.

I take up my seat in the lobby for the third period. It is clear the players still have a lot to give to the game. But like so much of life, now, hockey has become a digital fetish, one that fans in Lumsden have substituted for the real thing. They missed a good game, as the Monarchs win easily 4–1.

I follow Verne down to the dressing room. He goes in and comes out with two players: Kevin DuFour and Brody Luhning. Another player, James Beattie, steps out long enough to show me the 1970s Kawasaki snowmobile jacket he's earned as player of the game. An internal team tradition, it's never washed.

"From one sweaty player to another," Kevin tells me.

Two years ago, Kevin moved to Saskatchewan with his girlfriend and took a job in Regina. After four years of college hockey in the United States and then another four in minor pro leagues, including one season in the United Kingdom, he decided to call it a career. While settling into Regina, he signed up for beer league just to keep playing. Then he heard about the Monarchs, twenty minutes away. He called up and tried out.

"I thought it was going to be like pond hockey, just for fun," he says. "And then I come up and the first game there's elbows flying and fights and stuff, and I'm like, 'Oh, okay, it's intense.' But I love it. I like it intense. It keeps my edge for competition."

Unlike Kevin, who was born in Quebec City, Brody is a local boy, one of seven Monarchs Verne taught in high school. Brody lives on a farm five minutes up the highway. After junior hockey in Saskatchewan, he played five years for the University of Regina Cougars before coming home to the family farm to raise cattle with his father. He had offers to play in the United States and Europe but turned them down to play for the Monarchs, the final stop on his hockey career.

"I grew up watching the Monarchs, so I had to play here at some point, and I wanted to do it sooner than later," Brody says. "And I'm a homebody and a hometown guy, so I wanted to play here right away."

Brody is in his fourth year with the Monarchs and intends to play at least three more. As a kid, he came to games with his father and would play ball hockey with mini sticks between periods. The same arena, the same team, and now here he is, playing for his childhood team, with three championships to his name.

"Those three wins are probably more special than anything I've ever had in hockey, and I never thought that would happen in senior hockey," he says. "Just the feeling you got after those wins, it was the best."

From Lumsden, I head west on the Trans-Canada, meandering through yellow fields blanketed white and on past active and abandoned grain elevators, the architectural mascot of the Prairies. About half an hour from the Alberta border, I turn south on Highway 21 and follow it into Maple Creek, a square grid of bungalows and two-story homes dominated by an elevator on its northern edge, where the train runs through town. "Where Past is Present" is the motto of Maple Creek, Saskatchewan, a place where the momentum of its long history slingshots you outside town into the Cypress Hills, taking you along rolling roads lined with the trappings of ranch life: old Chevy and Ford trucks, haybales, irrigation lines, watchful cattle, and signs bearing the names of ranching families (the Bohnets, the Lawrences, and others).

I check into my hotel and drive to Maple Creek Arena at the edge of town. As the lobby fills up ahead of the big game, the line at the entrance begins extending outside into the blue twilight. Happy faces are stamped on every hand, and cowboy hats bob along atop the crowd, as if they're surfing aloft a throng of fans. One cream-colored Stetson sits on the head of well-seasoned rancher, Tom Reardon. Over his black-and-blue plaid shirt, he's wearing a black leather jacket bearing the words "Battle of Little Big Puck," the name he gave to Maple Creek's annual hockey game forty-five years ago at the town's old watering hole.

"The Commercial Hotel," he tells me as we walk outside to talk. "It's still standing, but it's empty."

Away from the growing din of the lobby, Tom takes out a cigarette, puts his pack on the hood of a pickup truck beside us, and recounts the day he came up with the name.

In midsummer 1978, Tom and his friend Nick Demchenko were having beers with their buddy Raymond Anderson from the nearby Nekaneet First Nation. The conversation started with a simple question. Who's better at hockey: the ranchers or the Nekaneet? What began as harmless barroom banter ended with a friendly wager and plans for a game.

"I invented the name at the Commercial," Tom says. "I was in the washroom, making room for more beer when I thought of it. I come out and Raymond and Nick were sitting at the table, and they both were just taking a drink when I said, 'And we'll call it the Battle of Little Big Puck.' Well, they both just sprayed beer all over the table. I remember that plain as day."

After that night at the Commercial, the three of them cut in Raymond's brother Wilbur to help organize the event. None of them were trying to be visionaries. They were just planning a Sunday afternoon of hockey. They thought the game would be a one-off, on that cold January day in 1979, but it went so well they had another the following year.

With each side winning one game, the founding fathers' attitude was, "'Well, that's good, let's leave 'er sit,'" Tom recalls as he pulls on his smoke. But then players began calling for a rubber match. So after a three-year hiatus, they held a third game. It wouldn't stop again until the pandemic.

Now seventy-five years old, Tom was born in Maple Creek, and he'll die in Maple Creek. He was gone for twenty years when he ran a community pasture elsewhere in Saskatchewan for the provincial government. But he never really left. No one here ever does. He came back for every branding, every weaning, every wedding, every funeral, any excuse he could find to come home.

"I was always a Maple Critter," he says. "It's a pretty magical place and good people, and a lot of them, well, they've been here forever, like this band here, the Nekaneet. The government tried for years to force them to move because of policy and whatnot. They just said no because they didn't wanna leave the Cypress Hills. To me, this band has the most interesting history in all of Canada."

In the late nineteenth century, the government forced many First Nations out of the Cypress Hills near the American border and onto reserves elsewhere in Saskatchewan. The Nekaneet stayed, without reserve land or treaty funding. It wasn't until 1913 that the Nekaneet First Nation received reserve status. By then, they'd formed strong relationships with the ranchers, working alongside them and learning to rodeo.

"Everybody here is a cowboy of some sort," Tom says.

I thank Tom and go back inside. The lobby is now overflowing, as are the stands. I walk toward the dressing rooms and run into Joe Braniff, who has Dale Mosquito and Bradley Goodwill with him. Joe and Dale are each wearing a black cowboy hat, while Bradley's thick black hair is pulled back in a braid. All three have on blue jeans and cowboy boots. Both Joe and Dale have played in so many of the games they've lost count, while Bradley, a third-generation player, is on his fifth.

To get away from the crowd, the four of us go into an empty dressing room to talk about the game and about the relationship between the ranchers and the Nekaneet. With few bodies to absorb our words, our conversation echoes off the concrete walls.

"We don't want to make it sound like we are this little Shangri-La community where everything is unicorn farts and fairy dust," Joe says. "But for the most part, there is that mutual respect. One thing I still laugh about, years ago when the Commercial was still going, I had a friend of mine that came from out of town, and he walked into the bar and he was looking for me, and he said, 'There were two cowboys, two Indians, and a biker sitting at the same table drinking beer.' He said, 'What's with that?' I said, 'Well, what do you mean?' He goes, 'Well, does that happen every day?' And I said, 'Yeah, pretty much.'"

The Battle of Little Big Puck is about remembering and recognizing a relationship that has carried on for more than a century. Many of the players, on both teams, have known each other their entire lives. Their parents knew each other, their grandparents knew each other and, for some, even their great-grandparents knew each other. Like all relationships, individual or collective, the ranchers and the Nekaneet have had their ups and downs, but they've found a way to make it work. The recipe is simple. All it takes is a town, two teams, a hockey rink, a game, and a long-standing tradition.

"It's an energy," Dale says. "There's a certain type of energy that gets emitted when people are in for the same cause. And for us, you can't define that. You have to be a part of it. That energy is there. I can feel it. It's hard to describe unless you're there."

Dale uses a Cree word to describe the relationship: *intchuwahm*. He says it means discussing anything as friends without offense, but with the mutual understanding of openness for teasing, camaraderie, and sharing. It sounds to me like the Cree word for chirping.

"At the end of the game, we have a major handshake that everybody has that camaraderie and that emotion in hand," Bradley says. "It could be the Cowboys beating the Indians, it could be the Indians beating the Cowboys, but at the end of the day we still shake hands. That's the best feeling in the world that, out of everything that we do, is that truth and respect for one another."

When I arrive over Family Day weekend, Maple Creek is celebrating the fortieth edition of the game. In all that time, there's never ever been a fight, just a hard-fought hockey game, albeit with a twist between the second and third periods.

"Never had a fight, and I don't ever wanna see one," Joe says. "But if it was to happen, heaven forbid, it wouldn't be because it's Cowboys and Indians. It would be because it's two Canadian teams playing each other, and it's hockey. It's hockey."

Every year, to make sure nothing gets out of hand, Joe and Dale give a speech to the players on their team before the game. "If you don't think you can stay in control," they tell their teammates, "maybe this game isn't for you."

"We're now at the point where people are trying to pattern this in other communities," Dale tells me. "And we don't say, 'No, no, no, you guys shouldn't do that.' We offer them a helping hand. 'This is how we do it, or this is what we do, and if you guys want to pattern yourselves after that, by all means have at it.' Because I think the world can use more battles out there."

"Good battles," Joe adds.

I leave the three of them to get ready for the game and go out to find a seat. There are none. I manage to find a spot to stand behind the glass at the near end of the rink, just outside the lobby.

The puck hasn't even been dropped yet and the energy Dale talked about is all around. The rink has a low metal ceiling, with gray, creaky, wooden seats on one side and standing room only, above the dressing rooms, on the other. "Definitely the biggest crowd that's ever been in here," I overhear someone say behind me. The Maple Leafs and Canadiens are playing at the same time on *Hockey Night in Canada*, but more than half of the town's two thousand people are at Maple Creek Arena for the Battle of Little Big Puck.

The announcer breaks the wait.

"Introducing first, the Cowboys!"

The ranchers, each of whom has to be a member of a rodeo association to participate in the game, come out wearing white jerseys trimmed in black and gray.

"And now, time for the Indians!"

The Nekaneet, who must either live or have lived on the reserve to play, wear navy jerseys with white and baby blue trim.

Both teams have nicknames like "Chipboy" and "R. J." and "Rubber Jack" on their nameplates, which the program explains is in memory of Robert Anderson, "a proud member of the Nekaneet band and a proud cowboy!"

Maple Creek's mayor and the Nekaneet chief both speak before the game, after which the national anthem is sung in both Cree and English. Then the good battle begins.

Right from puck drop, the energy of the crowd fuels the intensity of the players. Neither team is taking it easy. Although it is a charity event at heart, with strict no-hitting and no-fighting rules, both teams are playing to win. (To keep the game flowing, penalties result in penalty shots.) At one point, there is a flare-up at center ice. For a moment, it looks like it might ignite the first fight in the event's history, but Joe and Dale's pregame speeches win out.

The ranchers jump out to an early lead and carry it into the intermission. While the Zamboni is cleaning the ice, I walk around to the other side. I find the exit door propped open, with players from both teams standing outside, half-dressed and having a smoke together.

Before the start of the second period, I walk over to the concession stand to get some food. In the middle of the lobby, two "Welcome to Maple Creek" banners hang beside Saskatchewan and Canadian flags, along with various Maple Creek Hawks championship banners spread throughout the space. The town's hockey logo is almost identical to that of the Chicago Blackhawks'. Near the entrance, beneath a handful of jaundiced championship banners, is a wall of sponsors, both individual and corporate. Encased in glass are the jerseys of two players from Maple Creek who made it to the NHL: Barry Dean of the Philadelphia Flyers and his nephew Zack Smith of the Ottawa Senators.

There are more penalties, penalty shots, and flare-ups in the second period, but this time the Nekaneet control the pace and gradually cut into the lead. Then, with the game close heading into the final period, the real show is about to begin.

Before the game, Joe and Dale invited me to come into their respective dressing rooms during the second intermission. I go first into the Nekaneet's room and find the players in various stages of transformation. Wives, girlfriends, and children are helping the players paint their faces and get into headdresses and moose hides.

In one corner, Larry Oakes is sitting on the bench, half-dressed and dripping sweat, still trying to catch his breath.

"It's intense," he says. "You gotta keep your head up out there. But that's hockey. We're Canadians, eh! We're not just gonna go out there and give the other guys the game."

Larry is one of three players from the original game in 1979 who are still playing.

"Where you from?" he asks me.

"Toronto."

"Oh good, ho-ly, they should have one like this over there. Try it. We'll go help you organize it."

Other towns across the country have tried to copy Maple Creek's blueprint but couldn't make it work. I was told most don't even bother because there would be too many fights.

"The politicians will be against it," says one of Larry's teammates.

"Yeah, this would never fly in Toronto," I say.

That is when Dale, who's put his cowboy hat back on, pipes in to the conversation.

"That's where it's needed,' he says. "Maybe that's where it's needed."

I go into the ranchers' dressing room and find the players putting on their best western wear. Most are wearing flannel shirts and cowboy hats, but a few have added chaps into the mix, while one is wearing a buffalo jacket from the North-West Mounted Police, precursor to the RCMP, given to his grandfather. In previous years, some have gone as far as attaching spurs to their skates.

"How do you guys manage to skate in that?" I ask.

"Horribly," Joe replies.

"We all fall down about four times before we get used to it," adds one of his teammates.

I go back out and stand behind the benches as the players make their way back onto the ice. The score is almost inconsequential. This is what the fans have come to see. Hockey mixed with headdresses, war paint, cowboy hats, and plaid shirts. Even the referee, an RCMP officer, gets into the spirit, stripping out of his stripes in favor of a Stetson and red serge.

As the third period gets underway, I can't decide which team has it harder. Picture playing hockey in an elaborate Halloween costume. With the players in their respective regalia, the pace slows. The Nekaneet take over the game and go home with a 13–10 win. Just as Bradley said, the teams line up at center ice to shake hands.

After the game, I return to the Nekaneet's dressing room to congratulate them on their victory and then walk across to the connecting ranchers' room to see Joe.

"The wheels kind of fell off for us," he says. "We got lots of excuses, and they're excuses. This ain't our first time on this side of the battle. So where you headed after this?"

"I'm going to Regina tomorrow to see the Pats play."

"And the kid who can't hardly skate. You're gonna watch him, eh?"

That "kid" is Connor Bedard. From Joe Braniff in Maple Creek to Joe Daley in Winnipeg, who was being inundated with requests for the first Bedard hockey cards, it seems like all of Western Canada is talking about him. Bedard is only seventeen and hasn't played a single game in the NHL, but I couldn't escape a conversation about him wherever I've been in the Prairies. He's being touted as the best player to come out of Western Canada since Hall of Famers Joe Sakic and Steve Yzerman, perhaps even the great Gordie Howe himself. A lot of it is hype and hyperbole, but not by much. I have to see the kid play.

I leave Maple Creek and retrace my route along the Trans-Canada to Regina. My destination is a small bungalow, a short drive from the Brandt Centre, where the Regina Pats will be playing the Lethbridge Hurricanes later that afternoon. By the snow-covered stairs, still lined with Christmas lights, flutter two flags, one for the Pats and the other for Jesus, urging people like me to "Trust in the Lord with all your heart." As directed by a sign in the window, I walk around back. Out pops Kevin Shaw, all six-foot-six of him, ducking his head as he fills the doorway and welcomes me in. Sizing me up at his heels is his shih tzu-poodle, Brix, named after a former Pats vice-president from the 1920s, J. B. "Brix" Peebles.

"The guy eventually went to jail because he stole some money afterward," Kevin says. "But I didn't know that when I named her."

I follow Kevin into his basement, a wall-to-wall and floor-to-ceiling collection of all things Pats. These range from the typical jerseys, bobblehead dolls, and team photos found in any superfan's collection to more uncommon items, like a Pats pocket watch from the 1920s, a Pats golf bag, and Pats pillow covers Kevin's mother made for him.

"When I was younger, I knew I couldn't skate. That was it. I knew my dream was over when I was five," Kevin says. "But the Pats were my NHL team. People would be like, 'Are you an Oilers fan?' 'No, Pats.' When I was little, I thought the Pats could play against the NHL because I didn't know."

Named after Princess Patricia's Canadian Light Infantry, the Patricias, the Pats are the world's oldest junior hockey team, dating back to 1917, the year the NHL began. Although they ceased operations from 1934 to 1946, they've never changed their name, never overhauled their logo, and never left Regina.

Regina is in a tier of Canadian cities that are too small to hang with Canada's nine largest cities (Toronto, Montreal, Vancouver, Calgary, Edmonton, Ottawa, Winnipeg, Quebec City, and Hamilton), all of which have had an NHL team at some point, and too big to maintain the small-town feel of places like Lumsden. In this NHL-lite of hockey cities are some of the most storied franchises in the country, teams like the London Knights, Oshawa Generals, Chicoutimi Saguenéens, Saskatoon Blades, and the Pats. Although Saskatchewan has produced the most NHL players per capita, it is the only province that has never had an NHL team, nor an affiliate from the American Hockey League, the world's second-highest pro league. So for hockey fans in Regina, the Pats are their Maple Leafs or Canadiens (the same goes for the Blades in Saskatoon).

Born in Regina and raised on the Pats, Kevin started going to games as an infant with his parents. In his forty-four years of existence, he's missed only twenty games. Four of those were because he had his appendix taken out.

"Regina's home. It's part of me, it's in my blood," Kevin says. "The Pats are a part of me. Probably if I cut myself, it'd be red and a little bit of blue in there. Probably not too much white, though."

A Pats flag covers the window by his computer station, where Kevin spends much of his time piecing together the history of the Pats, compiling an all-time schedule, tracking trades and transactions back to 1946–47, and collecting a game summary for every Pats game ever played. He's also putting together an all-time Pats player list dating back to the team's first year, plus a player register for every Pats player. It is already thousands of pages thick.

Soon after Bedard came to the Pats and began breaking records, Kevin became the team's go-to resource for Pats stats. Fans and media would pepper the Pats' PR reps with questions about whether Bedard was the youngest player to do this or the youngest to do that. Eventually, the Pats started telling people to "talk to Kevin Shaw" and made him the team's official historian.

"The kid is once in a lifetime," Kevin says. "I've never seen anybody even close to that, even from any other team that I can think of, especially at seventeen."

Kevin throws on his Pats cap and we drive to the Brandt Centre. Before the game, the Pats run a highlight reel of Bedard's fifty goals so far this season. Then comes the Pats video intro, "Legends in the Making," to pump up the crowd, another sellout. The video starts with a kid playing on nearby Lake Wascana in front of the provincial parliament building. A beam of light shines down from the heavens and lures the kid. As he moves toward it, he skates over images in the ice of the Patricias, whose patch the players still wear on their shoulders. As he gets closer to the light, he starts skating through downtown Regina, passing under a banner of the Pats' 1974 Memorial Cup. His jersey evolves from when the Pats wore actual sweaters and then on through the years to the Pats' current jersey. When he arrives at the Brandt Centre, he is ready for war.

Late in the first period, the Pats pay tribute to Rob Vanstone, a longtime reporter for the *Regina Leader-Post* who's just taken a job with the Canadian Football League's Saskatchewan Roughriders. During the intermission, with the game still scoreless, I find him seated near ice level, wearing jeans, a blue hoodie, black jacket, running shoes, and a Winnipeg Jets cap.

"I had no idea they were going to put me on the screen," Rob says. "If I had known that, I would've dressed better."

Thanks to Bedard, these are the best of times for the Pats. But since the start of the season, they've been dogged with trade rumors. As a middling team in the Western Hockey League, the Pats could've traded Bedard to one of the league's top teams and brought back a king's ransom in return. But the Pats understand the significance of tying the franchise to Bedard forever. In a few months' time, he'll be drafted first overall into the NHL.

"I'm glad they kept him, because I want them to say, 'From the Regina Pats, Connor Bedard,'" Rob says. "I'm proud of the fact that I'm able to watch this. I've never seen anything like this, and I don't think I'm going to see anything like it again. I don't anticipate being here fifty years from now when the next one might come."

The crowd erupts in cheers. The Pats have scored, and Bedard has his first point of the game, an assist.

"It's not even the goals and assists," Rob says. "There's always this little Connor Bedard flourish. Just these subtle little things that he does that makes you think, 'Oh my goodness, I've never seen this before.' It's not necessarily what you see on the highlight reels. It's just the subtle little things on a shift. A pass could end up on the back of his skate and the next thing you know it's on his stick. It's unreal. I love watching him."

Bedard is so good he almost looks lazy, like he's drifting. But players of his type are so beyond their peers that the game comes to them. They don't need to chase it. Bedard is so skilled even his teammates don't know what he's going to do. In the first period, I watched him give the puck away several times, only because his teammates didn't know it was coming.

Back in the press box for the second and third periods, I watch as Bedard makes several more passes that his teammates aren't ready for. When he doesn't have the puck, the Hurricanes stick to him like glue, afraid of what he'll do if he gets it. But when he does have the puck, they give him all the space in the world, afraid of ending up on the wrong end of a highlight reel.

The game ends 4–2 for the Pats. With no goals and only two assists, it is an off-day for Bedard. For a moment, I consider following Kevin and the rest of the media down to the dressing room to ask Bedard what he sees on the ice that everyone else doesn't. But the kid is seventeen. He won't know how to tell me how good he is until he retires. So I make a mental note to ask him in twenty years and leave for Saskatoon.

The city that Gordie Howe built, Saskatoon is saturated with tributes to Mr. Hockey. There is the Gordie Howe Sports Complex, Gordie Howe Kinsmen Arena, Gordon Howe Park, and Gordon Howe Campground, all of which sit in or around the Gordie Howe Management Area. To the south is the Gordie Howe Bridge, while to the north stands a Gordie Howe statue outside the SaskTel Centre. There is also a monument that commemorates where the hockey gods delivered Howe to the hockey world in what used to be the village of Floral, about 30 kilometers (18 miles) south of the city. Howe is elsewhere in Canada, too. Once construction on the new border crossing between Detroit and Windsor is complete, Highway 401 in Ontario will end at the Gordie Howe International Bridge. In Chatham-Kent, Ontario, there is even a snowplow named after Howe. The Gordie Plow.

In any list of the greatest players of all-time, Howe is often placed third behind Wayne Gretzky and Bobby Orr. But neither had it harder than Howe. Orr came into the NHL in the late 1960s, just as the league was doubling in size, and by the time he retired it had nearly tripled. When Gretzky took over in the 1980s, the NHL had hit its highest level of scoring per game in the history of the league, a time when goalies were pylons who occasionally got in the way of pucks. Howe played his first twenty-one years when there were only six teams. Imagine having to beat one of the five best goalies in the world every given game. At one point in Howe's career, the NHL's six starting goalies were Jacques Plante, Glenn Hall, Johnny Bower, Gump Worsley, Harry Lumley, and his Detroit Red Wings' own Terry Sawchuk. All six are in the Hockey Hall of Fame.

It is a couple of hours up Highway 11 from Regina to Saskatoon, "from the ice box to the freezer," says P. J. Kennedy when I meet him at Merlis Belcher Place, home of the University of Saskatchewan Huskies. As planned, I find P. J. in the windowed lobby of the arena. As expected, briefcase in hand, he's come prepared.

"Let's take the elevator," he says. "Both my knees and one of my hips aren't mine, and I don't know when the warranty will run out. You a Leafs fan?"

"Against my better judgment."

"Well, I am too," he says as he strokes his white whiskers. "Sometimes, I tell people that this is a playoff beard from 1967."

On the second floor, P. J. leads me into Smuker's Lounge, named for Huskies player Cory Smuk, who died from cancer at age twenty-six. We grab a pair of foldup chairs and choose a table in the middle of the empty room. P. J. places his briefcase on the table and pulls out some handwritten notes, a syllabus, a bio, a publication list, and copies of three of his books. I wonder if there's going to be a test at the end.

Inside each book is a handwritten note. The one in *Words on Ice* reads: "For Ronnie, always keep your head up and your mind open!"

Keep an open mind. That was all P. J. ever asked of his students in his English 114 class, better known as "the hockey class," the first of its kind in Canada. Where skeptics would've seen incongruity between hockey and literature, P. J. saw connection. "Poetry on ice" is an oft-used expression for hockey, but in truth, when the game itself is narrated, the chaos of hockey comes closer to the auctioneer's tongue than the poet's cadence. Yet throughout Canadian literature, the pen has never strayed far from the stick.

"I discovered, boy, there's a lot out there, and people are just not aware of it," P. J. says. "That's really what triggered the course. So I put together a syllabus and presented it to the undergraduate committee. They went through it and said, 'Oh, look at this. There's some big-name Canadian writers.'"

Ken Dryden, Doug Beardsley, Peter Gzowski, Roch Carrier, Richard Wagamese, Donna Kane, Michael Ondaatje, Stephen Scriver, Richard

Harrison, Joan Finnigan—the list is long. Many are in P. J.'s anthologies of hockey prose (*Words on Ice*) and poetry (*Going Top Shelf*), including Al Purdy's poem "Hockey Players," which contains the best description of hockey ever written: "this combination of ballet and murder." But it is Bruce Meyer's "Road Hockey" that catches my eye, a poem about a man on a train who wakes up from a dream about playing road hockey as a kid:

> And as I woke just now,
> at some point in a journey
> I realized we'd all
> become grown men,
> and the waking, not the growing
> left me angry. Snow whirls
> by the coach car window,
> still clings to the furrows
> of pantlegs and fields
> as the journeymen continue on
> their battles of earthly overtime
> and the sudden darkness
> after.

At first, P. J. wasn't sure who was going to take his new course, Reading Culture: Hockey in Canadian Literature. But students flocked to it, with a near equal split between men and women. They came from every department: arts, science, commerce, nursing, engineering, even agriculture. Only ten percent were athletes. Every year, the class was full to overflowing. The course became so popular that P. J. taught it two or three times every year. During the first couple of weeks of each semester, other students would email, phone, or track him down in the hallways, trying to get into the class. Other universities came calling, too, leading to copycat courses across the country.

Intended, in part, as a way to encourage more students to take an interest in literature, P. J. discovered that hockey opened the door for people who wouldn't otherwise have given Canadian literature a chance. For fifteen years, from 2002 until P. J. retired in 2017, his students explored how hockey suffuses the Canadian canon. Along with his anthologies were poems on Don Cherry, books by famous players, biographies, autobiographies, and journalistic snippets from hockey writers. As an upper-level class, students had to write two essays and participate in a formal seminar. Anyone who thought it was going to be a bird course had to learn the hard way.

"People who knew me knew that I wasn't going to just offer a fluffy course," P. J. says. "Some of the hockey players, too, they'd come in and say, 'Gee, this is hard.' 'Yes it is, yes it is.'"

When he was still teaching, P. J. used to keep a photo of Howe on his desk. It was of them sharing a laugh after Howe received his honorary doctorate in 2010. At that graduation ceremony, P. J. remembered every student, whether they were a hockey fan or not, going up and shaking Howe's hand. Nobody told them to do it. They knew they were in the presence of greatness.

"We're standing up, and he takes his elbow, puts it in my rather obese belly, looks at me and smiles," P. J. tells me. "I'm thinking, 'Here he is, there he is, he's like the old guy, done so much, and he did the old elbow in the belly.' I thought, 'That's so cool, that's so cool.'"

Signs along Highway 3 in Saskatchewan advertise firewood and seeds for sale. In summer, the fields mimic the yellow and green of the provincial flag underneath the big prairie sky. But it is late February, and all that is buried beneath the snow. Stubble pokes through here and there like a patchy beard. Cattle stand behind huddles of birch trees, which are clumped together like animals trying to stay warm.

At the town of Tisdale, I turn north on Highway 35. About 30 kilometers (18 miles) up the road, I slow down as I near the intersection of highways 35 and 335, known locally as Armley Corner. My eyes go first to the six crosses on the southeast corner, with three blue wreaths on top and three pink wreaths below, in memory of six family members killed in a crash here in 1997. I then glance over to the northwest corner, to another memorial, which sits in front of a set of train tracks running from a grain terminal across the road.

When I get there, two men are standing in front of the memorial. I nod to one as he walks back to his car to get out of the wailing winter wind. The other, born in Montreal, is visiting from the United States.

"This touched the world, the whole world knew about this," he says, as we stand in front of the memorial. "International news, a little intersection like this all over the world."

On April 6, 2018, sixteen players and staff from the Humboldt Broncos junior hockey team died in a crash here, and thirteen others were injured. Like so many rural highways in Saskatchewan, the intersection is guarded only by stop signs.

"It was a day like today, too," the man says.

He turns and points east to Highway 335 and south to Highway 35, and then to the corner where a glade had blocked the drivers from seeing each other.

"The truck was coming from there, the bus was coming from there," he says. "They took the trees down."

In two feet of snow, a large green HUMBOLDT STRONG cross stands guard above all the white crosses below. The names and jersey numbers written in black stand out against the snow. A goalie stick lies half-buried in front of the memorial.

We stand there. Neither of us has anything more to add. Silence seems like the only thing to say.

"Well, enjoy your day," the man says. "Be safe."

"You as well."

I am now far enough north in Saskatchewan that it makes sense to turn northeast back across the Manitoba border to Flin Flon, named after Josiah Flintabbatey Flonatin, a fictional character in a novel by British author J. E. Preston Muddock. Flin Flon is a town of talkers. But it is a certain kind of talk that only happens here. It covers all topics but converges into one. History, tradition, people, the mine, the weather, music, sex—every conversation leads to hockey. They call it Bomber Talk.

I drive past the large statue of "Flinty" that greets people coming into town, and then another of him riding a submarine on the eastern edge of Ross Lake. I check into my motel and drive to the old Whitney Forum, built by Flin Flon's main employer, Hudson Bay Mining & Smelting.

When I arrive, the Bombers have just wrapped up their morning skate ahead of their game tonight against the Weyburn Red Wings. Players collect their shoes from the cubbyholes outside the dressing room (no footwear is allowed inside). Coach and general manager Mike Reagan, clad in a Bombers jumpsuit, comes out and leads me to one of the lounges.

"It's a lifestyle, it's a culture here, the Bombers," he says. "We'll have probably seven hundred to eight hundred people here tonight, and there are Bomber fans that don't come to the games but they follow it intensely, whether listening on the radio or just talk at the mine."

Flin Flon so self-identifies with its hockey club that to talk about the team is to talk about the town. The team actually predates Flin Flon, which wasn't incorporated until 1933, by six years (although it wouldn't be named the Bombers until 1936.)

The Bombers have a mythology all their own, one borne of place. It is impossible to export it beyond the borders of Flin Flon. You have to live or have lived here to be a Bombers fan, and you must love the team as much as the town, because the two are as inseparable as the Bombers' maroon and white.

"Bomber Talk is every day," Mike says. "The coffee shops, the theme is the Bombers. Even in the summertime, everybody's still talking about the previous season or the upcoming season."

Born in Flin Flon and bred on the Bombers, Mike was raised by a single mother who billeted players to give her young son male role models. Mike played four years for the Bombers in the late 1990s. After four years of college hockey in the United States and a short stint in minor pro leagues that took him through the Deep South and, briefly, Quebec, the Bombers brought him back in 2007 as coach and GM. He's been here ever since.

Flin Flon lies on the western edge of Manitoba and trickles over into Saskatchewan. The Bombers play in the Saskatchewan Junior Hockey League. For most teams in the league, road games are an hour drive out and an hour back home. For the Bombers, short trips are three to four hours away. Life is lived on the road aboard the bus. Their longest drive is Estevan, fifteen minutes from the American border, eleven hours away. Road trips often feature four games in five nights or three in three, getting back into Flin Flon anywhere from two to five o'clock in the morning. One of Mike's main recruiting requirements during the summer is to look for players who can handle the rigors of the road.

"Our road trips are long, and some people see that as a disadvantage," he says. "Don't get me wrong, it's tougher, but I also look at it as it prepares us for playoffs. When playoff time comes, we're used to the grind of the road, whereas some teams aren't. I also look at it from the perspective that our guys get an opportunity to come close together on the road."

I follow Mike back to the dressing room. Everything about the Bombers, their logo, the inspirational quotes on the walls, their blue-collar, fan-friendly playing style, the arena they play in—it all mimics the mining mentality of the town. On the inside door, a sign reminds players, "Through this door walks the heart of a champion." In the team's gym, "Nobody outworks the Bombers." Where the players dress, a large maroon rug, with the words "Built on Passion," covers most of the floor, mirroring the fluorescent sign above it on the ceiling. Above a large TV is a moose rack from a Bombers' super fan, Clarence Pettersen, who donated it to the team a week before he chose to get the shot to end his life because of cancer. The signatures of every Bomber who's ever graduated from the team as a twenty-year-old covers the plywood ceiling of the laundry room. Everything is in maroon and white, even the washer and dryer.

In the early days of the Bombers, the players did their laundry like miners. "In the mine, they used to dry their clothes using a pulley system with chains," Mike says. "They had a pulley at the top and they'd hang their underwear up there. Then they'd pull it up and the heat would dry out their stuff. They used to have that here. In the ceiling there were baskets, you put everything in there."

I leave Mike to prepare for the game and drive to CFAR, the local radio station, to talk with Flin Flon's professional talker, the Bombers' longtime play-by-play caller, Rob Hart. Although the walls outside his second-floor office are covered in posters of rock bands and musicians, Rob's tiny, windowless, half-wood-paneled, half-white-brick office is almost all hockey. It virtually enfolds Rob as he reclines on his swivel office chair, arms crossed, resting on his belly. Although a longtime Canadiens fan, he's wearing a Florida Panthers T-shirt, prescient since the Panthers would make it to the Stanley Cup Final this season.

"Flin Flon's got a mystique, it's a special place," Rob says. "We talk about the history of the team and the success of the team, but there's a lot of characters in the community itself. That makes it fun to go to the rink as well."

"Is it common for people who leave Flin Flon to keep tabs on the Bombers?" I ask.

"I get emails from people all over the world that listen to the Bomber broadcast. There's a pilot in Japan who used to send me emails regularly that he was listening and to make sure I put a shout-out to him during the broadcast. He lived in Flin Flon for a couple of years way back when, is a fan, and he just listens to the games."

In an age when cutbacks are keeping NHL radio broadcasters at home, Rob still travels with the Bombers to almost every road game. Even the Maple Leafs' radio crew no longer travels with the team, forcing fans to listen to them call "road games" off a TV in Toronto, even during the playoffs.

I go back downstairs and get talking with Austin Mattes and Raphael Saray, two of the station's other voices. I'm about to leave when the station's manager, Dianne Russell, pops out of her office.

"They used to say you're either a hooker or a hockey player if you're from Flin Flon," she says.

It isn't the first time I've come across this joke. Birk Sproxton wrote about it in his poem "The Hockey Fan Reflects On Beginnings":

Flin Flon? they say.
Why the only people I know are from Flin Flon are hockey players
and hookers.
My mother is from Flin Flon, you say.
Long pause.
And what position does she play?

"When the mine started, that wasn't totally untrue," Dianne says. "It was either you played an instrument, or you played hockey, or there was a red-light district, because there was a lot of single guys up here back then. It was like a shanty town."

Flin Flon is a lot like Newfoundland. It is rocky and hilly and has a similar vibe as a once one-industry town. Even though that lone industry isn't doing so well, the people still have hope that things will turn around for the better, that the town will find its way again. If nothing else, Flin Flon has the Bombers. People here are happy, content, and love to talk. If there is a difference, Newfoundlanders are born storytellers, while Flin Flonners are born talkers.

"Who are you talking to next?" Raphael asks.

"Brent Lethbridge, you know him?"

"Uncle Lefty!" Raphael says. "He used to have a TV show, the fabulous Bomber Show. That was kind of the Bomber hype show."

"He'll give you lots about the Bombers," Austin says. "He loves the Bombers, too. He's a really talkative guy."

"Retired insurance salesman," Raphael says. "Part-time rock star."

After dinner, I drive back to the arena to meet with Brent before the game. The concrete walls are half maroon and half white with a black stripe in between. The creaky wooden floor in the lobby, where we sit, is all maroon, as are stacking chairs piled along the walls. Brent has brought along his sister-in-law Jennifer Hanson, a former anthem singer for the Winnipeg Jets in the 1990s. I tell them I've just come from the radio station.

"So you've talked to all the professional talkers," Jennifer says.

"I was wondering if everybody in Flin Flon is a professional talker."

"Well, there's lots."

"People are happy to talk," Brent says.

Both Brent and Jennifer were born in Flin Flon, both are musicians, and both understand the analogy between being in a band and playing on a hockey team. In Flin Flon, music and hockey are intertwined.

As a company town full of miners, Flin Flon's only land link to the rest of the country used to be the train. No roads were built to it until the 1950s. It was a booming mining community back then, but it was isolated. Hudson Bay Mining & Smelting knew it needed to offer more than just jobs to keep people from leaving. They started to hire special miners.

"There's not much to do in the winter, so two things got a foothold," Brent says. "One was musical culture and musical theater, and the other was hockey. If you were a hockey player, a good hockey player, they would hire you to work at the mine. They'd work out a little deal where you'd get paid full time, but you weren't there when you're on road trips, and when you were there, you weren't working when you were practicing. So they got full pay. It was almost a little bit professional."

They would hire singers, too. Jennifer's father was hired as a tenor, and she became a singer herself. She left Flin Flon at eighteen when her career took her to Atlanta, Georgia. Bomber Talk followed her there.

"I had a house gig at this bar, and people would find out that I was from Flin Flon, and they would wanna talk about Bobby Clarke, about hockey and Flin Flon, especially if they were hockey fans," Jennifer says. "This guy walked up to me once, and he goes, 'I heard you're from Flin

Flon.' And I was like, 'Yes, I am.' He said, 'Bobby Clarke ruined hockey.' I was like, 'Hey, man, he is a national fucking treasure in Canada. I will not have you speak about him like this.'"

Bobby Clarke, the archetypal Bomber. His connection to his hometown runs deep. Clarke, whose father had been a driller in the copper and zinc mines, played three years for the Bombers before leaving for the Philadelphia Flyers. Although he lives in Pennsylvania, Clarke still has family in Flin Flon, owns property in town, and comes back to fish from his cabin some summers. He is all over the Whitney Forum, including the Bomber Hall of Fame, although a mural of him depicts the left-shooting Clarke shooting right-handed. The gymnasium at École McIsaac School in town is named after him, and tourists still ask to see his signature in the Bombers' laundry room.

At a team function in town, long after he retired, Clarke once referred to himself and other Bomber alumni as players who had "Made in Flin Flon stamped on our ass." In true Flin Flon fashion, Clarke made profanity an art form in hockey. If, as Gordie Howe once said, all hockey players speak two languages—English and profanity—Clarke was fluently bilingual.

"When I was a kid, the CBC came up with this great brain wave," Brent says. "Toronto's playing Philadelphia, 'Let's put a mic on Bobby Clarke.'"

Jennifer laughs hard. She hasn't heard the story, but she knows how it will end.

"They put a live mic on him, and Andy Van Hellemond, who used to come here and referee, was reffing the game," Brent says. "Bob's on the bench and something goes sideways and he says, 'Andy, you fucking cocksucker!'"

"Bobby, you're only supposed to say that in Flin Flon!" Jennifer says.

The name Flin Flon, the cast of characters and professional talkers, the combination of hockey and music, the unusual border-spanning layout of the town, the long tradition of the Bombers, and the lore of Bobby Clarke—it has all created a pop culture cult following of the team and the town. In the movie *Mystery Alaska*, Canadian actor Mike Myers plays a sports reporter from Flin Flon named Donnie Shulzhoffer, who describes the goalie in the championship game: "He looks like he's from the Flin Flon Bombers." The town and the team are also a favorite among low-budget, straight-to-video releases, like *The Road to Flin Flon*, a 1990s comedy in which a Californian travels to Flin Flon to find enlightenment, and *Santa's Slay*, a Christmas horror comedy in which the protagonist wears a Bombers jersey while trying to track down a murderous rampaging St. Nick.

Much has changed since the heydays of both Flin Flon and the Bombers. Once a city of fifteen thousand, Flin Flon is now a third of that. The mine's headquarters are still in town, but the mine itself has moved to Snow Lake about two hours away. The old Glee Club has closed, the red-light district is gone, and the Bombers haven't won a championship in thirty years.

"If there wasn't a fight at the bar on Saturday nights, there was nothing happening," Jennifer says. "It's not really like that anymore, but in the eighties and the nineties, it was like that. I don't know if it was the hockey bug, I don't know if it was the small-town vibe, but if you didn't get stoned, drunk, fucked, and in a fight, it just wasn't a good weekend, you know."

The three of us go out to watch the game. I look around the arena. Glass-encased Bomber jerseys of alumni hang on the walls along with old team photos. Across from us, I can see the bright white sign for the Bombers' wall of fame. Above us, Bombers banners hang the length of the rink. At the far end is written "Welcome to the Zoo." This is where Flin Flon's most colorful fans watch the games, while the queen looks over the ice from the other.

Flin Flon is a town built on people working underground, getting dirty, clawing a living from the earth. Fans demand the Bombers play the same way, and they aren't shy to remind the players of that.

"Hit him! Hit him!"

"Come on! Nail these guys!"

"Hit their goalie!"

As a mining community, the people in Flin Flon expect physical hockey, and the Bombers have rigged their rink accordingly. It is fifteen feet shorter and ten feet narrower than regulation size. It is blue-collar hockey played in front of blue-collar fans in a blue-collar town, and the Bombers send them home happy, with a 4–3 win over the Red Wings.

As is tradition after every home win, fans heft a couple of moose legs over the glass. I watch them slide to center ice, where a pair of Bombers pick them up to be placed with all the others in a freezer in the team's dressing room. Several years ago, the Red Wings kicked off a bench-clearing brawl with the Bombers when they tried to steal the moose legs after a loss.

I thank Brent and Jennifer and begin making my way to the exit. As I file out with the rest of the crowd, I understand something Raphael said to me back at the radio station.

"We don't have hockey fans here. We have Bomber fans."

I take the two-lane Hanson Lake Road for 362 kilometers (225 miles) through muskeg and rocky outcrops to Prince Albert and back down to Saskatoon, where I connect to the upper part of the Trans-Canada and carry on to Edmonton.

In the southern part of the city, I navigate Edmonton's maddening road grid to reach George S. Hughes South Side Arena on 72nd Avenue. The arena is small and old, but clean and well kept. I'm sitting in the lobby when Nelson Rego, all six-foot-five and 285 pounds of him, shaved head and Terminator sunglasses, walks in with his wife and daughter. He's wearing the sleek blue and maize colors of his hockey team, a jersey he designed himself. Eventually, he plans to add "SeeHawks" in braille along the arms.

A pair of half-ice high school broomball games are going on, making it too loud to sit in the stands to talk. Nelson and I grab a couple of folding chairs and go into the officials changeroom, while his wife and daughter watch the games.

A traditional hockey puck is 5.5 to 6 ounces of solid vulcanized rubber, about three inches in diameter and one inch high. Against plexiglass, boards, goalposts, even equipment on blocked shots, the audio of its impact is distinct. But on its own, a puck makes no sound. After we sit down, Nelson pulls out a large metallic puck and drops it onto the blue table in the room. Hollow and made of 22-gauge sheet metal, it is 5.5 inches in diameter, 1.875 inches high and weighs 7.8 ounces. When I shake it, the noise from the eight ball bearings inside echo off the concrete walls of the tiny room. The puck's once smooth circular edges have been dented and chipped after just two practices, leaving several sharp points exposed. To protect himself, Nelson wears a customized chest protector and a goalie mask as thick as the cage on a football helmet.

"I'd rather take a slapshot from an NHL player than a wrist shot from a blind player," Nelson says.

"How old were you when you lost your eyesight?" I ask.

Nelson pauses.

"Oh, geez, I don't even celebrate birthdays. I never give out my age either. When I lost my eyesight, my age kind of stood still. It's a weird thing. Time sort of stands still, because everything that I saw before I still it see it that way. I picture my wife the way I last saw her, because I lost my eyesight pretty quick."

It started as a gray-white blur, the way a bathroom mirror fogs up after taking a hot shower. After that, it became like the static on an old TV, a visual cacophony of black-and-white movement that came across as gray. Then it became white as Nelson lost all perception except light. Eventually, as his eyes atrophied and died and his optic nerve was severed, he lost that, too. Since then, everything has become different levels of textured black. So few people have Nelson's condition, uveitis, that little research has been done on it.

"I unfortunately got one of those eye diseases that there's not a lot of money in it," he says. "So I understand my lot in life is going to be blind till I die."

Yet Nelson can still see. Just not with his eyes. As he came into the room, ducked under the ceiling, and sat down in the chair, Nelson put together an image of the room in his head. The echoing off the walls from his voice told him the room was small and the ceiling sloped. The dull feedback from the ceramic tip on his white cane told him the floor was rubber. As he leans back in his chair, he can sense the wall behind his head.

"I just tell people I have to see through my brain, because that's the only way I can explain it," he says. "Normally, I would say my hearing makes up for the losses of the senses, but there's something else going on with the brain where it's just reconnecting senses or it's just using other senses in the body."

The last time Nelson was at this arena was November 14, 2021. He was filling in for a beer-league goalie on the Revolution HC in the Capital City Recreational Hockey League. When Nelson showed up, he was a bundle of nerves. He'd never played on a sighted team before. But the Revolution made him feel welcome. They even had a jersey made up for him, with REGO written on the back.

To hide his blindness from the opposing team, the Cheddar Hockey Club, Nelson had to find his own way to his net instead of being led there by a teammate, which is protocol in blind hockey. Once in his crease, he used his posts to gauge where to position himself. With the nets a foot higher than those used in blind hockey, he would have to stand instead of playing most of the game on his knees, like he usually did.

When he first became a goalie, a few years ago, Nelson tried playing at the top of the crease, the way any goalie would in the NHL games he used to watch as a kid. Until he realized that no sheet of ice is ever level. Even when he stood still, he would drift with the grade of the ice. He stopped playing that way and stayed close enough to the net to feel his goalposts. Then he came up with his own invention that let him stray farther out. He built a little beeper box, put a small magnet on it, and either clamped or stuck it to the top of the crossbar, a beacon for him to find the net.

When his game with the Revolution got going, Nelson's teammates helped him by yelling out how many opposing playing were coming into their end. Nelson also used the same audio clues he relies on in his practices with the SeeHawks: sounds from the puck, the players, the skates, and the sticks, all of it echoing off the boards and reverberating off the ice. But he'd never played at George S. Hughes Arena before, so it took him a while to figure out where everyone and everything was.

"Every arena plays different, it also sounds different as well," Nelson says. "The acoustics are important if you're a goalie. If I'm in a big arena, the sounds get lost in the air."

As the game wore on, and the score stayed close, the Cheddar began to clue in. They started shooting the puck slow, like a curling shot, so that Nelson couldn't use the sound of the stick to tell if someone had taken a shot. When the Revolution cut that trick off, the Cheddar began banking the puck off the boards, like they were playing Pong.

"That was one of the reasons why I didn't want them to know," Nelson says, "because they would start messing around."

Yet through all of the Cheddar's shenanigans, Nelson kept the Revolution in the game. With just over a minute left, and his team down just one goal, he was pulled for an extra attacker to try to send the game into overtime. The storybook ending didn't happen. The Revolution lost 9–8.

"If we had beat that other goalie, someone said he would've retired because the difference between me and him was that I couldn't see and he could, and that's a big thing," Nelson says. "We came close to winning."

At the end of the game, as Nelson found his way to his teammates, the Cheddar started tapping their sticks on the ice. At first, Nelson was confused. He'd never heard this being done in blind hockey. Then his teammates explained. "Hey, Nelson, that's for you." He'd become the first fully blind person in Canada to play in a registered sighted league game.

"It was a bit of an emotional moment for me, because I didn't realize how important that was," Nelson says. "I just thought, 'Oh, they gave me a chance to play.' But at the end, everyone realized I was blind, so everyone was shaking my hand. It was a really special moment. It was kind of like my little NHL moment, in this small way."

I glance at my cellphone. We've talked for two hours in this solitary cell of a room.

"That's the other thing about being blind," Nelson says. "You lose track of time."

"I wonder if that's a good thing," I say. "Time can be a tyrant sometimes."

"Well, ask my wife. Go outside and see her face and you'll see it's not a good thing. It's one thing that I hate about being blind."

It isn't until I leave Edmonton that I realize this will be my last chance to watch an NHL game on the road trip. Well out of the playoffs, the Vancouver Canucks are sure to be golfing by the time I get to British Columbia in mid-April, after another trip north. If I'm going to catch a game, it has to be in Alberta.

From Edmonton I drive down Highway 2 to Red Deer, which at a little over one hundred thousand people holds the cumbersome title of largest city in North America without a major pro sports team that is equidistant between two cities that do. I carry on to Calgary, where the Flames are in negotiations with the city to replace the old Saddledome, the last NHL arena to carry some civic pride.

At its origin, hockey is about impermanence. Before the invention of the arena, hockey could only exist part of the year. It came into being when the waters froze, and then disappeared into nothingness when the ice melted. Even when it was civilized and brought indoors, hockey wasn't able to circumvent the laws of physics until the advent of refrigeration systems. The irony of it all is that these systems built to bring permanence to the game have made hockey more impermanent than ever. Although they can combat the forces of nature, they cannot withstand the economics of entertainment. Build an outdoor rink by day and even nature can't remove it overnight the way an NHL arena crew can indoors to make way for a basketball game or a rock concert.

It used to be that NHL arenas were a locus for hometown fans and places of pilgrimage for those coming from out of town. They were mythic, shrouded in mystery and mystique, with a rarified air that translated into an atmosphere of allegiance that the home team could tap into and carry over from generation to generation. As places of worship, they were granted religious status as "shrines" and "temples" to which writers could attach words like "dignified," "grand," and "solemn." Like the Saddledome, with its saddle-shaped roof that only makes architectural sense in Calgary, these arenas could only exist where they were built. Now, each is as unremarkable as the next, and could just as well have been built in any other NHL city. All that can be said of them is their seating capacity.

With 19,289 fans in attendance, the Saddledome is a sellout when I arrive in town for a midweek game between the Maple Leafs and the Flames. The Flames come out in their alternate, black, nostril-flaring horsehead jerseys with a conspicuous Boston Pizza logo on their right chest, while the Leafs are wearing their road whites with a gaudy scrawl from the Dairy Farmers of Ontario on theirs, more milk money for a franchise overflowing in milk and honey.

Advertising has crept ever so slowly into every cranny of the NHL, from ads on the boards, to ads on the ice, to naming rights for arenas, to sponsoring division names, to brain-buzzing digital ads on the glass, to ads on practice jerseys, helmets, and game jerseys, and now to a bombardment of commercials for online gambling. The net, the posts, the crossbar, they're all coming too. And the NHL won't stop there. Having dislodged civic architecture and naming rights from their arenas, teams will eventually untether themselves from their cities. If Scotiabank Arena and the Bell Centre can stand as corporate arena names instead of community names like Maple Leaf Gardens and the Forum, what's stopping the Maple Leafs from being rebranded the BCE/Rogers Maple Leafs or, even better, the Montreal Canadiens the Molson Canadiens?

Blake Coleman scores in the first period to give the Flames a 1–0 lead. During stoppages in play, there are the usual in-game distractions, complete with hockey rock, although there are few actual hockey songs, that oh-so-Canadian genre of music. When Stompin' Tom Connors' "The Hockey Song," widely regarded as the best hockey song ever, was inducted into the Canadian Songwriters Hall of Fame, Ken Campbell of *The Hockey News* wrote that "being anointed the best hockey song of all-time is a little like receiving the award for best dressed at a leisure suit convention."

It is not for lack of options. "Big League" (Tom Cochrane), "Fifty Mission Cap" (The Tragically Hip), "Hockey Skates" (Kathleen Edwards), and "Hockey" (Jane Siberry) are among the hall of fame of Canadian hockey songs. But they're badly outnumbered by those in the beer-league of hockey tunes: "Uncle Gordie" (the Planet Smashers), "He Looked a lot like Tiger Williams" (the Hanson Brothers), "The Goal Judge" (Moxy Fruvous), "Two Minutes for Looking so Good" (Belvedere). Those are just a handful from Canadian musicians. Americans have gotten in on the fun, too, including a band called the Zambonis, who wrote "Bob Marley and the Hartford Whalers" as a tribute to the now-defunct Connecticut-based NHL team.

Still, for all of the advertising and game operations kitsch, there is nothing like watching the NHL. The speed of the game, the size of the players, the frenetic frequency that the puck changes hands and the play switches directions, it is a bewitching brew of virtuosity and violence. From ice level, it can look like chaos. From the press box, high above the ice, it is like watching speed chess, but with bodychecking and the occasional fight.

The Leafs and Flames aren't exactly painting a Picasso tonight at the Saddledome. But even the worst NHL games are the best of the game. Whenever I get a chance to watch one live, it is not lost on me that I am in the presence of the game's finest artists, and not just those who'll go on to the Hockey Hall of Fame, like Auston Matthews, who assists on the Leafs' tying goal in the second period. There are no bad players at the highest level of hockey, only degrees of great ones. So few players (only about 8,500) have ever made it to the NHL that even one-game wonders have to possess at least a hint of something special, whether through genetics and talent or ten-thousand hours of training, to summit hockey's highest peak.

The only time I've ever been on the same ice at the same time as an NHL player is when I played a pickup game with Dave Chyzowski, long after he'd retired. Projected by some to be the next Mike Bossy, injuries limited Chyzowski to 15 goals in 126 games in the NHL. Sitting beside me in the dressing room, he was in his late forties at the time, with a bad back that made tying his skates difficult. But on the ice, whatever it was that got him drafted second overall in the 1989 draft, behind only future Hall of Famer Mats Sundin, it hadn't left him. Surrounded by a pile of beer-leaguers, he went through us like we were pylons, as if he was playing another sport entirely. He had fun with it, too. At one point, I watched him deke through the defense without ever touching the puck, using only stick feints and head fakes.

Calle Järnkrok scores early in the third period, and the Leafs hang on for a 2–1 win. After the game, I follow the throng of media to the elevator and down to the dressing rooms. Right winger Mitch Marner and coach Sheldon Keefe come out for postgame interviews. I stand back from the scrums to avoid getting hit by a softball, having tossed my fair share over the years. Nearby, defenseman Mark Giordano and captain John Tavares are doing deadlifts in the hallway, while defenseman Jake McCabe rides a stationary bike. The Leafs are all smiles, unlike the Flames, who do their interviews inside their dressing room. Even though he allowed only two goals, goalie Jacob Markström looks like he just ran over the family dog.

I file out of the Saddledome with the last of the lingering fans, about an equal split between Leafs and Flames jerseys. By the time I finish the road trip, the Flames will have fallen just short of the playoffs while the Leafs will lose in the second round. For a few months, hockey will stop for both of them, but the game will carry on. Come September, the Leafs and Flames will return to the corporate caverns of Scotiabank Arena and Scotiabank Saddledome, and I to the cold, lonely community rinks back home.

Before turning north for the territories, I drive west to Invermere. Although it lies just inside the British Columbia border, the town may as well be in Alberta. Invermere runs on Mountain Standard Time and many Albertans own homes in the area. It also shares some of its politics with Alberta, judging by the large "F*ck Trudeau" sign on a parked pickup truck as I pull into town.

It is a perfect day for a skate. The sky is clear, the temperature hovering around freezing, and there is almost no wind. I grab my skates, leave Gumpy in the parking lot, and walk down to Kinsmen Beach on the shores of Windermere Lake.

Most Guinness World Records range from the ridiculous to the absurd: most toilet seats broken by the head in one minute (fifty-six), fastest hundred meters on a skateboard by a dog (19.65 seconds), most candles extinguished by a fart (five). Then there are records to be shared, enjoyed, savored, and skated. At 34 kilometers (21 miles) of groomed track, Lake Windermere Whiteway holds the record for the longest skating trail in the world. Sandwiched between the Rocky and Purcell Mountains in the Columbia Valley, the trail is made up of four interconnected loops, hugging the shore and, on occasion, crisscrossing to the other side of the lake. It stretches between the towns of Invermere (to the north) and Windermere (to the south) and is one of the few places on Earth to skate without boundaries. Every other form of locomotion is about getting somewhere. From the shoreline of the pond to the boards indoors, skating is containment. I would skate across the country if I could, for there is no better feeling than gliding on a straight sheet of ice. Here I can skate for miles.

The ice isn't as smooth as advertised, with large cracks and bumps to avoid, but it is wide, clear of snow, and not too busy. There are families, couples, parents pushing strollers or skating with their babies, and people with their dogs trailing behind. A group of men skate by with hockey sticks, although no pucks. An older couple on speed skates sweeps by me without much effort; another man rides past on a fat bike.

I was hoping to skate all of the Whiteway, but the southern half of the trail is closed. On my way back, I stop at one of the empty benches stationed along the trail and pause for a moment to take in the mountains surrounding the lake on all sides. There are ice fishing huts set upon the ice. A tourist plane swoops in and lands on the frozen lake, unloading its sightseeing cargo with smiles and laughter.

I eventually get up to skate back to Kinsmen Beach. I take off my skates and get into Gumpy. After a weeklong break to catch up on notes and writing, I'll head north. Time for the territories.

The Territories:
Call of the North

You can argue, with some justification, that hockey is a pedestrian and inconsequential subject. But, for me, it is the conversational access ramp to a highway that leads to more elevated topics and sustained relationships. —Jack Falla, *Home Ice*

I
T IS MIDAFTERNOON and −57°C when I land in Rankin Inlet. Welcome to the North. With the taxis all occupied, I decide to walk the half mile to my accommodation.

A large welcome sign of Jordin Tootoo greets me outside the airport. As the first Inuk to reach the NHL, there is a case to be made that no other player, past or present, has meant more to their hometown than Tootoo does to Rankin Inlet. He is to the Inuit what Maurice Richard is to Québécois, except Québécois can just as easily point to Jean Béliveau or Guy Lafleur or Mario Lemieux or any number of Quebec-born superstars. The Inuit have only Tootoo.

In every direction, as far as I can see, everything is white. The tundra is indistinguishable from frozen Hudson Bay. Just past Home Hardware, about halfway to the inn, I come to Williamson Lake in the middle of town. There my path crosses with a bundled-up fellow named Don, who's walking into town for lunch before his flight home to Arviat, 217 kilometers (135 miles) down the shore of Hudson Bay. Don is a Halifax, Nova Scotia transplant who took a detour into the North while doing research in university decades ago and never left. He asks what brings me to Rankin Inlet. I explain the hockey bag over my shoulder and the sticks in my hands.

"You've come to the right place," he says. "They play some pretty good hockey up here in Nunavut. The Inuit are serious about their hockey."

I make it to the inn, dump my backpack and gear in my room, and set out for Agnico Eagle Arena, a ten-minute walk. After being to places like Happy Valley-Goose Bay, Chisasibi, and Moose Factory, I understand how important a rink is to a small town in the middle of nowhere. In the isolated communities of the North, especially the fly-in-only territory of Nunavut, arenas are a centripetal force in winter, even for a kids' tournament.

I launch myself up the concrete stairs and into the lobby. I look around for David Clark, who is in charge of Rankin Inlet's hockey program, one unlike any other in the country. He told me to find him at the rink, but there is no sign of him. So I look around and find Quliit's Skate Shop, next to the bustling canteen. I wait for the kids to clear from the counter and walk over and ask the shopkeeper if he knows where I can find David.

"He's on the bench," he says. "He's coaching something like four teams today. The guy with the red hat. You need help with something?"

His name is Wayne Quliit Kusugak. Born in Winnipeg, Wayne has lived in Rankin Inlet all his life. He has on a black ballcap advertising his skate shop, a gig he juggles alongside his other job as a correctional officer. His time off goes to supplying territorial tournaments like this one for boys and girls ten and under.

"It's a hockey town, man," Wayne says. "Yeah, bigtime. Rankin's busy. I'm full because there's a tournament right now, but I'll be cleaned out by Monday."

A kid comes up to the counter and asks sheepishly for skate guards. I thank Wayne and sit down to watch a couple of games. Both are blowouts, and the third is looking much the same. I am about to leave when I catch sight of the man in the red toque jotting down scores on a large schedule near the dressing rooms. I introduce myself.

We jump into David's pickup and drive to his house on what feels like the edge of town, although I can't tell in the pitch-black minus-whatever night. David leaves his truck running and I follow him inside. I take a seat at the island in the kitchen while he throws on *Hockey Night in Canada* and makes us tea.

The house is unusually empty, he says. His wife is at a trade show in Ottawa, and two of their three kids are down south in school. Only his youngest son, who's playing in the tournament, is in town.

With the Maple Leafs game in the background, David walks me through life and hockey in Rankin Inlet. At the mercy of weather and surrounded by water and wilderness, life in Rankin Inlet revolves around the ice for most of the year and then, for a short time after hockey season, the waters outside it. David's life is eight months of hockey, two months of fishing, and a short break huddled at home when the bugs get bad.

"It's a cycle that doesn't stop," he says.

David calls the arena Rankin Inlet's "happy place." Throughout the hockey season, the two hundred or so kids in the town's hockey program, almost half girls, continually filter through the arena. For a population of around three thousand, those are some of the best numbers per capita in the country. About a quarter of the kids are playing in the tournament this weekend. When they get old enough, Rankin Inlet's best players often go down to Manitoba to pursue their NHL dreams, as Tootoo did. Some go on to play junior, college, university, or even minor pro.

"We need somebody to kind of push through to give those generations somebody that they can follow," David says. "There are people to look up to. But when you get that guy in the NHL, it's even that much more."

As president of the local hockey association, David works hard to keep the annual cost of registration down to just $150. The town runs the rink and donates ice time to the association. If a child's family doesn't have the money for gear, they get suited up for free.

"We want kids playing hockey because we see the benefit in it," David says. "It's not only the on-ice stuff but the off-ice stuff. They become better community members, better leaders in the community, healthy lifestyle, all that stuff. The more kids we have in hockey, the better our community is. It's that simple. You can see it this weekend. It's not so much about the game itself. It's about growing people as well."

That is the main difference between hockey in big cities and the game in small towns. In urban areas, hockey is too often a schedule slapped on the refrigerator, or an NHL pipe dream that parents push upon their kids. In places like Rankin Inlet, Labrador, Eeyou Istchee, and the Cree communities around James Bay, the game is part of the cycle of life, seamless and fluid, with the entire town pulling in the same direction.

"Everybody's invested because everybody's involved," David says.

Their greatest challenge is distance. The only way in or out of Nunavut, or even from place to place within it, is by air, except for the nearest towns to which people can snowmobile in winter and boat in summer. Travel costs for even a single out-of-town tournament can run to the tens of thousands, and total as much as half a million dollars a year. That creates a huge hole in the budget, one that takes a village to plug. But every year, the people of Rankin Inlet manage it. Whether through radio bingo, 50/50 tickets, bake sales, gear drives, summer beer gardens, applying for grants, or a Chase-the-Ace jackpot, the town finds a way to send its kids to out-of-town tournaments. While Air Canada, after years of paying multimillions to slap its name atop the Leafs' home arena in Toronto, is canceling many routes into the North, Calm Air is giving the local hockey association in Rankin Inlet steep discounts on charters so that David can take teams to tournaments in Manitoba, the Northwest Territories, and elsewhere in Nunavut. For many of the kids, the trips are the first time they'll fly on a plane, swim in a swimming pool, or eat at McDonald's.

"You hear Hockey Canada and all these associations saying hockey is for everybody, hockey's this, hockey's that," David says. "But I'll tell you right now, hockey's for rich people, in the South. I see it, and I'll tell you why I see it. I've invested in my boys a lot. They go to camps all summer long. So we travel in the summer, and my boys play spring hockey, my boys go to top-tier hockey camps, all summer long, because I know the investment I'm doing is going to benefit them to become better hockey players and better people and meet new kids and all the benefits that come with it. When I go to them, I look around and I just see rich people. But when I come to Rankin and I'm in my hometown, I see the poorest of poor kids in town still playing hockey, and that makes me happy, because I don't see it in the South. You don't see it in the big cities anymore. I think the South and these big corporations like Hockey Canada can learn from us and the way we do things."

Equipment manufacturers have a lot to do with it. Instead of selling less-expensive gear to more and more players, they're selling more expensive gear to fewer and fewer players. Fewer customers for larger margins. It is no coincidence that the drop in the number of kids playing hockey in Canada has corresponded with higher participation in basketball and soccer. Neither is taking the place of hockey. The game is giving it away.

I tell David about my attempt to get on the ice in every province and territory, and he suggests joining an old-timers game scheduled after the championship game. Although he'll be too busy wrapping up the tournament, David is still a regular in senior hockey. Like the Cree in Eeyou Istchee before the Billy Diamond Highway, going to a tournament means having to fly to places like Yellowknife and Iqaluit, at an annual cost equivalent to a Bentley or a Rolls Royce, or going overland to Rankin Inlet's closest communities.

"We're driving on a snowmobile for how many hours in minus-fifty weather just to go play hockey," David says. "I've been to Whale Cove for a senior tournament. We went on our snowmobiles, drove three hours, and played for the weekend, and then Sunday night, when the tournament's done, we're driving home and it's like minus-fifty-five. You're bundled up, you get home at like four in the morning, and you're like an icicle. I just remember crawling into my bed and never wanting to leave. You just do it for the love of the game."

David's phone buzzes. It is the rink. Duty calls.

"Alright, man, gotta go. They need scoresheets for the last two games."

The next day is a balmy −38°C. The kids must've cleared Wayne out early, because his shop is closed by the time I get to the arena for the championship game. The stands are packed, the lobby is full, and the hallways and aisles are obstacle courses of kids and parents. Half the town has to be here.

As I watch the game, I'm looking forward to playing later tonight. So far, I've gotten on the ice wherever I could: Deer Lake, St. John's, Marystown, Halifax, Summerside, Miramichi, Laval, Matagami, Chisasibi, Toronto, Burlington, Baker, Saskatoon, Red Deer, Invermere. I want to keep my consecutive-provinces streak going into the territories.

The championship game ends in a heap of ineffable smiles at one end of the rink and a line of dejected faces at the other. I walk back to the inn to grab a pregame meal and nap before the old-timers game later in the evening. Along the way, I realize I don't need to walk. I can slide my way there, or skate. During winter in Rankin Inlet, the ice surface never ends.

"Some of the guys I ended up playing senior hockey with used to get dressed at home and skate on the road to that old dome," David said, referring to the old Rankin Inlet Arena, where Tootoo forged his game. "It's just like really hard packed snow. Sometimes you see kids playing road hockey with their skates on."

In the taxonomy of hockey's off-ice offshoots, there doesn't appear to be any difference between street hockey and road hockey. Yet as all streets are roads but not all roads are streets, there is a careful distinction to be made. A subset of road hockey, street hockey is strictly an urban phenomenon, a game played on pavement between sidewalks on narrow streets and around parked cars and pedestrians. Road hockey, which includes its street version, knows no bounds. It can be played anywhere, on any stretch of asphalt, gravel, dirt, ice, or muskeg. Sometimes, it even spills over onto a highway. In 2017, a game broke out on the Coquihalla Highway in British Columbia when heavy snow and freezing rain caused a two-day traffic jam. The same thing happened in 2019 near Montreal while drivers waited for emergency crews to clear a forty-car pileup on Highway 40 just outside the city.

When I return to the arena a few hours later, the doors are open and the lights are on in the lobby, but the rink lights are off. The game has been canceled. One other player, wearing a Canadiens cap, has walked to the rink as well. I ask the attendant if we can just get on the ice for a quick skate, nothing more. We're turned away. Defeated, I walk back to the inn, oblivious to the cutting cold. My goal of getting on the ice in every province and territory has died in Nunavut.

After driving through Ontario and the Prairies on my own, and flying into Nunavut alone, I'm looking forward to having some company on the next leg of the road trip. Jobless and in the midst of a divorce, Stro from the Beer League Hockey Hall of Fame has decided to pull from his retirement savings to ride with me from Alberta through the Northwest Territories and the Yukon, still in the North, west of Nunavut. We barely know each other, but when he found out I would be driving a series of remote highways all the way up to the Arctic Ocean, he asked if he could come along. Call of the North, as I would later learn.

The first of those roads is the Mackenzie Highway, about four rural highways and half a day's drive up from Edmonton, where I returned with Gumpy to pick up Stro after he flew in from Toronto. Mile zero of the highway begins at a T-intersection about two-thirds up the province in the middle of the disappearing prairie. On our way up the Mackenzie, Alberta leaves us with a protestation to "Vote United Conservative Party," after which a makeshift monument wrapped in a Canadian flag declares "Freedom for All, United We Stand." In the middle of nowhere, we pass a yellow sign warning us to "Watch for Pedestrians on Highway." Where these pedestrians could come from, I have no idea, but I heed the "Bison on Road" signs and keep to the speed limit.

Upon crossing the border, the Mackenzie Highway goes from Highway 35 to Highway 1. From there, it continues on to the Yellowknife Highway, a 337-kilometer (210-mile) stretch that runs off the Mackenzie and wraps around Great Slave Lake, Canada's deepest, on its way into Yellowknife.

The stretch of lake near the town is home to an eccentric community of houseboats. Around mid-November, as soon as the ice is thick enough, residents of this ephemeral community in aptly named Houseboat Bay brave the Arctic chill to shovel off a patch within larger Yellowknife Bay in preparation for the upcoming hockey season. From then until about April, their wood stoves burn day and night as they hunker down for the long hard winter punctuated with trips outdoors to play hockey under the Northern Lights. Carefully and meticulously, residents shape and reshape a small patch of the bay into a rink, part of a bay-wide winter wonderland made up of dog teams, bush planes, cross-country skiers, and a giant ice castle for the Snowking Winter Festival, which comes complete with the annual Snowking Cup.

In the morning, Stro and I drive to Houseboat Bay and follow the Dettah Ice Road out to the rink. With city workers on strike, the indoor rinks are all closed, which means the rink here will be busy.

Cracks run across and along the rink, one nearly from end to end. More outline than full rink, the boards consist of two-by-fours running length-wise down the sides, while those behind the nets gradually rise upward in various sizes of plywood to a height of about four feet. The "nets" themselves are made out of wood and only four inches high to keep shots low. It is barely big enough for three-on-three hockey, much less four-on-four, but it is all any of us need.

On one side of the rink, dozens of houseboats line the shoreline. On the other stands the ice castle, with territorial, Pride, and Ukrainian flags flying from its frozen ramparts. There is an energy crackling about the entire town. It is mid-March, the best month to visit here in winter, I am told, when the North gets more light than the South, the winter festival gets going, and the Houseboat Bay rink is buzzing.

No one at the rink was born in Yellowknife, or anywhere else in the Northwest Territories. Most are from Ontario. Andrea, who pulls up with a Maple Leafs' flag flying from her vehicle, is from London, while her husband, Mike, is from Barrie. Jess is from Almonte, while her husband, Spencer, is from Kapuskasing. Tina is from Wainwright, Alberta, and her husband, Jay, is from Montreal.

I am teamed with Tina, Jess, and her daughter, Pontiac.

"We need a name, guys," Jess says. "What should we call ourselves?"

"It's St. Patrick's Day," Pontiac says. "So how about the Leprechauns!"

Yellowknife's houseboat community began in the early 1980s, when a couple of families built their own homes using old river barges. Others followed and the community now numbers a few dozen or more. The homes are colorful and energy-efficient, many using solar to power their electronics. Some of the houseboats are just platforms with a house built on them. Many have not only running water but hot water, fridges, propane heaters with thermostats, and generators. Others are old boats or river cruisers with no amenities, just a honey bucket for a toilet. Some of the homes float on old propane tanks, while small generators pump water from the lake into barrels to serve their daily needs. All the houseboats stick close to shore to protect themselves from the south wind.

Residents are a mixture of pilots, environmental workers, government workers, teachers, artists. Many have families. They are also a tourist attraction. Ice roads take visitors right to their front doors in winter, and boat tours giving glimpses of these floating homes in summer. In nicer weather, some of the tourists may see more than they bargain for—residents may wander around in their underwear and skinny dipping is not uncommon. It is an unregulated space.

Breakup and freeze-up are the most difficult times of year. Freeze-up is probably hardest because of the dark and cold. Many of the houseboaters go into town for a few days or more to wait it out. But once the water is frozen, everyone comes back to the bay and hockey returns for another season.

Several people at the rink tell me I should head to the ice castle and ask for Tony Foliot, better known as "Snowking." He'll know the history of Houseboat Bay. I leave Stro at the rink and wander over to the castle on the other side of the ice road. When I ask for Tony, I'm told where to find him, and then admonished never to call him Tony.

"Well, you don't go to the North Pole and say, 'Nick!' right?" he says after I find him and ask why. "All these children, they know me as Snowking, so you wouldn't wanna spoil the magic. That's what this is all about. This place, it's not for adults. It's magic if you're four-feet-tall or shorter."

"Are you Snowking outside the castle?"

"All year long."

"Even in summer?"

"In the summertime, I tell people I'm just a regular Joe. Joe King. Just jo-king."

Snowking chuckles under his thick gray beard. Like everybody I've met in Yellowknife, he too is a transplant. But unlike many on Houseboat Bay, he isn't a transient.

"I quit Quebec when René Lévesque was an asshole," he says.

"That's a long time ago."

"Yeah, it is. I'm pretty old. I moved up here, and this is God's country, eh?"

Snowking is among the last of the original houseboaters. He lives right next door to the castle, in a bright blue and yellow houseboat he built himself. With no mortgage, rent, or taxes to pay, he can take six months off to build a sprawling ice castle every year with his crew.

"It's like paradise," he says. "I can just step out my door in summertime, get in my boat, and go down the bay for half an hour and then I'm on a deserted island. I could nude sunbath or have a picnic or whatever, go fishing. And in the wintertime, I got a really big yard where I can build stuff."

That yard includes the Houseboat Bay rink, where the Snowking Cup takes place every year. Snowking himself doesn't play, but he did buy the trophy to crown the annual winner, and he still tends to the ice when needed.

"I went over there the other day to clear the rink because there was all this snow that had blown in and hardened up," he says. "Then I break my blower on a hockey puck. Two out of three pucks shot through, but the third one got caught and it just broke. All kinds of hydraulic fluid spilled out. It'll probably cost me a pile of money."

Out of the corner of his eye, Snowking catches someone under four-feet-tall making mischief and darts away to take care of it.

"You're not carving in the walls are ya, buddy? Looked like you were. I got my eye on you!"

When I walk back to the rink, Stro is taking off his skates. The parking lot is full of vehicles. On the ice are players of all skills, sizes, and ages, including a diehard Canadiens fan decked out head-to-skates in a Habs track suit, T-shirt, toque, and red, white, and blue gloves. It is a makeshift game going on at a makeshift rink within a makeshift community of transplants and transients. Bright sunshine, no wind, temperatures just below freezing.

"When you live in paradise, you wanna take advantage of it, right?" Snowking said. "I mean, look at this, beautiful sunny day. Can you imagine in the winter playing hockey right now?"

Stro and I take the "Fort" route to the Yukon, back along the Yellowknife and Mackenzie highways, and then on to the Liard and Alaska highways, looking for places to play wherever we can on our way to Whitehorse: Fort Providence, Fort Simpson, Fort Liard, Fort Nelson. We find rinks at all four, ice in two, and a beer-leaguer's heaven at the last of them.

For much of the four-day drive from Yellowknife, we listen to a ten-episode podcast about a little-known part of Canadian history. As we approach Fort Nelson, near where the Liard Highway connects to the Alaska Highway, Stro throws it on again.

The podcast is about Kosmos 954, a Soviet nuclear satellite that fell out of orbit and exploded upon reentry over Canada, spreading radioactive debris over 80,000 square kilometers (50,000 square miles) around where Alberta, Saskatchewan, Northwest Territories, and present-day Nunavut meet, all of it across the traditional lands of the Dene people. It happened on January 24, 1978, during the height of the Cold War and the on-ice rivalry between Canada and the Soviet Union.

I know all about the Canada-USSR Summit Series in 1972 and the first Canada Cup in 1976, and yet I know nothing of this story. But this is the North, where stories come to die, except among the people here who keep them alive. The cleanup, a joint Canadian–American mission, recovered the biggest pieces of the wreckage but left the rest to pollute the land and raise cancer rates among the people decades later.

"Oh, they must've missed something from the satellite," says Stro as we pass a mangled piece of scrap metal in the ditch.

He turns off the podcast as we enter Fort Nelson. Once a natural gas town, it is now reliant on government and tourism, much of it retired RV travelers on their way to or from Alaska. When the roof of the old Fort Nelson Arena collapsed in 2007, at the height of the natural gas boom, the Northern Rockies Regional Recreation Centre took its place. Flush with money, the town put in two rinks, a curling sheet, a pool, a rock-climbing wall, squash and racquetball courts, a walking track, and a gym. On the second floor, at the end of a long hallway, far away from the other dressing rooms, a collection of local beer-leaguers known as the Fort Nelson Old Wolves, many of whom work in the natural gas industry, added their own fun zone in this mall of play.

An employee lets us in.

"I didn't even check out this place for like six, seven months," he says. "I came in here because we had some issues with the piping, and I was like, holy fuck."

The door opens onto a shoe rack, where a handful of shower sandals are scattered about, and then a rack with several dozen hockey sticks neatly arrayed. Around the corner, sandwiched between a fridge and a locker, is the red glow of a repurposed Coke machine. I draw my finger down buttons for beer-league beverages: Bud Light, Coors Light, Steamworks, and then a few more for Canada Dry. On the walls are team photos and action shots, framed using wood from old hockey sticks. In the next room is a first aid kit above a table stocked with liquor bottles and disposable cups and plates. Above it is a sign with the Old Wolves' logo:

Players of this club have families to care for, mortgages/rent to pay, jobs to be at the next day, so let's keep every hockey game fun and safe.

"This is a dream," Stro says.

"Could you imagine playing here?" I say.

"It makes me almost wanna sell my house and move to Fort Nelson."

Beneath the exposed piping and ventilation systems, the spacious dressing room itself opens up. In every player's stall, mixed in among the gear, are both blue and white Old Wolves jerseys trimmed with gold. Above them, a line of black cubbyholes runs along the walls, stocked with skates, elbow pads, helmets, water bottles, and more than few beer cans and Captain Morgan bottles. Below are locked bins for players' personals. In the middle of the room, above a desk, table, chairs, and garbage bins, two big screen TVs hang from the ceiling, as do others in each of the four corners of the room. At the end of the room, where natural light floods in through a window, a mini-Canadiens jersey hangs from the piping above it. It is a dressing room akin to those of the pros, palatial compared with the cramped, echolocated brick changerooms Stro and I are used to.

"Imagine not having to bring your stinking equipment home," Stro says. "Aside from making money, that's the biggest benefit of playing pro hockey. You just get to show up to work, and then you can just walk out after work. Incredible."

When we arrive in Whitehorse, the capital of the Yukon, two days later, the parking lot at Takhini Arena is full to overflowing. Cars are double and triple parked; pickups have arced up onto the snowbanks. A few drivers don't care and just leave their vehicles wherever, blocking routes and making it a mess to navigate. I find us a spot down the road, at the end of a line of parked cars that extends more than half a mile.

Inside the arena, the lobby is as cramped as a mosh pit and the stands are literally standing room only. We make it in time to catch the opening ceremony, which has been held back until the second day of the four-day tournament, a Friday night.

Ceremonial puck drops are supposed to be nothing more than photo-ops. But Tshayla Nothstein is having none of it. She jumps over the boards, puts her stick down, and leans in, body tensed, eyes on the puck like it is a prey to pounce upon. When the puck is dropped, Tshayla lunges in to pull it back, hacking at the stick of her opponent like she's taking a draw in the final minute of a game with her team down a goal. She isn't here for photo-ops; she is here to win.

"I already had a plan," Tshayla tells me after the game. "I've been waiting for this since I was a kid."

Only about forty thousand people live in the Yukon, more than half in Whitehorse. Up here, as elsewhere throughout the North, people haven't forgotten about hometown hockey. Local games are weekly rituals, and annual tournaments are events that towns mark on their calendar months in advance, none bigger than the Yukon Native Hockey Tournament.

Whitehorse is where they meet, all fifty-six teams and more than one thousand players when Stro and I lumber into town. Most come from the Yukon, Northwest Territories, and northern British Columbia, but some are from Alberta, Manitoba, Ontario, even as far away as Newfoundland. To stay true to its roots, the tournament has a three non-Indigenous-player limit, but organizers have laxed the rule to get a new division off the ground. This year, for the first time since it began in 1977, the territory's biggest tournament features a women's division, with eighty-six players spread across five teams: the K'änächa Kodiaks, the AFN

Storm, the Nisutlin Knights, and then the nickname-only Vixens and Cougars.

After her team's 5–0 win over the Kodiaks, Tshayla comes out and sits with me in the stands during a men's game. She is all smiles underneath her brown fur trapper's hat, with its large black-and-white Cougars logo smack in the middle. If not for the Kodiaks' goalie, the Cougars would've hit the tournament's eight-goal mercy rule before the end of the first period. They looked like they'd been playing together for a while.

"No practice," Tshalya says. "That was our first time playing together."

Tshalya has been playing in the tournament since she was ten, always on mixed teams, except for 2019 when she was on a women's team that played in one of the men's divisions. That team didn't win any of its games, but the players were clear winners in terms of crowd support. Fans cheered them whenever they got the puck and booed the men for scoring on them. The whole experience sparked a conversation about creating an all-women's division.

"This is like the Native Stanley Cup," she says. "It's something that you look forward to every single year. It's number one. You don't get turnouts like this in women's hockey, at all."

Signs of the tournament are everywhere in Whitehorse as Stro and I walk around town the next morning. Businesses use their sidewalk signs to welcome back players and fans, who are all about the streets in their team jerseys, hoodies, jackets, toques, and caps. Many are eating brunch at our hotel's restaurant, under street signs on the wood walls for 99 Wayne Gretzky Drive, Maple Leafs Lane, Canucks Crescent, Senators Street, and Jets Street.

The women's games have moved to the twin rinks at the Canada Games Centre across the Alaska Highway from Takhini Arena. From the elevated seating high above the ice, the stands full again, I watch as the Storm mercy the Cougars, 8–0, and the Knights hold on to a heated 3–2 win over the Vixens.

At forty, Jodi Tuton is the oldest player on the Knights. Whitehorse-born-and-raised, she grew up watching the tournament, but never played hockey until she started in the local women's league ahead of this year's event. While her Knights were taking on the Vixens, her brother was playing on the other rink at the Canada Games Centre, while her two daughters were both playing at Takhini Arena, all at the same time.

As I wait for Jodi in the hallway after the game, one of the Vixens, fresh off the heartbreaking defeat, comes charging down the hallway, channeling hockey's bilingualism toward an unknown Knight.

"Fucking bitch," she says. "I wanna fucking kill her."

She's already thrown off her jersey and is about to follow with her shoulder pads when a teammate suggests she cover up.

"Fuck, who cares."

When Jodi comes out, she is in her gear, glistening with sweat, and still trying to catch her breath. With the win, the Knights will take on the Cougars in the morning for the chance to face the Storm in the final. The women are winning over fans, not for any novelty or for being the first women's division, but because they can play.

"We came earlier and watched some of the girls' games before ours," Jodi says. "I was standing there with men in the stands and they were like, 'Wow, these girls are actually really good.' And I was like, 'Yeah, we are.'"

On the last day of the tournament, hockey bags are stacked in the hotel lobby and blocking the stairwells. Teams that have been knocked out, including the Kodiaks and the Vixens, are checking out early.

Stro and I drive to Takhini Arena to catch the championship game. The Cougars have beaten the Knights to advance to the final and set up a rematch with the Storm. The fire chief must be on vacation, because the arena is a full-on fire hazard, as it has been the entire weekend.

The Storm manage to take a one-goal lead in the first period, but it is clear the Cougars aren't going to get mercied again. If not for an unfortunate own-goal in the second period, they would've only been down one goal heading into the third.

The Zamboni driver whiffs on his cleaning job during the second intermission, leaving pools of water around the nets and ignoring an obvious strip of uncleaned ice in front of the bay doors. I wonder if he would've done that for a men's game.

As the third period gets underway, I overhear a group of men behind me watching the game. Their eyes are glued to one player on the Storm, working herself into a whirlwind that has been frustrating the Cougars all game.

"That number twenty-two chick is fucking good," one of them says.

"Who is she?" asks another.

"Davina McLeod."

Born in Aklavik, Davina has been on skates since she was four, in hockey since she was five, and playing in the tournament every year since she was nine, mostly on boys' or men's teams. Like so many players throughout the North, Davina knew at an early age she would have to leave home if she were to go further in the game. That began a hockey journey that has taken her all across Canada: from the Northwest Territories to the Yukon to play for the Whitehorse Mustangs, the first all-female team she'd ever been on; to Saskatchewan to play for the Hounds at the famed Athol Murray College of Notre Dame; over to Ontario to play for a private hockey academy; and then to Alberta, where she played four years of college hockey. She is now back in Whitehorse, playing in the top rung of the local men's league, the only woman in the entire division.

Only twenty-five years old, Davina has played in the Gwich'in Cup, Arctic Winter Games, the National Aboriginal Hockey Championships, and countless other tournaments. But the Yukon Native Hockey Tournament, as it is for so many players in Whitehorse this weekend, is her Stanley Cup. Davina tops the women's division in scoring and leads the Storm to the championship.

"The final score: Storm 4, Cougars 0," says the arena announcer when the final buzzer sounds. "The Storm are the first ever winners of the women's division at the Yukon Native Hockey Tournament."

The Storm pour off the bench, leaving a trail of gloves, helmets, and sticks flung behind them. The ensuing pile is a mix of blonde, brown, black, and red hair atop a mound of mustard yellow jerseys, a collection of both Indigenous and non-Indigenous women from across Western Canada, as young as nineteen and as old as thirty-nine. At the bottom is their goalie, who didn't allow a goal the entire tournament. In four games, the Storm outscored their opponents 24–0.

After the game, I find Davina, still in her gear, celebrating with her aunt and teammate, Joyce Blake. The party has spilled out into the hallway. Amid a constant stream of hugs from family, friends, and teammates, some of whom have to rush to catch flights home, Davina is too busy, too happy, too tired to talk.

"All the hard work is done," is all she can say. "This tournament means a lot to me. I love everything about it."

I leave Davina to the celebration and walk back into the crowded lobby, bumping into people as I make my way outside. As I look around for Stro to head back to the hotel, I overhear another conversation going on around me.

"Did you see the game?"

"Which one? There are six divisions."

"No, not the men. The women. It was the best game of the tournament."

From Whitehorse to Dawson City is six hours along the Klondike Highway, which runs from the town of Skagway in Alaska, through the Yukon capital, and up to the old gold-rush-turned-tourist-town and trucking waystation. Paved for most of the way, the highway traces parts of the Yukon, Stewart, and Klondike rivers, surrounded by slash marks in the snow from the Yukon's "drunken trees," arrayed at odd angles atop the permafrost in the mountains and valleys. Along the roadside, spruce have begun to redden at their tips, while the ditches are dotted with abandoned vehicles; some will be retrieved, others will stay where they lay.

Partway to Dawson City, we stop so that Stro can take some drone footage at Five Finger Rapids, a four-island, five-channel stretch of the Yukon River. Minutes later, a pickup truck pulls in and out pop two men, who spread a feast of fried chicken and potato salad on their hood.

"Oh, it's a drone," one of them says. "At first, I thought it was a mosquito."

"Yeah, that's a big mosquito," Stro says.

"Well, I hope it comes back to you. You don't wanna have to walk down that mountain."

The man's name is Joel. Disheveled with a scruffy salt and pepper beard, black sweater and pants, he has on a baseball cap set slightly off-center.

"Where you guys going?" he asks.

"Dawson City," Stro replies. "Then all the way to Tuktoyaktuk."

"You gonna go to the Pit?"

"The Pit?" we ask in unison.

"You gotta go to the Pit, get into a fight, find a hairy bush chick to drag you off after the bar closes. You won't have been in Dawson if that hasn't happened to you."

"Sounds like a plan," Stro says.

"Westminster Hotel," Joel says. "Gotta go to the Pit, boys. Yup, good time. Check your rifle at the bar."

Joel and his silent friend are miners in Dawson City. They've just come up for the first time of the year to check out their camp and break trails.

"Couldn't stay away," Joel says. "Call of the North, it's just calling to ya."

Joel assures us we'll be able to get on the ice in Dawson City. He also advises us to check out the local senior league, which will be in the middle of its playoffs.

"You guys go to the tournament in Whitehorse?" he asks.

"Just came from there," I reply.

"Really good hockey," Stro says.

"I played once back in the day," Joel says. "Bribed my way onto the Dawson team. It was the funnest hockey game I ever played. There was a lot of energy going on, and the crowds were packed."

The conversation skips from the tournament in Whitehorse to the NHL playoffs, which are about two weeks away. The four of us stand there, a chance encounter at a slushy roadside stop in the middle of the Klondike Highway, meeting for the only time in our lives and talking hockey like longtime friends.

"Well, you guys, that's an exciting trip," Joel says. "Nice time of year. No mosquitos. But be careful of the Pit. Those girls are hungry, man, and they haven't had fresh meat all winter. You're gonna feel like a super stud. Some of those girls will fight over you."

"I'm feelin' it already," Stro says.

"Okay, well, safe travels, boys. Don't get the bug of the North or you'll never leave. If I see you here in a couple years, I'll be like, 'Yup, I told you.'"

Joel is right about Dawson City's senior circuit, the Klondike Hockey League (KHL). We arrive at the Art and Margaret Fry Recreation Centre just in time for game one of the best-of-three final between the Dominion Creek Regulators and the Midnight Sun Penguins. Neither team should've made it this far. After being up two games to none in their first-round series, the first-place Bunkhouse Bananas were bounced by the last-place Penguins, while the Skookum Skaters fell into a sudden slump toward the end of the regular season, losing their last five games to finish second in the league, and then were swept out of the playoffs by the Regulators.

The Regulators come out in matching camouflage jerseys with their red and brown masked outlaw logo. In contrast, the Penguins are a ragtag assortment, a mix of players wearing the team's baby blue jerseys bearing an old Pittsburgh Penguins logo alongside others in mismatched white jerseys. While the Regulators have a full bench, the Penguins have only nine skaters.

I have a rule when watching a game live. Never leave early. On May 13, 2013, with the Maple Leafs up 4–1 over the Bruins midway through the third period in game seven of their first-round playoff series, fans started flooding out of TD Garden in Boston. I remember the moment when Patrice Bergeron scored in overtime to complete the 5–4 comeback, and I often imagine the look on the faces of those fans when they got home and turned on the TV. With that loss, the Leafs became the only team in NHL history to lose a game seven after holding a three-goal lead in the third period.

Ten years later, in an old arena in the middle of Dawson City, two beer-league teams reenact that game. Their short bench does the Penguins in, as the Regulators come back from being three goals down late in the game to win 4–3 in overtime.

As we walk down the hallway to head back to our hotel, Stro and I see the Penguins' goalie come out of his dressing room with his equipment over his shoulder.

"That was fuckin' heartbreak," he says as he walks out into the night.

On February 28, 1911, Corporal William Dempster set out from Dawson City with two other constables from the North-West Mounted Police in a frantic search for a missing police mail patrol. They found the missing officers three weeks later, frozen to death. If not for their fur, wool, and sled dogs, Dempster and his crew would've fallen to the same fate.

Today, the 737-kilometer (458-mile) Dempster Highway traces that old sled dog route up through the Yukon and into the Northwest Territories. A handful of players had used the gravel road to get down to Whitehorse for the Yukon Native Hockey Tournament. Stro and I have driven to Dawson City to take the Dempster up to Inuvik and all the way to the road's end in Tuktoyaktuk on the shores of the Arctic Ocean. But when we arrived in town, just before the first game of the KHL final, we were told the highway had been closed for a week. A storm in the Richardson Mountains, near the border with the Northwest Territories, had shut it down, with no word on when it would reopen. Truckers I spoke with said they'd never seen it this bad.

Within minutes of waking up in the morning, I discover that all the hotels in town have been booked. I scramble online to find us a place to stay, then go to the front desk, looking to see if anything offline is still available. Nothing.

"Well, we can tough it out for a night in Gumpy, if need be," Stro says.

Even though the Dempster is closed, Stro isn't about to let the day get away. This morning, he received news about his pending divorce. It is also the anniversary of his family coming to Canada from Poland.

"And thirty-eight years later, I'm gonna play some goddamn shinny today in Dawson City because I'm a goddamn hoser," Stro says. "And the letter from my wife's lawyer lands on the same day. It's good news, though. It means we can both start to move forward with our own lives. I have nothing but love and gratitude for this world."

Without a room to put our stuff, Stro and I pile everything back into Gumpy and drive to the rink to mull our options over an early afternoon skate. A handful of others show up, including three teenagers from Inuvik who drove down the Dempster to play in the tournament in Whitehorse and another man, about our age, who shoots pucks around with us. He played in the tournament back when bodychecking was still allowed.

"It was pretty rough," he says in the dressing room afterward. "It just got outta hand. One game, the ambulance came on the ice twice. It was pretty rough at the end, just because it was getting more and more popular. It wasn't hometown hockey anymore. They were bringing in ex-pros and stuff like that."

After the skate, Stro suggests going to a local hipster café. While we were shooting pucks around on the ice, it dawned on me that we could just sleep at the arena. The rink attendant was game for it, but her boss wasn't. So while eating some overpriced food and sipping some overrated coffee, we start planning the logistics of sleeping in Gumpy until the Dempster opens. Fortunately, one of the baristas suggests we try Dawson Lodge. I call. Two single rooms are available across the hall from each other.

Each of the next four days will be Groundhog Day for Stro and me as we wait for the Dempster to reopen: wake up, check 511 Yukon for updates on the highway, discuss our options, eat breakfast, play midday shinny, have lunch, do some work, take an afternoon nap, eat dinner, play evening shinny, watch hockey, go to bed. We consider driving up to Eagle Plains, the only waystation on the highway. Many truckers are waiting there for road crews to give them the all-clear, as the road is open up to that point. But Stro and I decide we would rather be stuck in a place where we can still get on the ice every day than somewhere we can't. And we want to catch the rest of the KHL final.

Two nights and three days into our stay in Dawson City, the Regulators and the Penguins are back at it. A Penguins win would force a rubber match, while a Regulators victory would give them the championship.

With a full bench, the Regulators jump out to an early lead. Short on players again, the Penguins could've used Stro. Having skated with him a dozen or more times by now, it is clear he could've played some level of pro. He almost did some years ago. In 2007, Stro returned to his hometown in Poland, twenty-three years after his family had defected from their then-communist homeland. He tried out for the Gdansk Shipyard Workers in the Polish Hockey League as a walk-on during training camp. For nearly a month, Stro lived the dream. He had his own stall, his own jersey, a gym to train in, a team to play for, and all the ice time in the world. At thirty-two years old, he was realizing his dream of becoming a professional hockey player when a nineteen-year-old San Jose Sharks draft pick from Sweden by the name of Alexander Hult parachuted in last-minute and took his place.

"You see that Swedish kid?" the coach told Stro. "You're an old horse, he's a young buck. I gotta take him."

With the Penguins tiring, the Regulators add another goal in the second period. During the changeover into the third, I walk the hallway of the arena and take in more than a hundred years of Dawson City hockey. Along the walls are photos of men's, women's, boys', girls', mixed, and old-timers' teams, all framed and neatly aligned. Most are in color, some are in black and white, dating as far back as a women's game in 1904 between the Dawsons and the Victorias. Fourteen women, half in light tops and dark skirts and the other half in dark tops and light skirts, are standing on the ice in front of a full crowd at the first arena in Dawson City, their long skirts hovering just high enough above the ice to reveal their skates.

One of the photos was taken in 1997 in Ottawa, part of a long reenactment of the greatest road trip in Stanley Cup history. On December 18, 1904, the eight players on the Dawson City Nuggets began a 6,400-kilometer (4,000-mile) journey down to Vancouver and on to Ottawa to challenge the reigning champions, the legendary Silver Seven, for the Stanley Cup, back when it was still a challenge cup. The first leg was a 531-kilometer (330-mile) trek to Whitehorse. Some of the players began by dogsled, others by bicycle the following day. But the weather was so warm that it left the roads a muddied mess, so all of them ended up walking most of the way, sleeping in police sheds along the route. The next leg was the train to Skagway in Alaska, but they missed it because of bad weather in Whitehorse. That meant they missed their steamer to Vancouver, and the next one couldn't dock for three days because of ice buildup. The players did eventually reach Vancouver, after a roiling ride at sea and bouts of seasickness. When they arrived, it was too foggy for the steamer to dock, so they were forced to divert to Seattle and catch a train back to Vancouver. There, they got on the rails for the cross-country ride to Ottawa. When the players finally arrived in the capital on January 11, they had just two days to rest before the start of the final. They lost the first game 9–2 and the second 23–2.

That wasn't the end of their road trip. After losing to the Silver Seven, the Nuggets carried on with a twenty-three-game exhibition tour throughout Eastern Canada and the northeastern United States before returning home to Dawson City, on foot from Whitehorse. After more than five months away, they'd logged an estimated 21,000 kilometers (13,000 miles) on the road, the rails, and the sea.

Partway through the third period, I go back to watch the game with Stro. The Regulators are now up by four. The Penguins manage to break the shutout, but the Regulators roll to a 4–1 win.

When the game ends, the players jump over the bench, flinging helmets, gloves, and sticks everywhere as they mob their goalie. It is a camouflaged mound of sopping wet hair, sweaty faces, and smiles of the same sort Canada sees at some point every June on its national broadcaster—far less skilled but no less happy. They receive the Weldy Young Trophy, named after one of the players on the Nuggets, with whoops, hollers, and cheers in front of all twelve people in the stands. Then they pass it around to one another, every player grabbing the trophy, kissing it, hoisting it above his head, and doing a mini victory lap with it in the team's end of the rink.

As the Regulators leave the ice for the dressing room, I ask if any of them can speak with me in the hallway. A few minutes later, Spruce Gerberding and Dave Ezzard emerge from their dressing room, half-dressed, still sweaty, and smelling like victory, with the championship chalice in hand.

"It looked like your Stanley Cup out there," I say.

"For us, yeah," Spruce says.

"We don't take it that seriously," Dave says.

Oh, but they did, and I saw no reason for them not to.

"So how are you guys going to celebrate tonight?" I ask.

Spruce points to the trophy.

"Fill that thing a few times, then wait for last call and see where we go from there."

One night later, Stro and I go out to celebrate, too, at the Sourdough Saloon in the Downtown Hotel for a shot of Yukon Jack and a dehydrated toe, "garnished with courage," I'm told as the white-haired Sourtoe Captain writes out my membership certificate into the Sourtoe Cocktail Club. In homage to Joel, we end the night on the tilted beer-soaked floor of the Pit in the old Westminster Hotel. No one asks us to check our rifles, neither of us gets into a fight, and no Yukon women fight over us. We're almost disappointed.

Outside the Pit, Stro and I stumbled upon the lesser-known name of the Dempster. On the building's southern wall, marked in black stencil across corrugated sheet metal, was written "Mile 0. Joe Henry Highway." This name comes from the Tukudh Gwich'in elder who helped surveyors map the road.

We leave Dawson City the next morning. We're going to get to the Arctic Ocean, but not by the highway. Whichever name we invoke—William Dempster or Joe Henry—it will not let us pass. I am crestfallen. Of all the northern highways planned on the road trip, the Dempster or Joe Henry is the one I was most excited about. Aside from my flight to Rankin Inlet, I have made it this far without taking any trains or planes, and I don't want to take one now, so close to the end. But after five nights in Dawson City, with the highway still closed, the only way Stro and I are going to get to the Arctic Ocean is to fly to Inuvik and rent a vehicle to drive to Tuktoyaktuk. We find a pair of last-minute seats on Canadian North, leave Gumpy at Dawson City airport, fly to Inuvik, and catch a taxi to our hotel.

"That highway is a crazy highway," says our driver, Mohammed Alley. "Nobody know what time they shut, what time it's open. There's a section, about a hundred clicks, where it just blow and blow and blow. Hurricane Alley."

"That's where it was closed, right?" Stro asks.

"Yes. About ten years ago, I don't know how I made it, but I drove from Dawson City. When I got to Eagle Plains, the guy came, opened the gate for me, and asked me how I did it. I said, 'Don't ask me.' I drove all over the world, I never been scared. That day I was so scared. I was driving through snow drifts."

After checking into our hotel, Stro and I cross the street at Inuvik's only stoplight, walk past the Igloo Church and across an open field, where Grollier Hall, one of the town's two former residential schools, once stood. Next to it is the former Grollier Hall Arena, now the Inuvik Community Greenhouse. When we walk up to it, Adi Scott, a UK transplant who has been in Inuvik for four years, is standing in the doorway, smiling widely, and bathing in the sunshine and warming temperatures. Growing season will be coming soon.

"It's such a beautiful day," she says. "I was just taking it all in. Come inside."

Adi leads us past shovels, hoes, rakes, and pitchforks hanging from a wall near a stack of pallets. Along another wall, bags of fertilizer and potting soil lie beneath a green sign that reads, "Compost This Way," and a blue board that outlines what is and what isn't compostable.

We come to the edge of the second-floor space to look out onto the location of the former rink. Sunshine pours through the roof, made of clear polycarbonate plastic (with every other rib removed), filling the entire space with a warm late winter glow. It looks so much bigger because it is so much brighter. At 200 kilometers (124 miles) north of the Arctic Circle, Grollier Hall Arena went from being part of one of the last residential schools to becoming the world's most northerly commercial greenhouse.

Although Gordon's Indian Residential School in Saskatchewan is recognized as the last to close in 1996, Grollier Hall didn't close until a year later. It was demolished and Grollier Hall Arena, once the only arena in town, was slated for demolition, too, when a group of locals set out to save it.

"They decided to petition to the town to not knock this building down and instead to replace the roof and make it into a greenhouse so that it could be a third place in the community during summer," Adi says.

"Third place?" I ask.

"First place is your home, second place is work, and third is an open community space where you don't have to pay to be."

We follow Adi downstairs and out into the growing area. Except for the roof, the rest of the arena is just as it was when it housed hockey instead of herbs: the original black rubber mats on the floor in the front, the original floor of the rink where two rows of vegetable plots now stand, the original lights hanging from the roof ribs overhead, even the original white paint, peeling and puck-marked, with hundreds of scuff marks on the walls.

For more than twenty years, the people of Inuvik have been growing their own vegetables inside the old arena under the midnight sun. With three months of round-the-clock sunlight in summer, members are able to grow just about anything. Some have tried growing peanuts. There is even an autumn delight apple tree that bears a few fruits each year.

The greenhouse's growing season runs from about the second week of May until early October, extending a traditional growing season by a month or more on either side. Because of the twenty-four-hour daylight during summer, plants are usually ready seven to ten days earlier than usual. A year-round hydroponics trailer has been started out front, and the greenhouse also has a coffee shop, the Greenhouse Café, and a community classroom, where staff teach gardening and preservation techniques and give daily tours for tourists who, like Stro and I, are on their way to Tuktoyaktuk.

"Has anybody, if they were a kid here at the residential school, come back?" I ask.

"Elders will come in here when we've had free barbecues or stuff, and they'll be like, 'Oh, I haven't been in here since it was a residential school. I thought I would have really bad memories and bad vibes coming in here.' And they're really glad they came in because it reminded them of the times that were actually okay during that whole horrific experience. A space of growth and healing, I guess."

Canada is one of only a handful of countries whose coastline touches three oceans. With the Trans-Canada, getting to either the Atlantic or the Pacific by road is easy. But as with much of the North, reaching the Arctic is another feat altogether. The only options used to be flights year-round and an ice road in winter. In 2017, the Inuvik Tuktoyaktuk Highway (ITH) opened, the first all-weather road to the Arctic Ocean, connecting Canada from coast to coast to coast.

A marvel of modern engineering, the highway is a gravel road that runs 138 kilometers (86 miles) from the end of the Dempster Highway in Inuvik up to Tuktoyaktuk, the northernmost town in North America accessible by road and the first Indigenous community in Canada to revert to its original name. Wide, well groomed, well maintained, with no potholes, the road rises and falls gently as Stro and I drive through a wash of white hills on the rolling tundra. Signs tell us "You Are in Bear Country" and that there is "No Hunting Caribou," but we see no wildlife other than flocks of black-bellied plovers along the side of the road. Snowmobiles sit half-submerged in snow, awaiting hunters to return. Bony spruce trees grow outside Inuvik, but gradually decrease in number until they all but disappear about halfway to Tuktoyaktuk. From there on, all is white in the Mackenzie Delta, under a thin layer of cloud.

"Minus-twenty-five," Stro says as he checks the temperature. "Spring in the Arctic."

As we approach Tuktoyaktuk, about two hours later, a wide right turn takes us into town. We pass a group of kids, with a dirty husky in hot pursuit, playing road hockey with a puck on an ice-covered side road that resembles the hard, slick surfaces of Rankin Inlet. We pull into the snow-covered parking lot at Donald Kuptana Sr. (Malena) Memorial Arena and go inside to meet up with Donald Kuptana Jr. We find him busy cleaning the kitchen and mopping the floor of the lobby, while a pair of coworkers are hard at work doing renovations. Amid the piercing sound of a table saw and the rumble of a compressor, Donald offers us coffee.

"This is your first trip on the ITH?" he asks.

"First time in the Arctic," Stro replies.

"I was so excited the first time I was coming back home on the road," Donald says. "My wife and I were driving, and you go on top of the hills, and you see where you go fishing and where you go out hunting, and you're telling the stories about that area and you just can't believe you're driving to Tuk. Then when you come over that hill and you start turning and you see the town, you're like, 'This is crazy, man. We've got a road.'"

When the highway opened on November 15, 2017, the community chose to celebrate at the arena. For the opening, a local artist created a mural that spanned the length of the entire rink, depicting the drive from Inuvik to Tuktoyaktuk. Linking the road to the arena, the mural is made out of the same geotextile fabric laid down between the ground and the gravel along the highway to protect the permafrost. It has since been put in storage, but Donald plans to bring it out once all the renovations are complete.

"I need that compressor going," one of the workers says.

"Okay, we'll grab a coffee and go somewhere else," Donald says and then turns to us. "Come on, I'll give you guys a tour."

We move to a spot under a window in the main hall. Donald and his staff have only been at it for two weeks, but the place looks immaculate.

"Hockey is big here," Donald says. "The kids they all wanna be Wayne Gretzkys or Connor McDavids. They all got the shirts."

Hockey in Tuktoyaktuk, population 898 (2016), consists of a men's team and a couple of youth teams, one of which was called the Malena Selects. (Malena was Donald Sr.'s Inuvialuit name.) There is also an old-timers team that travels for tournaments in places like Victoria, Vancouver, Edmonton, Ottawa, and Yellowknife.

"I hate to say 'old-timers,'" says Donald, who is fifty-seven. "We're just old, or older."

"Or masters," Stro says.

"We're not even close to that. We just have fun playing hockey."

We follow Donald into the rink, past a large painting of a polar bear, seal, and beluga in the lobby painted by the same artist who did the mural. In the hallway to the two dressing rooms, one empty and the other full of arena supplies and hockey gear, hangs a bronze plaque in honor of Donald's father:

In memory of his dedication, encouragement and cheerful spirit to the game of hockey

"Put your jackets on," Donald says. "It's pretty cold in there. Some days, when I was a kid, when we were skating on it, it was so cold that whole chunks of ice would just break apart."

It is one of the things I love most about hockey, the cold. I hate the heat. The cold gives energy, the heat takes it away. When we walk out to the rink, it is like an icebox. Instant energy. In the *Divine Comedy*, the lowest

202

place in Dante's *Inferno* is a frozen lake, so if hockey players go to hell, there should at least be some puck to play when we get there.

Like the outdoor rink in Baker Community, the boards are free of ads. The only piece of advertising is a lone Gulf BeauDril sign above the players' benches. Flat wooden sculptures of various fish and whales, all painted, hang on the wall behind us. The ice glistens from the glare of the overhead lights, while the beams running lengthwise along the low ceiling give an illusion of speed.

"Beautiful," Stro says.

"Pristine," I say.

"Oh yeah, hard ice, fast," Donald says.

Once they finish cleaning and renovating the front of the building, Donald and his staff will turn their attention to the rink itself. Donald has big plans for it. He wants to put in new plexiglass along the boards, install heaters, and add stands around the rink to make it accessible for elders to come and watch the kids play. He also wants to fix the hiccup on the boards.

The arena was set up during the Tuktoyaktuk oil boom of the 1980s when 737s would land in this tiny village. But when the arena was being barged across the Beaufort Sea, two pieces of the boards fell off, leaving the rink a full section shorter than it should be. The blue line on the ice is sixty-four feet from the goal line, as it should be, but the one on the boards is several feet closer.

"You see where the blue line is on the boards?" Donald says. "You take a slapshot from here, look how close to the nets it is. So we have to make sure we move it back to where it should be."

"Would it be possible for us to skate on it?" I ask.

"You guys can if you want to," Donald replies.

Stro and I go outside and grab our frozen gear from the truck. My skates are rigid from sitting in the cold for a couple of hours. But this is what we've come for, to skate at the edge of the Arctic Ocean.

"Let's get the nets out," Stro says.

We guide the nets down along the top of the boards, placing them gently onto the ice so as not to scratch it, and then slide them to their respective creases. As I prep my phone to take some photos for Stro, I hear him drop a bucket of pucks onto the ice, like marbles being dumped onto a carpeted floor. Then comes the rapid *click-clack click-clack* of Stro's slick stickhandling, the *crack* from his heavy slapshot, and the reverberating *boom* from the puck hitting the boards, all of it made louder thanks to the rink's metal walls and roof.

Ever since talking with Nelson Rego back in Edmonton, I've been listening for the sounds of the game that have escaped my consciousness for so long. As Stro and I skate around, I can hear the bite and scrape of our strides as our blades cut into the ice. The rip of our turns sounds like a microphone being held up to a zipper and our stops like someone angrily shushing a child during a movie. The thunder of the puck hitting the boards echoes off the plexiglass and ricochets throughout the empty arena. After a few tries, I manage to hit the posts and crossbar. It may be my favorite sound in hockey, the *ting* of the puck hitting the pipe. I've heard all these sounds before, thousands upon thousands of times, but only now have I begun to listen to them.

We shoot pucks around for about half an hour and go back to the dressing room, where Donald is still busy cleaning. Stro pulls out a hockey card from his bag. It is Dave Keon, one of the greatest players in Maple Leafs' history. He hands it to Donald, a gift from one Leafs fan to another.

"Ever since I was a kid, I've been a Leafs fan," Donald says as he turns the card over in his hands. "Hopefully they'll do better this year. But every year it's been, 'This year, this year, this year.'"

"Well, this might be the year," Stro says. "I'm calling it now: Oilers and Leafs' final."

Both Edmonton and Toronto will lose in the second round of the playoffs, but it doesn't matter. Through that card, Donald and Stro are able to share a moment, two men of different backgrounds, living at opposite ends of the country, with little in common other than each having two sons, a loyalty to a team, a passion for the game, and a hope for the future, both on and off the ice.

Before heading back to Inuvik, Stro and I follow the road to the end, where a large sign stacks the English and Inuvialuit names for the world's most northern waterbody:

Arctic Ocean
Nunaryuam Qaangani Tariuq

As far as we can see, all is white, except for a couple of ice huts and a helicopter slicing the air overhead. A pole at the edge of the ocean tells us how far we are away from the North Pole (2,287 kilometers) and some of the places we've been to during our three weeks on the road together: Edmonton (2,054 kilometers), Yellowknife (1,139 kilometers), Whitehorse (987 kilometers), and Inuvik (129 kilometers). After returning to Dawson City, Stro will fly home from Whitehorse while I'll carry on to British Columbia. Nine provinces, three territories, and two oceans down. Only one province, one ocean, and one more northern highway left to go.

British Columbia:
The Last Game

But life on the road comes at a price. The energy it gives, the freedom you feel, it takes away, and more . . . A rhythm like any other rhythm, it is one you get used to; except this one is always changing and you never do. —Ken Dryden, *The Game*

THE STEWART-CASSIAR HIGHWAY runs 875 kilometers (544 miles) south from the Yukon down to Kitimat in northern British Columbia. Built for mining and logging, the road cuts through the most remote part of the province until it connects with the upper route of the Trans-Canada at Kitwanga.

I get onto the Stewart-Cassiar at Junction 37 near Watson Lake and drive past a large brown sign that reads, "South to Alaska." From there, I continue south to Dease Lake and then on past Iskut. Snow, sleet, rain, sun, clouds—the weather can't make up its mind, nor can the sea birds that like to camp out on the road and often refuse to move. Narrow, with no road lines, little cell service, but well paved for much of the drive, the highway dips and rolls past stunted spruce and poplar, like riding a kiddie coaster at an amusement park. When I reach the Meziadin Junction, walls of granite west along the Glacier Highway guide me into the town of Stewart, Canada's most northerly ice-free port, sitting on the border with Alaska.

As always, upon entering a new town, I head straight for the arena, which in Stewart is a large blue building without a sign. Inside I learn it is called the Al Lawrence Memorial Arena, named for a local hockey lifer. The lobby is full of figure skaters waiting to get their photos taken ahead of the town's end-of-season figure skating gala tonight. I interrupt the parade to the photographer long enough to find out that the last pickup game of the season is in two nights, after which the ice will be taken out for the summer. I find a room at a local bed-and-breakfast that has been converted from several of the town's old heritage buildings, including prospectors' cabins, stores, lodges, and even the brothel, from back when Stewart was a mining boomtown.

Hockey's long-standing connection to mining is often overlooked. When determining origins, talk always turns to which one of Canada's frozen ponds birthed the game, not the minerals that have allowed us to glide upon them better than our ancestors did. Skate blades have evolved from cattle and deer bones to (much later) wood, followed by aluminum, copper, chromium, carbon, iron, nickel, and steel, all extracted from the earth.

Throughout Canada, mines like those in the Coast Mountains around Stewart have given birth to both towns and teams, although, as in the case of Flin Flon, not always in that order. The mining roots of the game are sewn on jerseys in hockey towns all across the country: the Glace Bay Miners in Nova Scotia, the Noranda Copper Kings in Quebec, the Timmins Gold Diggers in Ontario, among many others.

Like many of these places, Stewart is no longer a busy mining town. When the gold, silver, and other precious metal mines were booming, the bars were full, the brothel busy, and the rink always occupied. At one point, Stewart numbered as many as ten thousand people; it now has fewer than five hundred. Some mining, logging, and mineral exploration remains, but Stewart has dwindled to little more than a summer tourist town for heliskiers and RV travelers and a trucking route that cuts through Alaska to the remaining mines in northern British Columbia.

It is about a two-minute drive from Stewart to the United States. A Canadian border guard comes out to greet me at the world's most pointless border crossing. Not even the American government thinks the ghost town of Hyder, Alaska, across from Stewart, is worth stationing.

"Can you take your sunglasses off for me?" she asks, then works her way through the customs official's usual tally of questions regarding alcohol, cigarettes, tobacco, and firearms before hitting me with "any outstanding warrants?"

It takes me a moment to stifle a chuckle and provide an answer. I want to ask, "Will shooting a hockey puck into the Salmon River get me arrested?"

"No ma'am," I answer.

"Alright, you're good to go. Enjoy your trip."

I drive slowly at first, until I realize that the "20" on the speed limit signs means twenty mph. Everything is closed, either permanently (Yankee Trader Self-Serve Gas Station, Canal Trading Post) or temporarily (Glacier Inn, Boundary Gallery). A gardening sign on what looks like a hoarder's house reads, "A dirty hoe is a happy hoe!" Another sign on the General Store reads, "Hyder Alaska: A town of about a hundred happy people. And a few old s--- heads."

Just over a dozen people now live in Hyder, but I see no one. Although they're full-blooded Americans, they don't pay US taxes and they get everything from Canada: electricity, gas, groceries, school, hockey. The town uses Canadian currency and has a Canadian area code. Even Hyder's name comes from Canada, the surname of a Canadian mining engineer. There are no American customs or police here, and the only domestic service is the United States Post Office, which is closed when I arrive.

I continue along the Granduc Road up the Salmon River Valley. It goes from pavement to gravel and then to dirt as it climbs the cliffside to the area's remaining gold and copper mines, back on the Canadian side.

I stop partway to let a dump truck rumble by me, then get out and grab a stick and puck out of Gumpy. I've done this at times throughout the road trip on a remote road where there is nothing and no one around. Hyder is the only place I take a shot, however. I stickhandle for a few minutes and then try my best to juggle the puck with my stick. Eventually, after looking out over the Salmon River, I send a souvenir to my American friends, lofting a wrister toward the river, watching it arc in the air until it kerplunks into the water. To the good people of Hyder, if you're ever short a puck . . .

On my way back to Canada, a sign declares Hyder to be "The Friendliest Ghost Town in Alaska." Why the sign points toward its own residents and not incoming tourists baffles me, but nothing makes sense about Hyder, not even its existence.

"So, was Hyder all that you hoped it would be?" the border guard asks on my way out.

"And then some."

"Did you buy anything?"

"I wanted to, but nothing was open. Is there any store that's open?"

"Not really. You're a bit early for the tourist season. Nothing will open up for another few weeks or so."

"By any chance, would you happen to know anyone from Hyder who plays hockey?" I ask.

"Yes."

"Could you put me in touch with them?"

"I don't feel comfortable giving out somebody else's information."

"Understood. Could I give you my information and you pass it along for me? I'm playing hockey in Stewart tomorrow night."

"I wouldn't have any way to deliver it to him. He's at work all weekend. But if there's hockey Sunday night, he'll probably be there."

No one from Hyder shows up for hockey the following night, although I'm told my defense partner's grandfather owns the Glacier Inn, where tourists come every summer to get "Hyderized" with a shot of 75.5 percent Ever-clear alcohol at the hotel bar. All the players are from Stewart, about a dozen or so, more than enough to play four-on-four, which is all that can fit on the ice (it triples as a hockey rink, curling sheet, and figure skating surface).

After the game, everyone hangs around for beer and hockey talk. I get talking with Jake Danuser, a Swiss transplant, the elder statesman of the group.

"Does anybody from Hyder ever play here?" I ask.

"Not today," Jake replies.

"Fuck those guys," one of the other players says as everyone laughs. "Fuck those idiots."

"It's hard to get them here," Jake says. "It's a long ways."

While I was in Stewart, the Prince George Cougars were in Seattle, losing the first two games of their second-round playoff series against the top-seeded Thunderbirds of the Western Hockey League. The Cougars then drove 895 kilometers (556 miles) back home to Prince George, where they would attempt to get back into the series. I drive 698 kilometers (434 miles) to watch them try.

Ralph Posteraro did the Seattle–Prince George route many times over his twenty years driving for the Cougars, nineteen of which were spent on one bus. When the engine finally blew on that bus a year before he retired in 2020, he'd put over 800,000 kilometers (500,000 miles) on it. The Cougars travel south to Victoria and the league's four American cities in Washington State, and as far east as Winnipeg. Mercifully, he never had to drive farther north than Prince George.

Lots of Canadian teams travel, but not like this. "I'm pretty sure it's the most," Ralph says. "Our closest team is five and half hours away."

Quiet, unassuming, and a man of few words, Ralph is wearing a Cougars spring jacket overtop an old Cougars jersey when I meet him ahead of game three. From Stewart, it took me eight hours to get to Prince George, back along the Glacier Highway, down the rest of the Stewart-Cassiar

Highway, and then east across the northern route of the Trans-Canada. I'm pleased to meet someone who's driven more in one hockey season than I have.

The Canadian Hockey League (CHL) is the umbrella organization for the country's three top junior leagues: the Quebec Maritimes Junior Hockey League, the Ontario Hockey League, and the Western Hockey League. Budgets aren't big enough for air travel, and trains are too irregular and slow. Bus is the only option. With more than thirty games on the road, plus preseason and playoffs, most teams drive anywhere between 11,000 and 29,000 kilometers (7,000 and 18,000 miles) over the course of a single season. Distances between rivals are shortest, like the half-hour drive between Kitchener and Guelph along Highway 401, or the forty-five-minute ride between Victoriaville and Drummondville in Quebec, or the two-hour trip up or down Highway 11 between Regina and Saskatoon. Many other teams aren't so lucky. For the now-defunct Kootenay Ice, every road game, whether east or west, ran through a mountain pass. For the Victoria Royals, on Vancouver Island, each road trip requires a ferry crossing. For the Cougars, who average more than 30,000 kilometers (20,000 miles) and up to sixty nights in a hotel every season, their closest opponent is the Kamloops Blazers, 518 kilometers (324 miles) down Highway 97.

Then there are the long hauls, many of them spent on the Trans-Canada and the lonely stretches of rural highways that crisscross it. Most come in the dead of winter. Blizzards, snowstorms, whiteouts, and black ice come with the territory in the CHL. Of all the teams in the league, those in Western Canada (and the northwestern United States) have it worst. For Prince George, the Regina Pats are a fifteen-hour bus ride away, and that is not even close to the league's longest haul. The Winnipeg Ice and the Royals must travel 5,021 kilometers (3,120 miles) round trip to play one another. For Winnipeg, that is about as far as driving to Quebec City, while for Victoria it is farther than Tijuana.

More than the ice, the dressing room, the weight room, school, or hotels, it is aboard the bus where players spend most of their time together.

These trips turn the road into a mnemonic device. Players who reach the NHL, where life is lived in the air, will often swap stories about the bus rides they took across Canada and reminisce about them after they retire. They'll ask each other about their longest trips, what movies they watched, what card games they played, what wildlife they encountered. Memories forged on the road never leave them.

In all those years driving for the Cougars, over all the miles he logged on the highways of Western Canada and Washington State, not once did Ralph hit an animal or blow a tire. Nor did the team ever miss a game, although they did cut it close once after driving through a snowstorm to Portland.

"We made it with just under an hour to spare," he says.

Ralph and I go our separate ways for the game. The press box at CN Centre is full. I'm told to just find an empty seat in the crowd. The seat is still cold when the Thunderbirds score first less than two minutes in and again a few minutes later. Before the end of the period, they score twice more. Down 4–0, the Cougars aren't coming back, so I break my own rule and leave early.

When I check the score in the morning, the Thunderbirds have won 8–1. By the time I arrive in Prince Rupert the next evening, after an eight-hour drive along the Trans-Canada, they've beaten up the Cougars again, 8–2, to sweep the series. The Thunderbirds will make the long trip back to Seattle in high spirits, while the Cougars will have to cancel their plans for another long haul for game five. Their season is over.

From the misty port city of Prince Rupert, I catch a ferry over to Skidegate on Graham Island, part of the Haida Gwaii archipelago. After a rollicking three-hour ride across the Hecate Strait, which sent plates smashing in the cafeteria, I drive up the island's east coastal road. At its end, a large, faceless, wooden yellow head greets me outside a shuttered visitors center. I've reached the end of the Trans-Canada.

The town of Masset has made something of a local industry out of calling itself the "Western Mile 0" of the Yellowhead Highway, the upper route of the Trans-Canada. There is the Mile Zero Laundromat, Mile Zero Tours, Mile Zero Pub, Mile Zero Inn, Mile Zero Motel, Mile Zero Taxi, and Mile Zero Dining Room, which serves a delicious Mile Zero Waffle. The entire Yellowhead, incidentally, is measured in kilometers.

In a country where hockey arenas seem as numerous as doughnut shops, there is not one indoor arena or outdoor rink in all of Haida Gwaii. It rains two-thirds of the year, about 152 centimeters (60 inches) on average, and winter winds can reach the strength of a tropical storm or low-level hurricane. Temperatures only fall below the freezing mark for maybe a week, at best two, a year.

Despite its lack of ice, natural or artificial, Masset is a hockey town, and Haida Gwaii a hockey isle, as much as any in Canada. There is the same Saturday night TV hockey ritual, the same hockey talk, the same group of people who play pond hockey whenever the weather permits. There is even an old-timers team, the Haida Gwaii Islanders, a collection of local scrubs who come together once a year to represent the archipelago at an off-island tournament in Prince Rupert.

I haven't brought an umbrella because I never use one, and good thing—Haida Gwaii is the kind of place so accustomed to rain that a tourist carrying one is called Mary Poppins. As clouds gather, I walk across town and over to Masset Bikes, where Terry Wallace is busy working at the back of his store. He pops out to greet me and hands me a huge mug of coffee in a company cup. He has on a Vancouver Canucks cap flipped backward.

Terry first came to Masset to surf the waves off the island's northern coast. Nine years later, married, with two daughters and a small bike sales and repair business, he is still here. It is easy to understand why. Haida Gwaii has it all: ocean, coast, surfing, hiking, fishing, forest, wildlife.

"But no hockey," Terry says. "That's the downfall of it, for sure. We have roller hockey here on the island, and that's what we mainly play, but our rink situation is not great. It's like a concrete slab with boards in an enclosed structure. It's pretty ghetto, for sure, if you're coming from Ontario. I wish we had hockey."

Growing up near Cambridge, Ontario, Terry played hockey all his life. One winter, after putting down roots in Masset, he wrote an opinion column in the local newspaper, the *Haida Gwaii Observer*. He'd been inspired by an unusually long cold snap that allowed people to play hockey for a couple of weeks straight, day and night, on local lakes, ponds, sloughs, and even mud bogs. Like so many others on the island, Terry didn't want it to end: "The road to an ice rink is going to be long and bumpy, but we will get there," he wrote. "Kevin Costner once said in *Field of Dreams*, 'If you build it, he will come.' If we build a rink, our islanders will come out in flocks and our youth will be given one more way to succeed."

Six years on, Haida Gwaii is still without an arena. Climate-wise, there isn't much difference between Haida Gwaii and Prince Rupert or Stewart, both of which are coastal towns that have rinks. And with nearly five thousand people spread across the archipelago, it has about ten times the population of Stewart.

"It sucks not to have it," Terry says. "But at the same time, whenever we do get skating here when the ponds freeze, it's really nice."

In the meantime, he and everyone else in Haida Gwaii's underground hockey community make do with the John Lalonde Roller Rink. "All the same gear," Terry says. "It's just hockey on concrete. It's fun, though, because it's like a bunch of old men who could have a heart attack at any time."

Tonight, the numbers and the conditions are perfect. Terry invites me over to his house to watch the NHL playoffs on *Hockey Night in Canada*. By the end of the second period, he's wrangled up enough players for a game.

The rain is rapping on the roof when we walk in. Cage fencing wraps around the entire rink. At center is a large Haida Gwaii Islanders logo, a slick scythe of the archipelago's more than two hundred islands.

The dressing room is an enclosed concrete room with a low ceiling and a mass of sticks outside. Seats plucked from minivans function as benches. Someone broke into the rink and graffitied parts of the room, giving it a ghoulish look. Posters of women's roller derby urge players to "Hit Like a Girl." Under the wood-panel ceiling hangs a golden roller skate for the Roller Hockey Champions 2010. Pawing through the mass of miscellaneous equipment strewn helter-skelter throughout the room, some of it left behind by RCMP officers after they rotated out of town, I'm able to find a set of roller blades that are only a touch too big.

There are just enough of us for four aside and a goalie each. A few of the players, including Terry, wear local Islanders jerseys. With no ice to keep us cool and wearing what feels like lead weights on my feet, I sweat like a hog and skate like a penguin. Terry has clearly completed the transition from ice to concrete, gliding around and playing the puck like he was born to do this. Eventually, I get the hang of it enough to start striding, using either the boards or wide turns to wheel myself around. At a certain point, I forget that I'm skating on concrete and just start playing with unpolished instincts carried over from the ice.

We play for about two hours, ten of us, a high schooler to middle-aged men, until we can continue no longer. In the dressing room afterward, talk turns to the Maple Leafs, who are in tough against the Tampa Bay Lightning in the first round of the playoffs.

"I've got a bet with my principal," says the high school student. "If the Leafs lose, he's gotta stand up in front of the school at assembly and say I'm the coolest kid there."

"What if they win?" someone asks.

"Then I have to say he's the coolest principal."

The Leafs go on to win the series in six games.

After the game, I start walking back to my room, my sweaty equipment slung over my shoulder. The rain has lightened to a drizzle, lit up by the lamps of the empty street. No ice needed inside the rink, and no umbrella outside it.

THE COUNTRY AND THE GAME

I don't know what to make of Canada's roadside landmark fetish. It is probably just a way for places to lure tourists to stop on their way down the highway. But it could also be something of a compensatory cultural reflex, a way for small towns to peacock some kind of king-sized kitsch to make them feel bigger than they are. Or perhaps it is just that harmless collective compulsion to fill up all that empty space that comes with being the world's second-biggest country with the thirty-ninth largest population and one of the longest national highways on the planet. Whatever the reason, Canada's road network is a largesse of the world's largest whatevers.

Some are official Guinness World Records. There is the World's Largest Egg Beater in Lauretta, Prince Edward Island, and the World's Largest Fishing Lure in Lacombe, Alberta, and the World's Biggest Hand Paddle near Golden, British Columbia. Many more are claimants to unofficial world records: the world's biggest bathtub, golf tee, peace pipe, and (presumably non-edible) Ukrainian sausage.

The list goes on through dozens of other less ambitious but larger-than-life attractions: a nickel, a UFO landing pad, a Ukrainian girl, a tomato, a coho salmon, and a mastodon.

Most of this colossal camp is scattered somewhere along the edges of the Trans-Canada, or within striking distance of it, but toward the west end of the line is the biggest of them all. It is surely the most Canadian. In Duncan, British Columbia, atop the Cowichan Community Centre, hangs the World's Largest Hockey Stick, known locally as the Big Stick, which comes complete with the World's Largest Hockey Puck. A tourist attraction to most, an eyesore to some, it is peak Canadiana, a supersized representation of the game's outsized place within the country.

I take the ferry from Haida Gwaii back to Prince Rupert and catch an overnight ferry to Port Hardy. For the second time on the road trip, I curl up on the cleanest piece of dirty carpet onboard and catch what sleep I can. From Port Hardy, I work my way down Vancouver Island on Highway 19 to Nanaimo, where I reconnect to the Trans-Canada. When I catch sight of the Big Stick, easily seen from the highway, I pull into the packed parking lot and lean back in my seat, coffee in hand, and twenty-five tons of steel-reinforced Douglas fir in full view.

At more than sixty-one meters (two hundred feet), the Big Stick is about forty times life-size. The federal government commissioned it in the lead-up to Expo '86 in Vancouver. Built in Penticton, in the interior of British Columbia, the shaft and the blade were made in separate sections, and the two pieces were then trucked to Vancouver. Two years after the fair, the stick was disassembled and shipped over to its permanent home in Duncan. Since then, the Big Stick has been distracting drivers on the Trans-Canada from its perch atop the arena, and for nearly thirty years it has been at the center of a good old-fashioned donnybrook between the people of Duncan, population 5,700, and the people of Eveleth, Minnesota, who number around 3,500. It is the kind of imbroglio that could only be found in the hockey world, or perhaps a philosophy conference.

For the Big Stick's first twenty-one years in Duncan, the coveted title of the World's Largest Hockey Stick had evaded it. Initially, the town didn't give much thought to the record. It wasn't until the Americans got in the game that Duncan decided to claim the title for Canada. In 1995, Eveleth built a 3,175-kilogram (7,000-pound), 32.5-meter (107-foot) stick made of white and yellow aspen, complete with a 317.5-kilogram (700-pound) puck 1.5 meters (five feet) in diameter, to take the Guinness World Record. In 2002, it upgraded its mark when it replaced the original stick with a 4,535-kilogram (10,000-pound), 33.5-meter (110-foot) design.

Duncan appealed to Guinness many times after it got word of its rival, but the town was repeatedly told that Eveleth was given the record because its stick was in one piece, not two. Then in February 2008, Vancouver billionaire Jimmy Pattison, who'd spearheaded Expo '86, bought the Guinness World Records book company. Shortly after his purchase, Pattison went about setting the record straight, and a few months later, Duncan was finally granted the official title of the World's Largest Hockey Stick.

That didn't deter Eveleth. The town pressed on in defiance, and in a fine bit of philosophy started calling its wood the world's largest authentic hockey stick and the world's largest freestanding hockey stick, citing the difference between a real stick (Eveleth's) and a sculpture (Duncan's). But it wouldn't matter. In 2023, with woodpeckers drilling holes into Duncan's Douglas fir, the town was forced to decommission its stick due to decay and give up the title as the World's Largest Hockey Stick.

I finish my coffee and pull out of the parking lot. Although I still have a few more stops to make before beginning the long drive home, the road trip is already beginning to retreat into the rearview mirror as I get back onto the Trans-Canada and head down to Victoria.

I could live out my golden years at Amica Somerset House, a short walk from Victoria's Mile 0 monument to the Trans-Canada. The sun-bathed exterior makes it look like a California beachfront property, while the windows and skylights light up the staircase and hallways inside. The rooms with ocean views look out over Holland Point Park on the waterfront of the Salish Sea, while those with the garden view, like Bill Brownridge's, look onto a courtyard. The dining and tea rooms resemble those of a private golf club, and it has a theater, a library, a swimming pool, a gym, even an in-house art gallery.

None of Bill's works are yet on display in the gallery, but he only moved in a month ago. Through a maze of renovations on the second floor, I manage to find his room, where he greets me from his wheelchair and welcomes me in. His white hair stands out against his heavy sweater striped in wide ribbons of green, red, yellow, and blue that pick up many of the colors in the paintings in various stages of completion lying about his apartment.

At ninety, Bill is still painting, three hours every morning. Across from his kitchen, under the bright afternoon sun of his garden view window, a painting of seven kids playing pond hockey on a prairie slough is nearing completion. It bears Bill's trademark style: an outdoor hockey scene on the Prairies, broken blues to give the effect of vibration and action, exaggerated yellow to reflect the sun off the ice, heavy texture to create excitement, "fat" paint for pixilation, the contrast of positive and negative space between the arms and legs of the players and the ice they're playing on.

When most people think of art, they think visual. Just stand and look at it. But Bill's paintings are invitations to touch. The blobs of paint jump off the canvas. Even though the puck barely registers, just a speck of black among the thick blobs of blue and yellow paint, everything points toward it as the center of the action among the kids playing hockey at its purist.

"Is this what fuels your paintings, that child-like grassroots hockey?" I ask.

"The heart of hockey," Bill replies. "Rather than all the glitz and glamor."

Born with spina bifida, a birth defect of the spinal column that can cause clubbed feet, Bill could wear a shoe only on one foot, much less skates on both. Doctors tried to reposition his right foot using a cast, but they put it on too tight, which caused blood poisoning and left him with a crippled foot. His leg eventually had to be amputated below his knee when he was fifteen.

"Because I had not been able to skate or anything or even run, I'm fascinated with movement," Bill says. "I'm a storyteller, but I'm also fascinated with motion and my inability to do it." Part of that fascination is also probably due to watching his big brother Bob, a former right winger with the New York Rovers in the long-defunct Eastern Hockey League. That spirit of motion is what suffuses his art.

To the untrained eye (which would be mine), many of Bill's paintings look like a mad scramble in any game of shinny. Yet where others see chaos, Bill finds coherence, patterns of innocence that pervade his paintings.

"I love the incredible patterns where you get two or three guys crashing together and stretching for the puck, especially around the goal," he says.

The net is special for Bill, because goal is the only position he could play as a kid. Although he was never able to wear skates, that didn't stop him from playing pond hockey as a boy with his buddies. Nor did it stop him from winning a championship in the only official game he ever played.

In 1954, five years after losing his foot, Bill was called upon to play for the local junior team, the Cougars, in his hometown of Vawn, Saskatchewan, after their goalie had been injured ahead of the league final against rival Meota. Bill had grown up playing pond hockey with all the players, so they asked their coach, who then asked the league, if he could fill in.

"The other team, they knew we couldn't come up with a goalie," Bill says. "So they said, 'Brownridge? Okay, let him play.'"

"So they had no problem with it?"

"I guess they thought, 'Forget it, these guys are dead.'"

Bill was in Saskatoon visiting his sister at the time. He bussed a couple hours to Meota for the game the next day. On an artificial limb, in full goalie gear, except for the moccasins he wore in place of skates, Bill backstopped Vawn to a 3–2 win and the title.

"It was quite the unforgettable time for me because of the fact that I wasn't able to play hockey," he says. "Then this sort of stroke of luck gave me a chance to play once."

That game and the shinny Bill used to play on prairie sloughs are the inspiration for his artwork. For thirty years, Bill painted around his job as a graphic designer doing "commercial art," as he calls it, at an advertising firm in Calgary. When he retired in 1995, he began painting full time. His work has been showcased at the Hockey Hall of Fame and in galleries across Canada. He is widely recognized as the country's foremost hockey artist.

Bill's paintings bring to life the game at its purest, overwhelming the senses with bright colors, thick paint on acrylic canvases, and the silent sounds of kids clashing sticks and cracking pucks as their skates slice the ice. Many of his paintings are drawn from a bird's-eye view, often of prairie landscapes.

"What I love about painting outdoor hockey is the fact that you're going to play regardless of the hostility of the weather or snowfall or anything," Bill says. "You were always fighting the elements in order to play."

Imagine, for a moment, it is game seven of the Stanley Cup Final. For the fourth time in their existence, and the first time since they reached the final in 2011, the Vancouver Canucks are once again playing for the Stanley Cup. The year doesn't matter, neither does the opponent. With the series tied at three games apiece, Canucks fans flood into the city to watch the game on big screens set up downtown and share their hopes that their team will finally bring the cup to Vancouver for the first time in franchise history. But by the end of the game, all hopes are dashed. The Canucks lose, yet again, in another game seven.

Now picture what happens next.

After taking the ferry from Victoria across the Georgia Strait, I drive to Vancouver's Central Library, between Robson Street and Georgia Street, in the heart of downtown. Outside the library, a city worker is pressure washing the area in front of the doors when I greet Michael Barnholden, who leans on his stylish brown cane as he makes a sweeping motion with his other hand.

"This was the center of the riots," he says. "This is where it all started."

Both Vancouver's Stanley Cup riots have been examined in great detail, including by a psychology professor from the University of Massachusetts who came to the conclusion that the Canucks riots, like all sports riots, were the result of a drop in testosterone levels among male fans, who then lashed out in vain attempts to regain their sense of manliness. The funniest part of his analysis is that it is probably true. But every take I've read of the riots has always left me wondering why. Why Vancouver? Why the Canucks?

"I can hazard a guess at that," says Michael, an author and historian who has written a book about Vancouver riots. "They always think they have a better team than they really do."

He is only half-joking. Michael grew up playing hockey in Toronto before coming out to Vancouver to go to school in 1970. Having lived in both cities, and having cheered for both the Maple Leafs and the Canucks, he understands an often-overlooked difference between Toronto and Vancouver.

"In Toronto, every corner park had an outdoor rink," he says. "You don't have that here because of the weather. So you have people here who would be your peers and would be hockey fans, but they can't skate, they don't know how to skate."

Vancouver, in fact, has a long history with hockey, dating back to the Vancouver Millionaires, the first West Coast team to win the Stanley Cup (1915). Even longer, as Michael points out in *Reading the Riot Act,* is the city's tradition of rioting: the anti-immigration riots in 1907, the dockers' strike known as the Battle of Ballantyne Pier in 1935, the Bloody Sunday strike in 1938, the Grey Cup riots in the 1960s, the Gastown riots in 1971.

Michael was living in East Vancouver when the Canucks lost to the New York Rangers in 1994, and in the Kitsilano neighborhood when they lost to the Boston Bruins in 2011.

The 1994 loss was by the slimmest of margins, falling 3–2 in game seven. The Canucks were underdogs in that series, but the moral victory of pushing the Rangers to seven games, and coming within an inch of tying the game when Nathan LaFayette's shot hit the post with less than five minutes to play, still wasn't enough for Canucks fans. After their narrow defeat, they proceeded to destroy Vancouver's downtown.

"You've got New York and Vancouver, you've got the metropolis versus the village, but what's happening in the village is the cops are basically harassing kids living in the streets," Michael says. "These kids are not wearing hundred-dollar Canuck T-shirts, they're poor. They're literally living on the streets. But the cops are harassing the hell out of them, and the kids are looking for a way back. It has nothing to do with hockey."

Seventeen years later, the Canucks were at home to face the Bruins in another game seven. As Michael tells it, inside Rogers Arena were twenty thousand people who could afford a ticket, including Premier Christy

Clark and Prime Minister Stephen Harper, while outside were one hundred thousand people who couldn't, many of them men aged eighteen to twenty-four, rocking hundred-dollar Canucks jerseys this time around. They weren't the hardscrabble poor from the city's east end, as in 1994, but they'd spent the previous ten years under a provincial government that had made deep cuts to health care, education, social security, and social safety programs, and introduced top-friendly tax reform. A new and unpopular joint-provincial-federal sales tax (HST) had come into effect less than a year earlier. As the Canucks' march through the playoffs was documented on the back page of the *Vancouver Province*, anti-HST sentiment was featured on the front page.

"It was like this clusterfuck, for lack of a better term, in 2011," Michael says. "You could feel the energy building. I was over at my house, and you could literally feel it in the air. This is not going to end well."

When the Canucks lost, this time 4–0, the downtown went up in flames and fury again. The only good to come of it was a photo of a couple caught kissing in the middle of the street as the riot raged around them.

"Don't get me wrong, this was not organized," Michael says. "This was not a bunch of anarchists. All the anarchists were at home watching the game on TV. But it's these kids, who have this pent-up rage that really has nothing to do with hockey. It's the haves and the have-nots, and you add alcohol and you're in a dangerous situation."

What's interesting about the 1994 and 2011 riots is that Vancouver had a trial run at this during the 1982 Stanley Cup Final. In that series, the Canucks were heavy underdogs against the two-time defending champion New York Islanders. The Canucks finished forty-one points behind the Islanders in the standings during the regular season and were dispatched from the final in four straight games. The city took it well, relative to the later losses.

"It goes back, in a way, to the history of hockey in Vancouver," Michael says. "These are not hockey players, these are hockey fanatics. You have to keep that in mind that 'fanatics' is the long handle for 'fans.' So these are hockey fans. They literally want to be part of the game, and by 'game'

I mean the larger game, and they're being shut out, in the earlier one by the cops and the later one by the economy and the political repression that's going on."

"Do you think the outcome would've been different at all had the Canucks won either of those games?" I ask.

"It would've become a celebration riot, if you will," Michael replies. "They would've been shouting, 'Go Canucks Go!' instead of 'Fuck the HST!' But they still would've done it. It's really not about hockey."

For all of hockey's distractions—the trade chatter, rumormongering, tribalism, armchair general managing, online gambling, crazy hockey parenting, game operations bombardments, and the occasional riot—there is still only one point to the game. Score. It never gets old, at any age, in any rink, at any level.

Ask any pro player about their first goal, and they'll recall it in great detail, like the birth of their first child. It could be Wayne Gretzky's slick backhand stick-side goal for the Indianapolis Racers, Terry Ryan Jr.'s lucky deflection off his skate with the Canadiens, or a beer-leaguer's snipe for a semipro team in Sweden. They'll know the date, the rink, the opponent, the goalie, the time, what led up to it, and what came after. They'll have the puck at home and they'll have watched the clip many times over.

Po-Yuan "Bryant" Tsiao remembers his like it was yesterday. When I meet him in Stanley Park, named for the same man who gave Canada the Stanley Cup, he's wearing a dark blue hoodie of his former team in Sweden, where he scored his first and only pro goal.

"And this is the hat, too," he says, pointing to his black cap. "I had to be in the zone to talk about it."

Born in Taiwan, Bryant has represented his home country at more than a dozen World Championships and international tournaments. Back in Canada, where he's spent most of his life, Bryant is a beer-leaguer, tearing it up around Vancouver. In 2022, a friend who'd played a year in Sweden put him in touch with the general manager of Hofors HC, a semipro team north of Stockholm in the Hockeytvåan, Sweden's fourth-highest league, about the level of the Ligue Nord-Américaine de Hockey in Quebec, but without the fighting. Bryant put together a highlight package from his most recent World Championship with Taiwan and sent it to the team. They liked what they saw and offered him a contract. At twenty-nine, he'd become a professional hockey player.

"I was like, 'You know what, this is six months of my life,'" he says. "Worse comes to worst, I just focus on hockey for six months."

While most of his teammates worked regular jobs or went to school, Bryant was free to just play hockey. He would wake up at the team hostel, where the import players all lived, practice, hit the gym, come back to rest and recover, and repeat it all the next day.

In fifteen games with Hofors, Bryant went goalless. After Christmas, he was transferred to Lerums BK, a team in Gothenburg in the south of the country. On a new team with a fresh start, he switched his jersey from 19 to 8, the first number of his favorite athlete, Kobe Bryant. The switch worked.

"I've probably watched the clip a hundred times," he says.

Lerums was on the road against Trollhättan, a top team in their division. With his team down a couple of goals, Bryant and his linemates entered the offensive zone. With his linemates in the corner, Bryant hovered around the high slot.

The next thing he knew, the puck was on his stick. It happened that quickly. It always does. Bryant had no time to think. There rarely is in hockey, at any level. Just react. The puck left his stick as fast as it came to it.

Everything went into slow motion. Bryant watched as his shot floated about a foot above the ice. It felt like it hung there forever, suspended in the air, as it sliced through a traffic jam in front of the net, squeaked past the goalie, between his arm and his body, and bulged the twine behind him.

"I immediately raised my arms," Bryant says. "My teammates knew it was my first goal, so they quickly skated over, and our bench was fired up, too. For me, it was such a relief. I felt I had gone through a few months of grind and adversity playing in a new country prior to that moment. My teammate scooped the puck out of the net after the goal and kept it for me after the game."

The puck is now at home, and the goal is registered on his Elite Prospects profile, which Bryant admits to checking online every once in a while.

"I thought, 'You know, if I love the game so much, let's get out of my comfortable shell and go halfway around the world to try this,' so I did," Bryant says. "Hockey wasn't the most successful for me, this past season, but I'm still proud of what I achieved. The fact that I got up and packed my shit and left home and just went on a journey myself, I'll never forget that."

The next day, I begin the long drive home from Vancouver, some 4,800 kilometers (3,000 miles) east to Toronto. Five hours in, I stop in Kamloops.

I arrive at the Hamlets at Westsyde, sign in, do a rapid test for COVID-19, and walk upstairs to my father's spartan room; just a bed, a chair, and not much else. The fewer the number of things, the less confused he gets. The staff are good to him, like he is their own father or grandfather. I told them I wanted to try to take him to a Kamloops Blazers game tonight, and when I walk in he's sitting quietly in a chair, showered and shaven, wearing his Blazers cap and jacket. I like to think he was waiting for me.

At least his pants are on right. When he was still living with my mother, in their downtown condo, he would sometimes come out of their room with his pants on backward. At first, I muffled my laughter, then I began letting it out and my father would laugh, too. We would laugh together, me knowing what was coming and him knowing nothing at all. When it got so hard that he needed full-time care, I would do and say all the things any son blessed with a good father wished he'd done and said years earlier. I would hug him fiercely, kiss him on the cheek, and tell him I love him.

It started out harmless enough, back when my parents were still living in Cedar Valley, a hamlet just north of Toronto. "Mild cognitive impairment," the doctors said. Then came the ghosts my father started seeing at home while my mother, an air ambulance nurse, was away picking up ill and injured tourists in some far-flung part of the world. The ghost tales were easy enough to shrug off in a century-old farmhouse with untold stories in its walls. But then came the day when my father called my younger sister from a parking lot, telling her he couldn't find the car. Then came another, a few years later, after we'd sold the family farm and moved my parents out to Kamloops, when someone from the YMCA, just a few hundred feet from my parents' condo, called my mother to tell her my dad couldn't find his way home while walking the dog.

Every unwritten rule of life goes out the window when dealing with dementia. The only option is to figure it out as it goes along and treasure the rare moments of lucidity. You hold onto those for your life, as long as you can. Like the time my father looked me square in the eyes as we sat at the kitchen table and said, out of the blue, with a lucidity and clarity I hadn't seen from him in years, and haven't since, "You know, son, I've always loved you." For those who suffer from the disease, it is almost always something non-linguistic that brings them back, however fleeting it may be. For many it is music, for others it is some other activity or hobby, like painting, baking, gardening, or arts and crafts. For my father, until even it lost its magic, it was hockey.

For whatever reason, from whatever region in his deteriorating brain that somehow remained intact, hockey became a brief reprieve from the dementia, whether it was watching the Maple Leafs or Canucks on TV or catching the Blazers live in Kamloops. When the game was on, the hallucinations disappeared. Gone were the conversations with ghosts, the phone calls from the news anchors on CNN, the boats floating down the middle of street, the robbers trying to steal his stuff. He stopped trying to stick a knife into the toaster "to check if it's alive" and didn't stare at the chair cushions "waiting for them to move." Normally he would've struggled with even basic commands, like "sit down" or "put your shoes on." Yet when hockey was on, he seemed to understand concepts like offside, icing, powerplay, and penalty kill. For a few hours, it was nice not having to pluck the Raisin Bran out of the refrigerator or the butter from the dishwasher. It was just father, son, and the game.

For years, my father had been a loyal subscriber of *The Hockey News*. As his dementia got worse, he began poring over every issue, like he was under some kind of deadline, as a former journalist, marking up the margins and taking notes—pages and pages and pages of notes.

"I know, I know," he would say to me. "Who's that crazy goof who never gets anything done? That's me, right?"

Winter road trips were a staple of my childhood. Like most hockey dads, my father's days off were spent schlepping his son to long-distance road games or tournaments. When I wasn't practicing at some god-awful early morning hour on weekdays before he went to work or playing games on weeknights and weekends, he was taking me door-to-door throughout our neighborhood so that I could raise enough money selling cookies, baked goods, or whatever else kids guilt their neighbors into buying just so they can play on the ice at Maple Leaf Gardens for the Timmy Tyke Tournament. My father knew that his son would never be one of the 0.00025 percent of kids who make the NHL. He was never a deluded hockey dad. He sat in the stands among the crazy hockey parents and never pretended it would ever amount to anything other than his son having fun playing the game, learning whatever life lessons hockey has to teach. He never yelled at me after a game, never told me what I did wrong, and never cursed any coaches, although he did give it to a referee once during a road game when I was crosschecked headfirst into the goalpost and the hometown officials said play on. I'd never seen my father, as meek and mild a man as I've ever known, get angry before. He screamed at the officials so loud and so long, he got kicked out of the arena.

Our family never could afford tickets to see the Leafs play, not even in the 1980s when the team was comically bad. Instead, my father took me to American Hockey League games when the Leafs' farm team was briefly housed in Newmarket, a short drive from the farm. The closest thing to any NHL game we ever went to was an exhibition affair between the Leafs and Moscow Dynamo at Maple Leaf Gardens, and later an intrasquad game that the Leafs played in Newmarket during training camp. I remember that game for Wendel Clark, who wallpapered teammate Brad Smith into the boards and sent him out on a stretcher. It was *preseason*, Wendel.

After picking up my father, I drive us downtown to the Sandman Centre and walk him to the ticket gate. As we cross the road, a young man takes my dad's hand and helps me get him across. You would think being around all these people would make my father anxious or agitated, but crowds seem to calm him. He doesn't stray, unlike the time he left the condo in the middle of the night in the dead of winter and the police brought him home.

When I find our aisle, the usher lets us sit in a pair of seats at the end of an empty row, where I won't have to keep getting my father up and down for others to walk past. To keep him from wandering, I've brought four blueberry muffins. By the end of the first period, they are gone. A couple behind me, Alex and Stephanie Bell, can tell I need help. Over the next two periods, as my father and I watch the Blazers run away with the game, Alex and Stephanie keep bringing my father food, including three hot dogs, a bag of popcorn, and a supersize Coke. For every drill sergeant coach, overzealous hockey parent, or deluded beer-leaguer, there are a thousand good people in the game. I can't thank Alex and Stephanie enough.

Kamloops is set to host the Memorial Cup after I return home from the road trip, so the Blazers are stacked with talent. They aren't the Blazers of the late 1980s and early 1990s, when the team had such future Hall of Famers as Mark Recchi, Scott Niedermayer, and Jarome Iginla, but they've assembled one of the best teams in the Western Hockey League. They win easily tonight, giving me the victory I was hoping for.

After the game, the crowd starts filing out of the building. Sensing I need help, a security guard stops people from coming up the stairs in our aisle so that I can get my father out of his seat. No one protests. Everything went right that night.

I walk my father back to the car and fasten his seatbelt around him, much the way he did for me as a kid before I could manage on my own. I pull out of the parking lot and wait patiently for a break in the dispersing crowd. I look over at my dad. He looks calm and quiet, warm and puffy in his Blazers jacket, with his Blazers toque tucked tight around his ears. I don't know what he is thinking, but he seems peaceful and happy. I smile as I pull onto Mark Recchi Way and drive him home.

Epilogue: The Road

FOLLOW ANY ROAD in this country and it will lead you to the game. Both naturally and artificially, like a birthmark you come to accept or a tattoo you occasionally regret, hockey is everywhere in Canada. It is inscribed onto its lakes, rivers, ponds, bays, and sloughs, where the game was born, and written into the land, where it evolved to skate upon. It is part of Canada's history, art, literature, film, and music, and inseparable from its climate and geography. It is carved into the country's architecture and infrastructure, bound to its corporations, imprinted on the currency, illustrated on its postage stamps, and in bed with its beer and coffee. It is in dive bars and bowling alleys, crash sites and plane wrecks, ancient arenas and abandoned mines, restaurants and even restrooms. It is in think-tanks and universities, coffee shops and hotel rooms, schools and churches, greenhouses and grocery stores, and in a national mosaic of memorials, museums, monuments, and murals. Most important, it is part of the people who watch and play and talk about the game: pilots, truckers, tour guides, players, fans, police officers, farmers, carpenters, hotel managers, hunters, adventurers, restaurant owners, Zamboni drivers, architects, curators, mechanics, loggers, memorabilia collectors, high school teachers, cowboys, beat reporters, professors, radio hosts, roughnecks, miners, gardeners, bus drivers, painters, even prime ministers. I know this to be true, because I saw it all and spoke to many of them after eight months and more than 48,000 kilometers (30,000 miles) on the road.

In Canada, the road is a rite of passage in hockey, a ritual every player goes through, both for the few destined for the NHL and the many bound for the beer leagues. It is there, at every level of hockey and in every part of the country. Road hockey is a timeless Canadian tradition played on streets in cities, roads in rural towns, and even highways in between. Road trips to out-of-town games and weekend tournaments are a staple of youth hockey, running the gamut of the country's roadside waystations, from coffee shops and greasy spoons to gas stations and motel rooms. A little way up hockey's hierarchy are the long bus rides of junior hockey, where teammates spend more time together than they do in the dressing room or even on the ice. For those who carry on with their careers, many end up eking out a living on the road in minor pro leagues, playing for and against teams in Canadian and American backwaters. Within the game's moneypuck community is an invention called the Royal Road, an invisible highway that runs lengthwise down the middle of the rink from one net to the other. It is the most trafficked route anywhere on the ice. The road also features as metaphor, as the phrase of choice for "road games" but also in the annual "road to the Stanley Cup," which takes over Canada's national public broadcaster every spring, a time when fans across the country lay claim to a downtown street in their city to either cheer their team to the cup or die inside trying.

Canada's roads themselves are laden with hockey lore. On welcome signs, small towns preen with pride over their NHL offspring, from skilled shooters who scored their way to the bigtime to grinders and grunts who ground their way there. In both small-town and big-city Canada, street cred is dished out to hometown players in the form of roads, streets, avenues, lanes, and ways named after those who got a taste of the NHL, with bridges, parkways, and highways reserved for those who dined there for years. Throughout the country, the local arena is often the center of the community, so all roads in Canada do eventually lead to a rink.

One of those roads is Canada's highway of hockey, the meandering and schizophrenic Trans-Canada, which runs through six of the country's NHL cities (all seven if Highway 401 through Toronto were included) and dozens of NHL-lite cities in the Canadian Hockey League, as well as hundreds of hockey towns across the country. But there are many other roads: the Trans-Labrador Highway through Labrador; the Billy Diamond Highway in northern Quebec; the Wetum Road in Northern Ontario; the Mackenzie Highway in Alberta; the Yellowknife Highway and Liard Highway through the Northwest Territories; the Klondike Highway and Dempster Highway in the Yukon; the Inuvik Tuktoyaktuk Highway to the Arctic Ocean; and the Stewart-Cassiar Highway in northern British Columbia. When strung together with the Trans-Canada, these roads resemble something of a kindergarten's drawing of a figure-eight or a toppled-over snowman, forming a drive that touches three oceans and runs through every province and two of the three territories, leaving out only Nunavut until roads are built connecting it to the rest of Canada. Mix in a few flights and a slew of ferries, and the route would reach into every part of the country. And at every point along the way, there would be the game.

Acknowledgments

S O MANY PEOPLE TO THANK.

The entire team at Sutherland House Books: Ken Whyte, for taking a chance on me. Ian Coutts, for his seamless editing. Serina Mercier, Shalomi Ranasinghe, and Jordan Lunn, for shepherding the book from draft to press and beyond.

The Hockey News: still the bible of hockey. A special shout-out to managing editor Edward Fraser, for always being offside. It was a fun five years in the trenches together.

Everyone who got Gumpy on the road and kept him on the road: Jon Keto, Eugene Mercier, and the service team at Richmond Hill Subaru, and Scott King at Richmond Hill Honda.

Fiorenzo Arcadi at Toronto Hockey Repair: thank you for suiting me up and christening the Black Knight. Best hockey shop in Canada.

All of you who shared their stories with me: Junior Humphries, Roxanne Dyson, Craig Penney, Noah Burnett, Rob Carter, Matt Howse, the Ryans, Todd Pardy, Fab Guérin, Arnaud Briand, John Hanna Jr., Kevin Morrison, Mark Pottie, Craig Smith, Danny Dill, Cornelius Van Ewyk, Carl and Suzanne Watters, Jason McAllister, Danny Braun, Gerald Allain, Gerald Clavette, Paul Levasseur, Didier Leroux, Christian "Bill" Allard, Roy Neacappo, Richard Hamel, Charles Hester, Adil El

Farj, Ralph Metki, Qais Hafsi, Adam and Annie Sherlip, Jean-Pierre Tanguay, Bobby Baril, Chad Calaiezzi, Kevin Vincent, Wayne Bozzer, Mike Mulryan, Doug Higgins, Rick Eaton, Peter Austin, Bill Leithead, Jimmy "Iceman" MacNeil, Dean Bevan, Howard Shubert, Alex Brown, Zach Anderson, Darryl Deller, Brian Clarke, Charlie Cheechoo, Bradley "Beuf" Cheechoo, Jassen Metatawabin, Jussi Kuokkanen, Kenny Luhtala, Kari Jämsä, Aarno Peura, Joe Daley, Travis Daley, Chris Maendel, Nolan Waldner, Philip Waldner, Tirzah Maendel, Wayne Quliit Kusugak, David Clark, Verne Barber, Chris Fisher, Kevin Dufour, Brody Luhning, Tom Reardon, Joe Braniff, Dale Mosquito, Bradley Goodwill, Larry Oakes, Kevin Shaw, Chris Clark, Rob Vanstone, Mike Reagan, Rob Hart, Austin Mattes, Raphael Saray, Diane Russell, Brent Lethbridge, Jennifer Hanson, Nelson Rego, Scott Bell, Tom McLennan, Mike Mitchell, Snowking, Tshayla Nothstein, Jodi Tuton, Davina McLeod, Spruce Gerberding, Dave Ezzard, Adi Scott, Donald Kuptana Jr., Jake Danuser, Ralph Posteraro, Terry Wallace, Behn Cochrane, Bill Brownridge, Michael Barnholden, Po-Yuan "Bryant" Tsiao, Alex and Stephanie Bell, and the late Don "Branks" Brankley and Charly Washipabano: you are the kind of people this great game is built upon.

All the beer-leaguers, shinny stars, and pickup artists I played with on the road trip: it was a pleasure sharing the ice with you.

My travel companions Adrian, Stro, and (in studio) Chippy: the best things to come of the road trip are the friendships I've made with you. Thank you for sharing the road with me. I'll ride with you anytime, my brothers.

The ever revolving crew at midday hockey in Aurora: our games are my weekly Zen.

Coach Fip: thank you for showing me that hockey can and should always be fun.

My father, Ronald Shuker, the gentlest man I know, and my mother, Jill Shuker, the strongest woman I know: I know where I'm going because I know where I've been and I haven't forgotten who got me here. Thank you for having been the kind of parents to let a kid find his own way.

And K, the GWOAT, with whom I share the game of life: thank you for encouraging me to go "do that hockey" for the better part of eight months. Coming home to you was the highlight of the road trip, and you coming home to me is the highlight of my every day. And now a new game dawns for us.